"Fo... ...-
tions ... ...
He ... ...ive up to those
epics ... ...moral courage established by
those who preceded him. He believes that the Corps is
truly unique—that it is the most elite military organization ever devised and that he, as an integral part of that
organization, must never bring disgrace or dishonor
upon it. His is an unsworn oath, an unspoken promise,
a conviction that he must never betray the trust of his
comrades and that his individual safety, his very life
must be secondary to the attainment of the unit's assigned objective. To have it said of one, *He* was a *good
Marine!'* is far preferable to the award of the highest of
battle decorations, for that accolade will have come
from the heart of a fellow Marine . . ."

—Gerald P. Averill in *MUSTANG*

"Averill displays a rare ability to capture the thoughts,
words and actions of Marines in combat and in training
for combat. His experiences include the most authen-
tic descriptions I've ever seen of the ways of combat
Marines from the beginning of World War II through
the Korean War."

—Colonel William E. Barber, USMC (Ret.),
Congressional Medal of Honor

"Well-written with vivid descriptions which give the
reader the impression that he is participating in the
combat actions described in the book."

—Colonel Carl L. Sitter, USMC (Ret.),
Congressional Medal of Honor

"*MUSTANG* is rich reading because it rings so true."

—Lt. Gen. Victor H. Krulak, USMC (Ret.),
author of *First to Fight*

MUSTANG
A COMBAT MARINE

GERALD P. AVERILL

POCKET BOOKS

New York   London   Toronto   Sydney   Tokyo

Map of the Solomon Islands, page 66, from the *West Point Atlas*, Department of Military Art and Engineering, the United States Military Academy, West Point, New York. All other maps courtesy of the Reproduction Section, Marine Corps Schools, Quantico, Virginia.

POCKET BOOKS, a division of Simon & Schuster Inc.
1230 Avenue of the Americas, New York, N.Y. 10020

Published by arrangement with Presidio Press
Library of Congress Catalog Card Number: 86-30485

ISBN: 0-671-64909-4

First Pocket Books printing October 1988

10 9 8 7 6 5 4 3 2 1

POCKET and colophon are trademarks of
Simon & Schuster Inc.

Printed in the U.S.A.

For Lieutenant Colonel Ernest Leo DeFazio, United States Marine Corps, one of the truly great ones of the mustang breed.

For my wife, Helen, who never for a moment forgot that the Corps must come first, who never once stood in the way of a campaign, an expedition, or a war that I needed to be in.

And for my sons, who kept the faith and fought the good fight in the battle for Vietnam—Mike, a Marine rifleman who survived, and Craig, a rifleman of the 101st Airborne Division, who did not.

A CONSECRATION
John Masefield

Not of princes or prelates
  with perriwigged charioteers
Riding triumphantly laurelled
  to lap the fat of the years,
Rather the scorned—the rejected—
  the men hemmed in with the spears;

The men of the tattered battalion
  which fights till it dies,
Dazed with the dust of the battle,
  the din and the cries,
The men with the broken heads
  and the blood running into their eyes.

Not the be-medalled Commander,
  beloved of the throne,
Riding cock-horse to parade
  when the bugles are blown,
But the lads who carried the koppie
  and cannot be known.

Not the ruler for me, but the ranker,
  the tramp of the road,
The slave with the sack on his shoulders
  pricked on with the goad,
The man with too weighty a burden,
  too weary a load.

The sailor, the stoker of steamers,
  the man with the clout,
The chantyman bent at the halliards
  putting tune to the shout,
The drowsy man at the wheel
  and the tired lookout.

Other men sing of the wine
and the wealth and the mirth,
The portly presence of potentates
goodly in girth;
Mine be the dirt and the dross,
the dust and the scum of the earth!
Of the maimed, of the halt and the blind
in the rain and the cold—

Of these shall my songs be fashioned,
my tales be told.

AMEN

Contents

PART THREE

SAND AND BLOOD

PART FOUR

THE LEAN, MEAN, IN-BETWEEN YEARS

PART FIVE

THE LONG WALK

PART SIX

THE SECOND DECADE

PART SEVEN

CLOSED CIRCLE

Foreword

The title of this volume, "Mustang," descriptive of one who rose to commissioned status from the ranks, has never impressed me as being a particularly significant term. Such importance as it does possess is confined largely to the minds of the people who come into the Corps by that route. It is not by chance that the term describes some of the Marine Corps' greatest.

When first I met Gerald Averill I had no idea of his antecedents—whether he came from Yale, Annapolis, or the street. Nor did I care. What I wanted from him was performance. That is what I got, as did every commander he served in the next twenty-five years.

The classic portrait of a Marine is one who has an unshakable belief in his country, his Corps, his associates, and himself; one who eschews the easy life and sees, as the ultimate, service in combat. That is the religion of the Corps, reflected in its apocrypha, its recruiting posters, its book titles: *Retreat Hell, O'er the Ramparts We Watch, Fix Bayonets, First to Fight*. That is really the burden of the story Averill tells, in this book. In words that are eloquent in their simplicity he tells the reader that the battle is the thing, that everything else is secondary, at best a necessary evil. And then he proceeds to illustrate that conviction in a stirring recital of events in his own career.

It is rich reading because it rings so true. Averill accepted, with great reluctance—more often than not, under protest—assignments not in the main stream of the combat forces, and he never concealed his impatience with such assignments. On one occasion he said unhappily: "Sitting behind a desk, flipping papers all day, was not my forte, but I was stuck with it." A fitness report entry pegged him precisely, "He finds it difficult to go from a war situation into a garrison situation"—which is not all bad.

Disdain for those not similarly motivated stands out like the trees on the skyline. He refers to "a non-combatant captain who knew nothing and did not want to know" or "an inexperienced young lieutenant from the Confederate aristocracy." Combat, combat experience, and combat skill were the criteria for membership in his fraternity.

Averill saw a lot of combat, and has the rare ability to describe the adrenalin-packed movements in a way that brings the reader into the middle of the action. He tells of exciting service as a platoon commander in a seven-day seaborne raid in the Solomons, where the Marines were outnumbered ten to one. He went through the whole of the wrenching battle for Iwo Jima in a rifle company, and his recital encompasses all of the starkness, intensity, and blood in one of our bitterest battles. He also gives a mud-level view of the interaction of personalities stretched to the physical and psychological breaking point.

The same incontestable realism undergirds his recital of battle experiences as a company commander and battalion executive officer in Korea, where he exhibited his basic philosophy of leadership: "The average trooper wants to see rank running around when things turn hot. That is what rank gets paid for. . . ."

A famous Marine of three-quarters of a century before Averill—Littleton Waller Tazewell Waller—boasted: "In thirty years in the Corps I never accepted a desk job without a protest."

Waller was a warrior. So was Averill.

Lt. Gen. Victor H. Krulak USMC (Ret.)

MUSTANG

Introduction

In the naval service, one who is commissioned from the ranks is known as a mustang. To the Naval Academy graduate or the direct commission officer from the nation's colleges and universities, the word may at times be spoken with a hint of scorn. To the former enlisted man, quite the reverse is true, for no greater honor could be given him. There is no doubt in the mustang's mind that he must lead, and lead exceptionally well. Leadership, in every connotation of the word, is expected of him. He cannot fail to accept and carry out that responsibility; therefore the field manual dealing with tactics is no more a stranger to him than the technical manual from which weaponry is taught. What he might lack in formal education he makes up for in troop sagacity and empathy, and, because he comes from the ranks, he considers it mandatory to excel in all things military. The mustang knows that he has been placed in a position where his every move will be carefully scrutinized and evaluated by both his seniors and his contemporaries. He understands very well that his chances for promotion are infinitely less than those of the direct commission officers. He is equally aware that he

1

may not be as socially acceptable to his senior officers as his direct commission contemporaries.

Comprehending these things the mustang perceives that he must be openly competitive with those contemporaries, must strive to out-distance them, must be willing to accept and succeed in missions which they cannot or do not wish to accomplish. He stands alone in the scheme of things, with only his initiative and native ability to see him through. He has no academy ring to knock, no school tie to wear, no sheepskin on the wall to proclaim his intelligence. Instead, he possesses the one thing that the direct commissions may pretend, but can never attain: the sure knowledge of what goes on in the heart and mind of an enlisted man—his feelings, his reactions to particular words or deeds, his innate pride in himself as a Marine, his pride in unit and Corps. Never having served in the ranks, not having felt discipline as enlisted men do, not having been humbled as enlisted men are, the direct commissions only can surmise what may be in the minds of the men when a particular situation arises. The mustang knows instinctively, and that insight provides him with that extra bit of confidence, that positive feeling about the outcome of a given mission, that sends him forward with the troops to ensure success in battle.

During the time I spent in the Corps, I came into contact with many mustangs. Some pursued their trade diligently, as did the direct commissions who trained with them and fought the wars with them. Other mustangs did not, and fell by the wayside for a variety of reasons. Some were adequate to lead platoons, but lacked the organizational capacity to serve as commanders of larger units, or as staff officers. Some mustangs, like their direct commission contemporaries, had no appetite for ground combat, nor did they have the desire to acquire a taste for it. Others, upon commissioning, took off on a protracted ego trip, rendering themselves useless to themselves and to their troops. The weak-kneed and the egomaniacs did not linger overly long and were permitted to return to enlisted rank or asked to resign for the good of the service.

The units that I served with were officered by a high percentage of mustangs. I understood them, worked for them and with them, respected them, admired and disliked them, loved them with the love that brothers feel for each other. I had to, you see, for I was one of them.

Some of our civilian friends would have us imagine that they are *very* religious. To prove it they attend church almost every Sunday; for surely, if one does not attend services he cannot be religious, can he? Some are devoted enough to participate in the activities of the church that require additional time. Some lead lay services, read the word, sing the hymns. They exhibit piety and devoutness calculated to give the impression of saintliness. No matter how volubly or how fervently they pursue their sacred duties, few stand ready to *die* for the propagation and survival of the religious persuasion that they have entered upon. They say that they are *totally* obligated, pledged to give everything in their power for their religion, everything, that is, except for that most precious of all things—life! Would they give up their lives for their brothers if they would not for their religion? Not likely. Involvement is a wondrous thing, up to a point. Personal survival has become the strongest of all emotions—stronger than devotion to duty, devotion to a creed, stronger than honor, stronger than love. The average citizen of our country accepts this as a viable fact and lives his life accordingly.

To the Marine, the *Corps* is his religion, his reason for being. He cannot be committed up to a point. For him, involvement is total. He savors the traditions of his Corps and doubts not the veracity of them. He believes implicitly that he must live up to those epics of physical and moral courage established by those who preceded him. He believes that the Corps is truly unique—that it is the most elite military organization ever devised and that he, as an integral part of that organization, must never bring disgrace or dishonor upon it. His is an unsworn oath, an unspoken promise, a conviction that he must never betray the trust of his comrades and that his individual safety, his very life must be secondary to the attainment of the unit's assigned objective. To have it said of one, *"He was a good Marine!"* is far preferable to the award of the highest of battle decorations, for that accolade will have come from the heart of a fellow Marine, infinitely qualified to voice it, and not from the typewriter of a professional awards writer.

The Marine does not *want* to die, but he is not afraid to die if he must. Perhaps it would seem inconceivable to an outsider, but often a Marine is far more fearful of the judgement of his peers than he is of the knowledge that he may well be killed in the action that he must take. It is this very simple fact that makes the Marine the superior fighting man that he has been and always will be. No particular magic. Just his unshakeable belief in his Corps and in himself, and the generous ration of pride and self-confidence that the Corps dispenses so freely to those who wear its uniform.

The Marine Corps is good to all men who embrace it. It was especially good to me. It took me in as a five-foot-six-and-three-quarters "sand blower" at $20.80 per month, and nearly twenty-five years later cut me loose as a lieutenant colonel of Marine infantry, drawing forty-five times that $20.80. In that quarter of a century the Corps gave me a chance to lead all of the infantry units—the squad, platoon, company, and battalion. It gave me the opportunity to serve as the operations officer of battalions and regiments and a combat-deployed Marine Corps Expeditionary Unit; it allowed me, too, the command of the Marine Corps Cold Weather Training Center. The Corps sent me to the Junior and Senior Amphibious Warfare Schools as a student and was gracious enough to have me serve as an instructor in the Junior School, teaching offensive and defensive tactics and counterinsurgency operations. Between classes at the Junior School, I spent the summer months as senior instructor in the Air Observation School.

There was duty, too, with a "sister service," the United States Army, where I met professionals who would have brought credit to the uniform of any service. My first duty station was Fort Benning, Georgia, where, after a fourteen-year layoff, I went back on jump status. The Airborne people were very kind to me. Nearly every time an aircraft was manifested for a troop jump, my name was listed. One hundred jumps in twenty months testifies to the regularity with which my name appeared on the manifests. At Fort Benning I qualified for and was awarded the senior and master parachutist badges. I was the first Marine to be so honored.

My second tour with the Army took me to the John F. Kennedy Center for Special Warfare at Fort Bragg, North

Carolina. During this tour my service was again with Airborne people—people who shared my judgement that the American fighting man can outmaneuver and outfight any other man on earth provided that he is instilled with the spirit to win and is given the proper weapons and equipment. These were the Special Forces people that I had known on Okinawa—the six-month temporary duty troopers who had fought in Laos and Vietnam during the early sixties and the ones that I would be associated with closely in Vietnam for nearly five years.

To make the circle complete, the Corps assigned me, a product of Parris Island, to duty at the Marine Corps Recruit Depot, San Diego, California, for my final tour with Marines. There I served as operations and training officer, Recruit Training Regiment; commanding officer of the 1st Recruit Training Battalion; and G-2/Inspector of the Recruit Depot.

I noticed a peculiar thing as I came along in the Corps. There were very few people suited to be troop handlers—the unit leaders at all levels of command. As a matter of fact there were damned few people who wanted to get involved in that business. It was too accident-prone, too easy to receive congressional interest, too easy to become a fall guy. In the early years of my time in the Corps, when platoon leaders, company commanders, battalion commanders, and staff officers from the Great War were rotating through the job of commandant one after another, a prerequisite for promotion was to have commanded the unit of one's rank—platoons for lieutenants, companies for captains and senior lieutenants, battalions for field grade officers. The old-timers, in their wisdom and their wealth of practical experience, still believed that an officer should be able to shoot, to salute, and to lead troops with a flair on the battlefield. They had little respect for those who could not. You may be sure that during the tenure of these general officers as commandant, there was an overt attempt to become *qualified,* but for promotional purposes only, not from a great affection for line duty.

Much of my time in the Corps was spent where the real Marines were and are—in the operating forces—the Fleet Marine Force. From 1943 until 1951 I spent all, or portions of, each one of those continuous eight years in the Fleet Marine Force. In 1954 I was back again for two years and in 1961 was

overseas with a Marine division. When I was not assigned to
the Fleet Marine Force, I was being trained, or training
others, for duty in it. The Fleet Marine Force was where I
wanted to be, where I wish that I could have spent even more
time. Troops and troop handling were for me. Nothing else
really mattered.

My duties as a platoon and company officer brought me
very close to the Marines of World War II. We had not
allowed ourselves then the doubtful luxury of *rotation*. We
knew nothing of R and R—rest and rehabilitation. Few in the
lower ranks were married. If they were they were still required to maintain a bunk and a locker in the barracks, were
expected to be aboard throughout all duty hours. Perhaps
they made it home on weekends, perhaps not. Overseas there
was little leave or liberty, and the training days and nights
were long. During those days and nights we got to know each
other very well. Many Marine Corps units averaged more
than thirty months in the Pacific area of operations, so it was
not surprising that we were rather "family" oriented. We
knew nothing but war and getting ready for it. That sort of
environment tends to produce a close-knit organization in a
minimum amount of time.

As a battalion and regimental operations officer during
parts of two winters and a summer in the Land of the Morning Calm, I was exposed not only to the old-time Regulars
and Reservists of World War II but also to the new breed of
Regular Marine who had enlisted in the late forties, and
whom I had helped to train between the end of the Big War
and the beginning of the police action. In later years I came
into contact with the Marines who came along during the
time of the first Lebanon show, and those who made the run
from Okinawa to the bend of the Mekong, at Udorn. I worked
with the lads who had gone ashore in the Dominican Republic and with the young men who came out to northern
Indochina, to mix it up with the Cong and the regular main-
line units of General Vo Nguyen Giap.

There was little difference in any of those lads. They
were for the most part competent, their attitude was good,
and they comported themselves as professionals should. If
there was a weakness anywhere, it was not in them. It never

is. If they were well supplied and armed, provided with adequate food and shelter, and *led* the way that Marines *should* be led, there was no stopping them. They could, in fact, do without shelter and for a time exist without food. They could survive even a temporary shortage of ammunition. But when leadership came up short or failed entirely, they fell flat on their faces, just as they have ever since the Corps began. Marines are trained to believe in their leaders, both noncommissioned and commissioned officers alike. If those officers show weakness or fear or, worse still, a lack of interest in the safety and welfare of their troops, the individual Marine loses not only confidence in his leaders but also in himself, and that lack of confidence is transmitted to his peers. It is then that failure instead of success, defeat instead of victory may be the end result of combat. Fortunately, during my time, we had comparatively few losers playing the leadership game, although they were ever present in varying numbers. Had those numbers been greater, I surely would not be around today to tell this story.

What follows is an account of life in *my* Marine Corps—the Corps as I perceived it to be, through the eyes of a mustang—and the stories of some of the Marines I knew during the quarter of a century that I served them and the Corps. You will not find sadism, cruelty, or savagery in these pages, for in my time *example* and not fear was the prime motivator. I cannot argue with those who paint a more vicious picture of the Corps. I can only state that in my training, at all levels of stress, I was not beaten, was not tortured, was not physically abused. I was humbled as I never have been humbled before or since. From that abject and total humiliation emerged an acceptance of things as they *were*, not as I might have liked them to be. The ability to accept any circumstance, to cope with it, to live with it—all the while actively scheming to overcome it—is in my opinion what keeps a Marine going, what gives him the stamina, the steadfastness, the moral and physical courage that produce success in battle.

Part One

BOOT

1

The Island

The nonrated slop-chute was jam-packed, full of noise and smoke. Over the incessant wail of the jukebox came the hum of animated conversation, punctuated by roars and cackles of laughter. Coke and beer a nickel a bottle, take your pick. If you could stand the wear and tear on the kidneys and bladder, the 3.2% would eventually loosen your tongue and run your spirits high. Coke loaded up your stomach and your bladder. Period. The swinging doors of the head never stopped swishing. There was always someone going in or coming out.

At a corner table, taking in all this local color, sat Bowles, Hardage, and myself, three out of the five left on the island for duty. Motelewski, the fourth, now an artilleryman, was stuck with the weekend duty. Johnson, the fifth, a rifle range coach, was preparing to receive an incoming platoon. We were old-timers now, two months out of boot camp, home leave behind us, salty, wearing cut-down khaki shirts and service green trousers. In actuality we were about as salty as the peanuts we were munching by the handful and popping down the necks of our Coke bottles. It was the first time we all had been together since our return from leave, so there was much to palaver about. Bowles had gone home to Kentucky, Hardage to Georgia, and I way down east to the state of Maine.

We watched the others in the slop-chute, listened to snatches of lyrics from the jukebox music, and talked. We felt *good*. All of us were Pfc's, making $36 per month plus shooting pay. To put the frosting on the cake, all of us had passed the test for corporal and were on the promotion list. We already could visualize the wide red stripes down the seams of our dress blue trousers, the mark of an NCO—and the $42 a month base pay was not to be derided. We had it knocked up tight and we knew it. All of this good fortune *almost* made up for being left behind on the island while the rest of the platoon went rolling off to freedom over the Horse Island bridge. Almost, but not quite!

I have never known a Marine who did not want to reminisce about his recruit training, to talk about it from his first day off the grinder until that final day when they planted him in Arlington or some other bone yard of his choice. As soon as another Marine learns that you have been exposed to boot camp, the queries commence. What platoon? What year? What months? Who was the senior drill instructor? We have an unreal thing going about all this. I suppose that this inordinate curiosity must stem from the fact that everyone who ever entered the system had been given the same message by the drill instructors. "You will *never* make it! You are not *good* enough. You don't have guts enough to be a Marine! You *never will be* a Marine!"

Somehow the majority of recruits survive, do go on to be Marines—good Marines—but the mystery of why *they* survived, why *they* did not fail is always present, tucked away in that special recess of the mind where all the other flaky things that one cannot understand hide out. When the questions start they come crawling out into the sunshine to be recognized, to be compared, to be shared. It is a compulsion that never can be ignored and we all react to it. Who had it toughest in terms of weather, of training? Who suffered most from the attitudes of the drill instructors? It is in all of us to try and prove that it was *our* platoon that bore the unbearable, *our* platoon that endured beyond endurance, *our* platoon that outlasted the most tenacious efforts of the drill instructors to grind us down. There never has been, there never will be any sort of device or badge awarded to any platoon for having overcome these things, but we surely try to make it appear that way. It must be some kind of screwed-up, far-out pride in the act of survival that prompts us to be this way: the surviving of mental and physical pressures never encountered elsewhere, surviving to make liars out of the drill instructors, surviving to become a Marine, the thing that the drill instructors had said you never could be. It is an inexplicable aberration with us, this boot-camp syndrome, affecting young and old alike, quite without cure.

During the afternoon, between head calls and ordering up more peanuts and Coke, we skirted the subject religiously knowing full well that it would end up as the meat and potatoes, the main course of the day's conversation. We talked about the peculiar way that the civilians had stared at the forest green uniforms with chevrons outlined in red that we wore. Puzzled and curious they had asked, "Are you from the Canadian Army?" It was not their fault. The average American did not recognize a Marine in any other uniform but dress blues. We talked about the home-cooked food, the long hours sleeping in, the warm and tender glances of the home-town girls. We talked on into the midafternoon about other aspects of that other world that had once been ours, and then the small talk dried up. There was no more avoiding it, no way to turn except inward, to recall the days and nights spent with the platoon, to relive in memories still bright and sharp that summer and autumn, those few blistering weeks that had seared us, body and soul, had changed us all in so many ways.

Everyone at the table realized that we had been extremely fortunate to have drawn the drill instructors who took our platoon through recruit training. An old salt and a neophyte. A buck sergeant and a private first class. No physical resemblance. Different ways of handling recruits. Neither felt the need to beat on us with their hands. Both of them figured that they were smarter than we were and that brain power was the way to go. There might have been instances in which provocation could have brought them close to violence, but seldom, very seldom. They made a team that ran a smooth, efficient operation, with a minimum of wasted motion. They got the most out of us and every training day.

The sergeant had considerable time in. He had completed three cruises and was working on his fourth. He had been a member of the rifle and pistol team, was a distinguished marksman. He came to us from seagoing, from one of the big carriers. Seagoing Marines were known for their sharpness in dress, deportment, and demeanor. The sergeant was a cut well above the average seagoing Marine. He had been out where the water was deep. We knew this because he never tired of reminding us of that fact.

His head was not shaved as ours were, nor did he wear his hair in a crewcut. You may be sure, however, that its length did not exceed the three inches on top specified by the Marine Corps Manual. The sergeant *knew* that book, and he lived by it. He was of medium height and build, and carried himself in such a manner that he seemed to strut rather than walk. He always reminded me of a thoroughbred show horse prancing, but in a mannerly and well-disciplined way. His uniforms, cut to perfection by the ship's tailor shop aboard the carrier and kept in immaculate condition by the sergeant, were the source of instant envy, coveted by recruits and other drill instructors as well. His hallmark was his web trouser belt, always freshly scrubbed, its original light tan color bleached nearly white from repeated laundering but with never a frayed or worn spot visible along its length. The brass tip of the belt and belt buckle glistened from endless polishing.

When he first came before us the sergeant exuded the very essence of calm superiority. We had much to learn about him, and this we did quickly, for beneath that cool exterior there lurked a wild wickedness that he refused to curb completely. Sarcasm was a favorite weapon of the sergeant, a weapon utilized with a relish. He cut us down to size, ripping our self-respect to shreds systematically without the use of a single word of obscenity or profanity. His tongue lashings were almost physical in their effect upon us. He made us cringe inwardly and tremble outwardly. His vivid imagination, his ability to employ it against us, played havoc in the ranks and kept us perpetually, nervously on the defensive.

We openly admired his appearance, his professional knowledge, and ability. On the one hand he inspired us. On the other he induced in us a sense of apprehension, desolation, and despair.

One other thing about the sergeant. This was not his first tour on the drill field. He knew precisely what to do with us.

The junior of the team was different from the sergeant in all respects but one—they both wanted to be good Marines and they both worked at it. The junior drill instructor stood six foot plus, barefooted, and weighed close to two hundred pounds. He was big in the chest and shoulders, slim-hipped, and long-legged. He was a Texan with all of the sureness that breed carries with it. Though not as smooth and flashy as the sergeant, his appearance was equally impressive. Mainly because of his size he moved with just a shade less snap and precision. He had played football in college, had been an ROTC cadet. He could have—at least that is what he told us—finished his schooling and received a commission as a second lieutenant in the Army of the United States. He told us that he had foregone the easy way, had chosen to come into the Corps as an enlisted man, which right then made some of us wonder just a little bit whether or not he was playing with a full deck of cards.

We should not have had any doubts. He had his ducks lined up, fully intended to have that commission the hard way, by correspondence courses and eventual selection to an officer candidate course. He had in his possession the officers' basic course and was well into the first section. Out of recruit training but a short time himself, he seemed able to relate to our problems directly. Instinctively, as frightened animals often do, we trusted him.

His hallmark was bestowed by mother nature—a patch of curly black chest hair, never invisible, always creeping up and over the collar of his snow white skivvy shirt.

These two, salt and boot, senior and junior, skilled craftsman and apprentice, would manipulate, dominate, regulate, and direct every movement that we would make during recruit training. We would know them as father and brother, as common taskmasters, as judge and jury. We would love them, fear and hate them. Sgt. Don Keown. Pfc Bill Kerr. They owned us, could make us or break us as we attempted to become Marines. There was no future, good or bad, without them in it.

Platoon 116 was split into almost even segments, half Yankee, half southern, half city boys, half from the farms and backwoods areas. As luck would have it most of the drill instructors were southern and country reared. They had no use for Yankees, especially those from the big cities. I had spent time in a small city and was about as Yankee as one could ever be. You can't get much farther north than the state of Maine. For those two reasons and I suppose for a multitude of others then not readily apparent to me, I was chosen to be the prime example of the damn Yankee, someone to take it out on, to lean on, to ridicule. The drill instructors came down on me hard and often. That could have been the spur that drove me, that urged me on, that helped me to struggle through. Perversity works both ways.

Keown dubbed me "sand blower," a term of denigration bestowed as a matter of course on short recruits, a term indicating that one's posterior was so close to the ground that sand would fly under the pressure of a flatulation. I had been born with a long waist and short legs, which made the appellation even more appropriate.

Some of the other terms used to describe us by Keown were far more devastating.

In spite of being stumpy I was far more fortunate than my platoon mates in many ways, better equipped to cope with the everyday humiliation and contempt heaped upon us by our trainers. I had the advantage of being born and raised in Maine, where, in my youth, except for a very few wealthy families, the simple process of existence was formidable. My father worked hard, was a man of few words, who could find fault with almost everything that I attempted. I expected to be wrong and was seldom disappointed. A superb rifle and pistol shot, he somehow found the patience and time to teach me the rudiments of those skills. He taught me, too, how to cruise the woods and hills silently; how to find game trails and identify their makers; how to gauge the wind correctly; how to apply leads—Kentucky windage they used to call it; how to stalk painstakingly, sometimes not moving at all for long minutes, waiting for the optimum moment as a cat will hunch itself into position, muscles tensed for the final running leap of the hunt. He taught me how to use all of the senses as well. His teaching was to serve me well, better than he ever would have thought.

The high school that I attended—much to the chagrin and horror of the pacifistic clergy of the town who preached vehemently against such open criminality—featured in its curriculum that tool of Lucifer known as compulsory military training. Mandatory for the first two years, elective for the second two. Within this fascist program, youngsters of thirteen or fourteen were taught the martial arts and drills, according to the Reserve Officer Training Corps master plan. In spite of what the parish leaders might have screamed about tender stalks of manhood being molded into killers, it was all quite harmless. We learned the manual of arms with Springfield rifles from which the firing pins had been removed. You couldn't fire one even if you had the ammunition. We never saw a bayonet, although we were purported to be under instruction in the use of "cold steel." A canteen cup was about as close to cold steel as we ever came, no matter what the clergy said.

We did learn to march, to drill, to do the old squads-right-about, left-about, squads-right-into-center line, a drill that took some concentration to learn and perform correctly. On Saturday mornings, those of us who could qualify for the rifle team practiced small-bore shooting. After two years of this I was able to execute the manual of arms in an adequate manner, even though the Springfield was almost as tall as I, and able to do the squad and individual movements to the satisfaction of the French-born Army drill sergeant who was responsible for our military education. Years later, at the university, I would learn the new drill, the right flank, left flank, to-the-rear-march drill. By the time I reached the island I was discipline prone, unable to get upset too much by the routine verbal abuse and the continual harassment by the drill instructors.

I was *not* prepared for the high temperatures and humidity found on the island, nor for the enthusiasm and stamina exhibited by the drill instructors in the daily performance of their training duties.

We learned a lot in the first weeks of our training. How to clean the interior of the barracks. How to clean windows.

How to clean toilet bowls, urinals, shower heads. How to scrub the time-worn wooden decks of the barracks with toothbrushes. How to launder clothing using scrub brushes and bars of yellow soap. How to iron. How to spit shine our leather. How to linseed oil the stocks and foregrips of our rifles. How to saddle soap the slings. How to shine brass until it glowed. How to use the blitz cloth. How to preserve the patina by washing the brass in hot, soapy water; rinsing it; and drying it immediately.

Sergeant Keown believed in demonstration. For each thing that he taught us he demonstrated—just once. If you missed his instruction the first time around, you had better learn from another recruit. Keown did not fancy repeating anything.

As a part of the daily routine, we originally spent about three hours each morning and afternoon on the drill field, learning by repetition the manual of arms; counting cadence aloud and slapping the rifle slings for punctuation; doing endless to-the-rear marches, to-the-right flank, left flank, to-the-rear march again; forming files and columns; doing column movements; stacking arms and breaking stacks; forming for inspections; opening and closing ranks. We finally doped off in sheer weariness, were caught, and were punished in the standard manner: loping around and around the perimeter of the drill field with the rifle held high overhead—high port, as it was called—running until no breath remained and one could feel his nose and cheeks go numb and prickly from lack of oxygen and inadequate circulation, running until one of the drill instructors would see you start to drop, and the game would end for that particular drill session.

It was hot on the island that summer. Hotter than usual in a place that compares favorably with Hades at all times. The heat spread its mantle over instructor and instructed alike, driving them panting into the ground, into the shade of the barracks. Three recruits died on the drill field that summer from heat-related causes. It was hot enough to force a change in the training schedule after the third recruit dropped dead, and we were secured from the drill field daily at 1500—the time when the days were at their most wicked temperatures. We lost no drill time because of this schedule change. We made up for it after evening chow. It was nearly as uncomfortable to drill on a full stomach at the end of the day as it was to brave the midafternoon sun. It had its compensations. Nobody died from belching.

Sergeant Keown's rifle inspections were object lessons in psychological warfare. He would prepare the platoon for inspection, dress ranks, and order us to parade rest. He had a good reason for this. He wanted the other inhabitants of the island to soften us before he took over. Often he would call Kerr forward to watch over us at close range. Then he would saunter over into the shade of the barracks to observe our tribulations in relative coolness and comfort.

By the time we were formed for inspection, the sun had climbed just high enough to slant directly into our eyes. Even in the early hours of the day it generated intense heat, which struck at us savagely in our exposed position. At that time of day, as in the early evening, myriads of tiny flies floated through the air seeking sustenance. The ever-present sand fleas had burrowed into the sand to stay warm at night, but with the arrival of the sun's rays they popped out of the earth to commence the day's depredations. The combination of heat, flies, and fleas was a flail against our hides. Perspiration formed above the sweat bands of the pith helmets that we wore, dripped steadily into our eyes until they were full, and then coursed down our cheeks. As the drops of sweat hit our eyeballs, the salt stung and burned them, causing us to blink rapidly. About then the flies hit us, crawling into every opening of our heads, buzzing and whining as they entered our ears and moved up our nostrils. They dive-bombed our eyes, flying straight in, fluttering their tiny wings, drowning in sweat and tears, completely obscuring our vision. It was then the turn of the sand fleas, surging up out of the sand, swarming over the tops of our field shoes, running up the calves of our legs, biting deep into the tender flesh behind the knees, hopping even higher from knee to thigh and crotch, there to inflict even greater misery. The parade rest position—legs spread apart, left arm locked behind the small of the back, right arm extended forward holding the rifle, chest out, head erect, chin in—gave every advantage to the insects and to the sun.

Keown watched silently and patiently, until he was certain that we had been driven nearly frantic. Smiling his most benevolent smile, he emerged from the shadows, ordered us to attention, and commenced his inspection. By that time we were beyond caring what he found wrong as he inspected, which is the attitude he set out to foment. He whipped us once again without ever touching us.

Our days on the range were far from disappointing. We had been briefed by returning members of other platoons on the more casual attitudes of range personnel. We were heartened to see that this was so. We found that communication with the coaches was far simpler than with the drill instructors. The coaches had a specialty to teach us. If there could be no conversation, no questions asked or answered, that specialty could not be learned. Therefore there was a dialogue, stilted though it might be.

Marksmanship was the most important phase of our training. Although we were not aware of it then, our scores on the range would have a pronounced influence on how our first year of service would go. The weapons proficiency page of the service record book was almost always the first one to be examined by the first sergeant and the commanding officer when a new man reported aboard. A man who had failed to qualify with his basic weapon was held immediately suspect.

In a Corps made up of riflemen, of what use was an individual who could not master the tools of the trade? For decades before I came into the service that had been the attitude. For decades in the future it would remain. Failure to qualify attached a stigma to one that could not be shrugged off or easily removed. One found himself ostracized by his fellow recruits, looked upon with disdain by the drill instructors. Pressure to produce a high percentage of qualified shooters was on everyone—us, the coaches, the range officers, the brigadier commanding. Marksmanship was all important. It was the bedrock upon which the Corps had built its reputation. The ability to deliver a heavy volume of *aimed* fire was what had given the Marines the edge over the Germans in the Great War. *That* fact was always before us. It was not to be forgotten. It was one of those things that set us apart, made us better than any other military organization.

We were not the highest scoring platoon on the range

that year, but we were not the worst. We were stuck in the upper third of shooters—not a bad place to be. The coaches knew their trade and taught it to us well. They made shooters out of most of the platoon and, more than that, they made it enjoyable. They taught us a lot about the weapon, taught it to us as if it were a living thing, which in a way it was—the U.S. rifle, cal. .30'06, Model 1903—the same rifle that had torn up the Germans so badly in France. As we learned about it, we learned a lot about ourselves.

If you were afraid of the '03—"that mean old bitch!" my father used to call it—that rifle would fight you to a standstill. It would kick you senseless; move you back four or five inches when you were firing prone, if you did not have your toes well dug in; knock you over backwards from the kneeling position. The coaches told us about these inherent dangers, demonstrated just how they could happen, and then pleaded with us, jibed at us, and irritated us into snuggling up to that hard and treacherous beast like two lovers on a cold night. The closer you got to her, the less terror you let her see, the better she treated you. Make no mistake, she wanted to be conquered and once you did that she spit those rounds right where you aimed them. The '03 was one of the most consistently accurate rifles ever produced anywhere in the world. But before we got her tamed, there were a number of bloody noses, black and blue lips, badly bent and broken thumbs, and bruises of assorted dark colors under our right eyes.

The thing we all worked the hardest for, watched for, prayed for, was to see the target come up for mark with a white spotter in it and a white disc showing. Bull's-eye. Five points for the shooter. It didn't matter whether the round struck dead center in the "V" ring or was trailing on the edge of the black. As long as that white disc came up, we were in the money, quite literally, for an expert drew five whole dollars a month extra pay, and a sharpshooter two. That white disc was sheer magic. It could do more for a man's ego than a strong drink. A heavy dose of the white disc—four or five consecutive exposures—might make a man so overconfident that he might blow the remainder of the string, might never see another white disc that day. On the other hand, if one was shooting poorly the sudden appearance of a white disc might just provide the impetus to pull one out of a slump. Keeping those white discs coming up was sort of like learning to drink—get used to that good feeling, but don't overdo it; cut it fine, just on the edge; and proceed with infinite caution.

Our platoon might not have made the highest in qualification percentage, but it did have some very high individual scores—scores that stood very close to existing range records—and we did have the highest ranking visitor to grace the island that year to watch us shoot.

The hottest marksman in the platoon was a lad from Florida named Johnson. Tall, heavy, handsome in sort of a girlish way, like myself he had become one of Keown's prime targets back on main station. Johnson had attended military school, where he had become a very proficient rifle shot. This proficiency was apparent to the coaches, to Kerr, and to the range officer. Johnson's success had already been reported to main station operations. Everyone had an eye on him. He looked like potential coach material, perhaps even a candidate for the rifle and pistol team. The range personnel were pulling hard for him, which seemed to make him even more adept.

On the day before record firing, Johnson's scores were phenomenal. The rest of us were caught up in the fever too. Although we could not match his scores, we were all catching sight of enough white discs to make us feel right good. At the 500-yard line, Johnson became the epitome of concentration, taking his time, making sure that every round he squeezed off counted. He had dropped only three points on the way back to the 500. A possible at 500 would put him high on the range standing. One by one the rest of us completed our ten rounds, cleared our pieces, got our scores from the coaches, and moved back to watch Johnson finish his string. He fired the sixth round. Down went the target. Up it came, a white disc floating in the center. Six in a row.

Movement to the rear of the line distracted us. A black staff car was pulling off the road, easing in towards the firing line. On each fender small flags fluttered—red background with two white stars. The sedan stopped. The driver opened the rear door, and two tall men stepped out. They walked toward Johnson's firing position.

On the line, Johnson loosed his seventh round. He was now the only one firing. Coaches clustered around him, urging him on. The target came up for mark. Seven straight bulls. He was riding high.

The two tall men approached the group surrounding Johnson. The range officer broke from the group and trotted to meet them. He guided them toward the line. As the three men moved, a coach or a drill instructor came to attention, saluted, and came forward to be recognized, to converse briefly with the two visitors. The party moved close up behind Johnson to observe the firing.

Johnson was unaware of the two visitors. His back toward them, he was totally immersed in the business of shooting. Exposed to our view were the two officers. One was very tall and slim, wearing the bursting bomb of a Marine gunner on the collar tab of his shirt, his head covered by the Stetson field hat decorated with the scarlet and gold officer's cord. The other officer was of equal height but stockier in build, wearing full summer service with blouse, the two silver stars of a major general pinned to each shoulder strap. On the blouse, just below his battle decorations which included the Navy Cross, was pinned the badge for distinguished marksmanship. My eyes opened wide. Who could *these* people be? I had never seen an officer of higher rank than second lieutenant. I wondered how Johnson would feel if he turned and saw all that rank standing there. It froze me, and I wasn't even close. Johnson fired. The target went down. The white disc flashed again. Eight consecutive bulls!

The group behind Johnson came alive, pointing, talking. We could see Johnson roll over onto his left elbow and glance back, could see him take a second fast look and roll back into the firing position. We felt for him, every one of us. What a kick in the head! Johnson fired again, this time much more quickly than with his previous rounds. The target disappeared. When it came back up, no white disc—a red disc and a black spotter—a four, just out at six o'clock. All that rank standing right behind him had broken his concentration, had spooked him, wound him up too tight.

Then we saw the Marine gunner touch Johnson on the shoulder, talking to him as he did so. Johnson loosened his sling, slipped the loop off his left arm and passed the rifle up to the gunner. Johnson's coach held out a round to the gunner. We could not hear a word. It was all pantomime. The gunner turned and offered the rifle to the general, who shook his head in the negative.

There was no sound all along the line. The attention of everyone was focused on that lean figure.

The gunner inserted the round into the chamber, closed the bolt, locked it down, and very deliberately placed the butt of Johnson's rifle in the hollow of his right shoulder. Then, holding the rifle in place with his left hand, he arched his right arm to the rear and swivelled it upwards, bringing it down and forward, grasping the small of the stock with his right hand, right elbow high and canted slightly upwards, in the exact manner that the coaches had taught us for the offhand position. He stood there in the morning sun, field hat tilted forward to cut down the glare, sling hanging below the rifle. He looked like a bronze marksmanship trophy—transfixed, no movement at all. The rifle spoke. The target went down. It came up rapidly. The white disc was in the center. The white spotter covered the center of the bull. At 500 yards, offhand, with no sling, a "V" ring! The target went down to be cleared.

Murmurs and exclamations of admiration for such magnificent shooting rippled along the line. The gunner handed the rifle back to Johnson, said something to him and then to the coach. The coach nodded, reached into a cartridge carton, and handed Johnson an extra round. Johnson slipped his arm into the sling loop, tightened down on the keeper, rolled up into the firing position, and held. He didn't hurry. The piece bucked back into his shoulder. The target went down. When it reappeared one could think that the gunner's round had never been cleared. Precisely the same. Disc centered for mark. Spotter in the center. Johnson looked back at the gunner, reloaded, held, fired, and sent another round through the same hole.

There was a grin, a huge smile on the general's face. He touched Johnson on the arm, patted him on the shoulder, said words that we could not discern. Then he spoke to the range officer, pointing to Johnson as he did so. A nod of affirmation, a salute given and returned, and the gunner and the general were moving towards the sedan, followed by an entourage of range personnel.

That night, between Johnson and Kerr we got it first hand. Johnson had gotten the shakes *bad* when he saw those two strangers behind him, had yanked the trigger instead of squeezing it, had bucked the round into the four ring. The gunner had told him to relax, that he and the general were sorry that they had spooked him, that he wanted to try Johnson's piece to see if there was any fault in it. Of course his shooting had guaranteed the rifle, so he had the coach give Johnson an extra round, one that could be scored if he bettered the four he had just shot. It was a fair thing to do, the gunner said, and there in front of the gunner and the general, with all that pressure, Johnson had proved himself.

The general? Oh, Kerr said, *that* was General Holcomb, already major general commandant for a full term, and now two years into his second—a team shot from the old days and a battalion commander in France during the Great War. The gunner? A man named Harris, who had shot with the best of them, military and civilian; a shooter of world renown, Olympic status yet!

None of us would ever forget that day in September when we saw our first general, nor would we ever forget that fantastic shot—offhand at 500 yards.

At 1400 we stood at parade rest. The final formation of the final day. Make this parade and we would all be free men—free to go back across the bridge, free of boot and all its restrictions.

The late October sun was on us, warm enough, but minus the deadly bite of August. A fitful breeze rustled the fronds of the palmettos lining the parade ground; toyed with the guidons, fluttering them spasmodically, and then letting them droop inertly.

We have never seen so many officers and senior NCOs in one place at the same time. We had seen a lieutenant on pay days, had been inspected once during the training cycle by another. Beyond that, with the exception of the major general commandant, we were virgins as far as officer contact was concerned. The sergeants, the corporals, and the Pfc's had brought us through all of our training.

To our right the post band stood ready. We had faintly heard the echoes of its music daily, but had never seen it. Its members were dressed in spotless, sun-bleached khakis. The bills of their barracks caps were jet black. They wore wide white belts with brass centerplates. Attached to their belts were scarlet music holders with golden fringes. The drumsticks were tasseled in crimson and gold, the brass instruments burnished until they too took on the look of precious metal. The drum major was tall and thin as a reed, his baton catching the rays of the sun on its gleaming head, its length wrapped in twisted cord of gold and scarlet. Looking at all that color, at the impeccable uniforms, filled me with a deep sense of humility, of pride, a sense of family which grew stronger as the minutes passed.

Orders rang out. The ceremony of the battalion parade was underway. The reports were made, the band trooped the line, the officers and NCOs were called front and center. The guidons dipped; the officers and NCOs saluted, about-faced, and returned. As they went up and back, no one stood out more than Keown. For this parade he had broken out his saltiest, seagoing khakis and an old-issue field scarf with square ends, heavily starched. His pistol holster shone like glass. His high-top dress shoes, even after the abrasion of the sandy parade ground, still glistened. We watched him prance and strut, his facings precise, his step jaunty, in perfect cadence, every movement exuding self-confidence. We watched him, remembering how he had looked that first day on the drill field. Nothing had changed. He had been without flaw then. He was even more flawless now.

Both Kerr and Keown had schooled us thoroughly on the Hymn. We were required to memorize the words, to recite them, to sing them. We were told that all Marines were required to stand when the Hymn was played, go into a brace, in uniform or out. We knew what the Hymn was all about, the message it carried, but we had not learned about the inner power that came from the Hymn, or what that power could accomplish.

The band played "Colonel Bogie" to get us moving, then dropped to the drum beat as we closed on the reviewing stand, where the brigadier commanding stood ready to accept our salutes. As we rendered them and passed on by, the band struck up "Semper Fidelis," turned out of line and marched back to face the reviewing stand, finished "Semper Fidelis," and let the drums carry the cadence.

We were safely by the brigadier now, sliding along, relieved of the tension that had been in us, moving in a happy daze. The drums rolled, and rolled again, and then a burst of music shattered the air. Those opening bars knocked us completely out of that daze, brought us back into focus instantly. The short hairs stood up on the back of my neck; my skin went cold, crawled, and prickled as the goose bumps rose on its surface. My back stiffened. That music struck at my ears, having the same effect as the sight of the globe and anchor—they were symbols of the Corps that I served. Others reacted the same way. I could see their heads come up, shoulders go back, could see a new spring in their marching step, one that had not been there moments before. Their chests went out, their chins were drawn back and tucked in as Keown had taught us. Elbows were locked tight against rib cages to ensure better rifle alignment. No person made us do this. No order was given. It was the witchery of that music casting its spell, filling our minds, our bodies. We could no more refuse to react to it than we could refuse to breathe. Oxygen and symbolism. Two elements the men of the Corps could not live without—the oxygen life-sustaining in the physical sense, the symbolism life-sustaining in the moral sense. Lost in the music of the Hymn, we breathed deeply of both.

And now we were clear of the parade ground, our final evolution nearly complete. Keown turned and marched backwards. We could hear the final bars of the Hymn in the distance. The music stopped. The drums took up the marching beat as the band moved off. Keown faced forward again, let us come up on him, and took his field position, centered on our flank. He picked up the beat from the drums and started calling cadence. It would be the last time we would ever hear his clear, vibrant chant, though its echoes would resound in memory on down the years, for as long as we might live.

There were still surprises in store for us before that last day was over, for me a most unpleasant one.

Mustered in the squadbay we waited for Keown to call us to his room to receive our orders. Since I was in the *A*'s I found it strange that my name had not been called early. Perhaps Keown had mislaid my orders. Then in the *B*'s he failed to call Bowles. Bowles and I exchanged questioning glances. Then Hardage, Johnson, and Motelewski were not called. Johnson had been selected for coaches' school, but what about the rest of us?

The platoon members returning from Keown's quarters were in different moods, some pleased, some doubtful, but all positive of one thing. They would be off the island by nightfall. The buses that would take them to the railhead were already outside the barracks.

As we waited impatiently to learn what was in store for us, the lucky members of the platoon were called outside by Kerr. Down the ladder they clomped. On the opposite end of the squadbay we heard footsteps coming up the ladder. A driver, with transportation to take Johnson and his gear to the range.

Keown entered the squadbay, four sets of orders under his arm. He gave us that sardonic smile he always displayed when the knife was about to go in. "*Special* orders for you lads. They want you to stay on the island a while longer. Motelewski, artillery—to the cannon cockers. Sand blower to Maintenance Company. Hardage and Bowles to Headquarters Company. I *know* that you are going to enjoy the island life even more as permanent personnel. Better get your gear together and start moving. You will have to hike it to the main station!" He passed out the orders, chuckling to himself as we ruefully accepted; spun on his heel; and headed back to his room. He had much to do. In less than forty-eight hours he would pick up another platoon for training.

Surprised? Talk about a good kick in the crotch! It *hurt!* All of the anticipation, the euphoria, the happy glow that had started that day vanished abruptly. Trapped again, still on the godforsaken island! We said nothing, could say nothing. We put on our packs and rifle belts, slung our rifles, heaved our seabags up onto our shoulders, and went down the ladder. We looked wearily towards the red brick barracks, some thousand yards away, that would be our new home, and trudged off towards them. We did not look back or stop moving until we reached them.

Weeks later my section chief told me why I had been selected to remain on the island. During my initial recruitment I had listed four years of draftsmanship as my specialty. How was I to know that prior to my enlistment extensive construction had been approved for the island? How was I to know that Maintenance Company needed draftsmen and blueprint makers to support that construction? How was I to know that Headquarters Battalion personnel would be screening service record books looking for my specialty? That service record book could trip you up so easily, and more than once, as I would learn before my time in the Corps was over.

In some circles, it does not pay to advertise.

And now, until the next retelling, those days in the platoon were over. We came back to reality. The day was almost at an end. Bellies distended from too much Coke and too many peanuts, we made one last head call and went outside. The sun was low, long shadows starting to crisscross the area. Our living spaces were in different barracks, but there was a common approach, so we stayed together.

As we closed on the living spaces we noticed a strange thing. There were no troopers outside, even though it was almost time for evening chow. And there was yet another strange thing. Radios were blaring loudly from every deck, but there was no music. Many of the sets had been moved to the windows for better reception. Startling, unbelievable words came floating down to us from the radios, filling us with consternation as the meaning of the words became clear. "Pearl Harbor has been attacked by Japanese air units. Part of the Pacific Fleet has been destroyed!" A pause and then again the same voice. "It is reported that Manila has been bombed and that Clark Airfield is under enemy air attack. Midway and Johnson Islands have been struck. The Japanese air attack continues!"

It was inconceivable. We stared at each other blankly, stunned. Like all other Americans growing up in the late thirties and early forties, we had been fed the national theme—the Japanese were stumpy, bow-legged, half-blind. They could not shoot; their ships were made from melted-down American beer cans; their aircraft, made of wood and cloth, without armor or armament, had no striking power. Yet in the span of those few hours that we had whiled away in nostalgia, these same inferior people, with their substandard war machinery, had devastated major United States naval and air bases.

Suddenly we were no longer the carefree, salty Marines of a few hours ago. We had been reduced to the least common denominator—three well-disciplined young men, highly trained in the basics of their trade, but totally ignorant of the ways of combat—three youngsters looking their first war straight in the face. The fact of our woeful inadequacy came down on us like a thunderbolt. We could forget the relative rigors of boot camp for a long time. Wordlessly we turned from each other and raced into the barracks to report to our section chiefs.

It was the afternoon of Sunday, the seventh of December, 1941. On that day we had completed just less than four months in the Corps.

We should not have become so agitated. The United States had been attacked, had been dealt a most humiliating blow, but in spite of that, in spite of the long-term machinations of the British prime minister and the president of the United States to commit the country to open warfare in Europe, the country was unable to do battle with anyone, anywhere, except with oratory. That was a lesson well-learned by me in the winter of 1941–1942, a lesson that I would rather not have learned, but one which I would relearn over the years and through the other battles yet to be fought. The United States had given up its belief that eternal vigilance was the price of freedom; had brought itself to believe that it was not necessary to be capable of instant retaliation; that preemptive action never must be taken, no matter what the provocation; that the enemy always must be allowed to have his chance to blow us over the edge of the earth and then hope that Divine Providence would help us scramble back on in time to fight the winning round.

Following President Franklin Roosevelt's stirring oration concerning that day of infamy, and his formal declaration that henceforth circumstances would preclude the successful conclusion of scrap-metal contracts between American businessmen and the empire of Japan, things on the island eased back to just about normal routine. Two provisional rifle companies had been formed from Headquarters Battalion and rushed north into the wilds of Quantico, Virginia, and the recruit input surged upward dramatically. Beyond those two things one must stretch his imagination to believe that a state of war existed.

December passed. I caught the duty on Christmas Eve and New Year's Eve. A new man on the duty roster always caught the duty on the year-end holidays. Still, it was better than sitting around the barracks hating yourself, remembering those special days of childhood.

I learned a lot in those days and nights at the main station, more than I would have admitted then, but knowledge that I fully recognize now. The huge squadbays. The spotless mess hall. It was all so different from what we had known in the recruit area that one could hardly believe that both areas existed on the same island. To be sure, the troops were still double-decked in the squadbays, but the distance between bunks was far greater—more room to breathe, more elbow room.

In those brick barracks a young private was exposed to much of the earthiness of Marine Corps life. With beer but a nickel a throw in the slop-chute and only a few pennies more on the outside, there were still those in the barracks who craved a stronger, swifter-acting libation. Aqua Velva, strained through a loaf of post bakery bread, provided a nectar at once strong in impact upon the senses and economical in procurement. Between paydays the escapist desires of some of the oft-promoted, quickly demoted corporals, a few with more than sixteen years of service, were satisfied in this manner. Status to them was a relative thing, and responsibility a burden too heavy to bear. Enough Aqua Velva, belted down in a secure area of the squadbay, promised instant relief and release without the men ever having to leave the safe haven of the barracks.

It was in the evenings that I was taught the lore of the Marine Corps. The "shanachies" of old Ireland had nothing on those of the Corps, I can assure you. Sea tales and snow jobs were told nightly until lights out. There was always an audience. We made no money to speak of, so between paydays the barracks were full. In the squadbays were Marines who had served in the Philippines, San Domingo, Haiti, Nicaragua, and on the old China Station. There were many who had served aboard the cruisers, the carriers, and the

battlewagons. There was even one buck sergeant who had
come in for the First World War, his tunic decorated with
ribbons of the Purple Heart and the Victory Medal with four
engagement devices upon it. Old "Gabby" never spoke of his
wartime service, but after an evening at the NCO Club he
would return to the barracks and, before the bull session was
over, would invariably turn out his own version of the flight of
the flying fish—standing precariously balanced on the toes of
one foot, the other leg extended to the rear and held very
high, his head and neck stretched forward, his arms flailing
the air in a grotesque parody of the little fish that leap, skitter,
and fly alongside the vessels that transport the Marines.

I listened to the sea tales, digested them, put the best of
them away in my mind for future recital, watched the camaraderie of the old salts as I sat hunched on the edge of a
locker box, if anyone allowed me that liberty; more often
than not I sat on the tiled deck, legs pulled up tight to form a
rest for my chin. The storytellers all had me snowed. I was
enchanted by what they said and how they said it, by the
stories that they wove. I was envious, wondering if I should
ever have the good fortune to visit those distant stations, to
sail on those ships of war, to share those escapades described
with such animation and relish by the old-timers.

It was in the evenings, too, that I first saw the nonrated
Marines preparing themselves to go up for promotion to
corporal, the corporals studying to go up for sergeant. All of
them were intent on mastering the pages of the handbook,
the old Red Book, the question-and-answer manual cleverly
devised by two senior Marine officers who understood well
the needs of the leathernecks of that day, a book that could
be learned by heart, memorized, and re-memorized until it
was virtually impossible *not* to know the answer to every
question in that book. Every question of the written exam
was taken from that book, every question of the oral exam
based upon its contents. There remained only the ability to
give commands, drill a platoon satisfactorily, to exhibit command presence. Admitting to myself that my chances were as
good for promotion as any of my bunk mates, I, too, took up
the practice of devoting a portion of each evening to study.

During recruit training all of us had heard the morning
and the daytime bugle calls—loud, strident, demanding—

portending movement of one sort or another. The late evening calls, heard vaguely through a fog of perpetual fatigue, never had been fully appreciated. In those main station barracks I heard them really for the first time, and they became a part of the memories of the Corps that I would savor always—the haunting beauty of tattoo, the perpetual gentleness, the infinite sadness of taps sounded each night outside the brick barracks. Each note true and steady, every tone emerging in perfection, to be echoed and chorused the length and breadth of the main station; each bugler delaying momentarily before taking up the call; the sound overlapping, swelling, spreading like an ever-widening ripple, washing over the entire island, signifying the closing of another day, the respite, the solitude of another night.

January passed. February arrived and things finally started breaking my way. I made the corporal's list, and about the same time a letter came down from Washington inviting qualified personnel to apply for parachute jump training at the Parachute Training Center, Naval Air Station, Lakehurst, New Jersey. Just as soon as my warrant had been issued, my Pfc stripes pulled, and my corporal stripes sewn on my uniforms, I requested an audience with the company commander, to enlist his aid in getting a jump training assignment.

He cheerfully approved my request and included a written recommendation to help me along the way. I underwent a modified flight physical and passed all the requirements, including depth perception, but came up one quarter of an inch short of the specified height requirement. A friendly corpsman blithely brought me up to standard with a minor forgery on my physical examination papers, and my request went on up to Headquarters, U.S. Marine Corps. Almost by return mail, orders for Lakehurst arrived.

2

The Naval Air Station

Parris Island had been set apart physically from human habitation, which contributed greatly towards the monastic effect. The Naval Air Station at Lakehurst was located in the center of the lush New Jersey countryside, surrounded by some of the more elegant resort towns of the state, yet as we approached the main gate of the station, the same feeling of desolation so prevalent on the island swept over us. The terrain upon which the station was built was a flat tableland. Just inside the gate rose the gaunt, unadorned, massive dirigible hangars that once had housed the *Hindenberg*. They were sharply outlined against the February sky, adding to an already pervasive illusion of remoteness. A ten-foot-high, chain-link fence, topped with barbed wire, marked the station limits, completing an image of incarceration. A layer of gray clouds hung low overhead, blotting out the feeble rays of the winter sun. There was a decided difference in temperature between the Garden State and the Palmetto State. It was *cold* at Lakehurst.

When we checked in at the security detachment, we became aware of another chill, one not attributable to weather or temperature. Hostility towards us was openly manifested. It had nothing to do with the training we were about to undergo, but rather with the fact that our position entitled us to incentive pay—corporals on jump status drew more cash each month than a line platoon sergeant. People tend to get uptight where money is concerned. Fifty extra dollars a month was a lot of loot back in 1942.

The Parachute Training Detachment's trainee squadbay brought back memories of the rifle range barracks at Parris Island—much newer, tile decks and bulkheads instead of rotting wood, but no wall lockers. Seabag racks, clothing racks, and foot lockers. Bunks double-decked and even closer together than on the island. There was a reason for the crush. Much to our surprise, and subsequently to our dismay, we discovered that we were not the only platoon under instruction. Due to the miserable winter weather, the platoon ahead of us had been unable to complete their live jumps and would remain aboard until the weather improved and their jumps could be executed.

The people in that platoon had been under instruction too long. They wanted no more calisthenics, no more long-distance runs, no more parachute packing, no more Navy mess hall. They wanted to finish jumping, pin on their wings, and leave. Since they could not actively vent their spleen on the instructors, they took out all of their unhappiness on us. No band of brothers here! No helpful hints on the training. Aloofness. Sarcasm. Scorn. Spite of the most bitter variety. All of this would vanish, good friends would be made, brotherhood would return with the advent of good flying weather and the arrival of the jump aircraft from Quantico, but until then we were in a hell of a position, caught in a cross fire between two enemy forces—the instructors and the members of Platoon 14.

Once our platoon had been mustered and formed into provisional squads, we were made aware of another disturbing fact. We were all, regardless of rank or time in service, right back in the recruit game again, back to the zero point, worth nothing.

"You will hang up your stripes when you join the detachment. They will stay hung up until the day you leave. *If* and when you graduate, your rank will be returned. During

your training you will be identified by the stencilled last
names on your dungaree jackets. You will respond to the
instructors when that name is called—understood?"

The morning after our arrival the field music of the day
showed us exactly how the security detachment felt about us.
At 0545 sharp, he stepped noiselessly through the swinging
entrance doors of the upper deck squadbay and into the
overcrowded living space. With rapt attention to every note
he sounded first call, and then slipped back out. In the
confines of the squadbay the notes of the bugle were ear-
shattering, nerve-jangling. We groaned, twisted, and turned
about on our narrow racks, unwilling to accept the birth of
another day.

In strange surroundings, with our clothing and gear not
properly secured, we floundered, were clumsy, slower than
we needed to be. It was the first morning and the last that our
platoon ever would sleep in until 0545. From then on we
would greet the day much earlier.

On that day we learned other things, mainly about the
course of instruction. The training was divided into three
segments—physical conditioning and parachute packing
conducted at the station, tower training at Hightstown, and
live jumps from aircraft over the station airfield. Built into the
course was a detachment-manufactured handicap, a ten-de-
merit system, applied against all students, commissioned
and enlisted alike. Ten demerits, awarded for any reason,
entitled a student to a set of orders to the 1st Marine Division
at New River, North Carolina; a station wagon ride to Whit-
ings; and a free train ride south on the Seaboard Line. Pack
your gear and go!

The detachment commanding officer, when my platoon
went through training, was a naval aviator with the rank of
major. In the beginning, and for years to come, there was
always a question in the minds of Marine organizational
planners as to where parachutists should be—with aviation,
where the aircraft were, or with ground troops from which
the manpower came. In the early days a naval aviator ran the
business. Along with command and administrative duties, he
often flew the aircraft for the indoctrination flight and for the
live jump segment of the training. He was seconded by a
ground officer, a line captain. The operations officer was

likewise a ground officer, commissioned from corporal and now a line captain. Logistics were handled by ground and supply types and a ground first lieutenant was the parachute officer. We learned to know all of these individuals during the course of the instruction, would grow to know them better in the battalions later on. There was one on the staff who we never might know well at all, but one who we never would forget, for he left his mark, his brand, upon all of us. The senior outside instructor. Outside, as opposed to rigging, classroom work, and the like.

Though he might have given that impression, he was not the highest ranking man in the detachment nor was he the best educated. He was, as we soon would observe, the most dynamic, nit-picking, dedicated man on board. He exercised complete control over every student, over every instructor under his supervision. His leadership was by example. Nothing was asked of a student that he could not do in a superior manner himself. He was unaware of the word patience, stayed wound up tight from before dawn until after darkness, feeding on a diet of nervous energy. He wanted everything *right*. Right *now!*

We knew him first as a gunnery sergeant and few weeks later as a marine gunner. He was tall, long-legged, not carrying an extra ounce of flesh. He wore a pencil-thin mustache, had his hair trimmed close and high on the sides and the back of his neck. His eyes were those of a falcon, never still, piercing, seeking always to find a student in error, ready to pounce, to sink his talons into his prey. He was in excellent physical condition and pushed himself to the limit. Six years older than the average age of the platoon members, he made it a point to run us into the ground regularly, loping backwards and shouting cadence at the top of his voice as he wore us down.

No one could doubt that he knew his business, that he took great pride in that fact. His junior instructors had been indoctrinated thoroughly in his ways. They knew what he wanted from them. They transmitted those wants to us with maximum speed and efficiency. His seniors deferred to him, trusted him implicitly, and let him run the training without undue interference. Hershel Don Carlos Blasingame. As a gunnery sergeant he had been a supreme being to us. As a

Marine gunner he became just a little lower than the angels, just a little higher than Lucifer himself. Within the inner circles of his acquaintances he was called "Cheesey." To this day I never have dared to ask why.

The first two weeks of training contained more than just a touch of hell. The daily schedule was without variation. The first afternoon, after gently introducing us to calisthenics done in the Lakehurst manner, Cheesey elected to test-run the platoon. The choppy, short-stride lock step was new to all of us. We did not know how to breathe correctly, how to slap our boots down on the pavement to aid in maintaining cadence, or how to keep interval. We pulled together, jamming the formation, and then stretched apart. Cheesey, running backwards, watched us with a sneer of contempt clearly mirrored on his face. He shook his head in derision and ordered us to run at maximum speed back to the barracks. Once there he halted us and, in terms terse and menacing, informed us, *"I* don't like the way you people run! You have just bought yourself a new reveille. I want you outside every morning at 0400, ready to run to the main gate and back. *Every* morning! *Dismissed!"*

The days followed a general pattern. Back from the main gate run, it was shave, shower, police call, and change into greens without blouse for morning chow. At 0800 to parachute loft for instruction in parachute nomenclature, functioning, and packing classes. No student could touch a parachute until he had been inspected by Cheesey or one of his delegates. Inspection for a clean shave. Inspection of uniforms. Our shirts must be pressed with military creases front and rear, collar wings pressed flat, with a battle bar beneath the knot of the field scarf holding them together. Trouser belts inspected for cleanliness. Belt tips and buckles inspected for shine. Inspection of hands, palms up, palms down. No *dirty* fingernails. No *long* fingernails. It made one feel like a grade school boy being checked out by his parents just prior to the arrival of special guests. Trouser legs pulled up one at time so that the shine of boot uppers could be checked. If we passed inspection we could pack parachutes. If we failed, it was good for a demerit and reinspection after the close of working hours.

Noon chow; then at 1300, in full greens, rifles, rifle belts, and bayonets, it was outside for troop inspection and close-order drill. Upon completion of drill, back inside, secure weapons and equipment, change into dungarees, and back outside for tumbling and harness drill. Then inside once again, to the barracks basement for weapons instruction. Marine Corps General Order Number 10 said that weapons instruction would be given daily everywhere in the Marine Corps, no matter how specialized one might become. Then back outside for calisthenics and the afternoon run.

The calisthenics must have been developed especially for us, designed, I am positive, to ensure the highest degree of physical discomfort. Little gems like hopping up and down on one foot, in cadence, until the calf of the leg became one huge knotted tendon. Four-count deep knee bends, repeated in cadence, subject to a halt in count at any given part of the sequence—halts that exerted so much pressure on the thighs and calves that one's legs would shiver and shudder involuntarily, might even refuse reaction of any kind, in which case the trainee might fall over or remain locked in place, halfway up or down. The number of repetitions increased daily in increments thought suitable by Cheesey.

Cheesey allowed no one but himself to supervise the afternoon runs. He made each of them a memorable event. The student runs started at a half-mile, the goal to be five miles or better, the distance to increase every day. Since Cheesey was a tall man and needed to stretch his legs to run comfortably, he placed the taller students at the head of the column to pace him. Those of lesser height were placed in a graduated manner towards the rear of the platoon. Stumpy students like myself ran twice as far, twice as fast, just trying to keep up with the longer strides of the tall men. If we started to drop back, Cheesey had a sure cure. The assistant instructors would come alongside, step directly into position to the rear of the laggards, and let the toes of their boots come down on the heels of the student runners.

There was *no* falling out on the runs. We ran until we collapsed, and even that was not effort enough, for then Cheesey would demand that the platoon run around the fallen man until he had rejoined the ranks. The longer he stayed down, the longer we ran and the more distance we covered until we were as angry with him as Cheesey was.

From time to time Cheesey would endear himself to the casualty by having the platoon run directly over him as he lay panting and vomiting on the ground. If anyone tried to step *over* the victim instead of *on* him, Cheesey would shout, "NO! NO! God damn it! Run straight onto the sorry bastard! That will force him up. If you don't I will have *you* down there!"

Usually the fallen warrior would drag himself out of the way of the oncoming herd after the stampede had hit him, lurch to his feet, and join up rather than be trampled into the sand and gravel at the edge of the main service runway. Many of us learned to finish those runs half-conscious, mouths dry and full of fuzz, eyes filled with tears of sweat and frustration, hearts banging like bass drums, knees aching, thighs as hard as stone, noses and cheeks numb from sheer lack of oxygen, for we knew that if we ever fell out, it was the beginning of the end. The instructors and particularly Cheesey never would let up on you after that. We weren't guessing about that. Some of the platoon members who had fallen out were already in New River.

The most memorable event of our early training was the indoctrination flight. After a week at the station, the weather cleared and a DC-3 was flown up from Quantico to accommodate the remaining jumps of the 14th Platoon and to provide us with our first military airborne experience.

The indoctrination flight accomplished many things. It was a stress device, one that gave the instructors a close look at the airborne reactions of the individual student, and provided an opportunity for the student to decide rapidly if further airborne training was his desire. The flight itself was very simple—an approach over the service runway of the station, which served as a drop zone for student jumps, from several directions in order to orient the student from the air and to familiarize him with the drop zone. Each student was scheduled for two runs, one kneeling on the aircraft deck in the door, the other standing in the open door.

The morning of the flight we were on the field at 0600. It was March and still very cold. We shivered; our teeth chattered. The platoon was broken down into the eleven-man sticks utilized by jumpers at Lakehurst.

Our stick was airborne. The aircraft shuddered and

bucked in the wind, the sound of the port-side engine reverberating, echoing inside the fuselage. We huddled deeply into the canvas of the bucket seats, stretching them downward to the limit of the fabric. The cold, as well as the engine noise, seeped through the open cargo door, negating for all practical purposes the heating system of the aircraft. We looked at each other, examined the interior of the plane, watched the swaying of the anchor cable. We looked at the open door, then at Cheesey and the assistant jumpmaster, a salty gunnery sergeant by the name of Ettenborough. Cheesey wore a leather aviator's helmet with chin strap and a leather cup over his chin. Sergeant Ettenborough wore then, and on every flight, a green fore-and-aft cap. How it stayed on was his secret alone. Both jumpmasters wore a quick attachable parachute harness, but no parachutes.

We wore green cloth helmets and quick attachable parachute harnesses.

The aircraft banked slightly to the left, turned, and commenced its run. Three students already had gone to the door, had performed there as instructed, and, speechless, had returned to their seats. Number four coming up. ME! Cheesey dropped to his knees with his elbows on the deck, crouched in the door watching the drop zone. He looked up, nodded his head to Ettenborough, and motioned me to the rear of the plane. I went aft, struggling to maintain my balance. Ettenborough met me, snapped a length of safety line into the QAC harness, and led me to a position to the rear of Cheesey. The other end of my safety line already had been secured to an anchor point in the deck. Once in position I was pushed down onto my knees until I was alongside Cheesey.

He turned towards me and pointed downwards. The wind tore at his face, distorting it, giving him the look of an angry gargoyle. I peered down carefully. I never had been in a large aircraft before and did not know *what* to expect. We were just a few seconds out from the station. I saw the V of the service runway, the X of the secondary. On my left the barracks area suddenly came into view and quickly disappeared. To my right, the dirigible hangars loomed. It was like watching a film. I was taken in by the panorama below, unafraid except when the aircraft skittered and yawed. I was absorbed in what I saw, could not take my eyes from it. The aircraft, moving at a speed of 90 knots, seemed to be standing still, the earth rushing past it. Then we were again beyond the station limits, over the town of Lakehurst, and turning for a second run.

Cheesey motioned for me to move to the right, to stand alongside Ettenborough. I stood, hastily backed away from the door opening, and crowded in on Ettenborough. Cheesey arose and took his initial station, just to the rear of the cargo door opening. The aircraft turned again. Once more Cheesey dropped to his knees for a look, but this time stood quickly and motioned me into the door.

This was a different feeling! It seemed to me that the door opening had grown perceptibly larger. I looked down, could see the aluminum and plywood decking, could see my safety line securely anchored. I felt Ettenborough's hand push me forward. I looked at Cheesey, who over the roar of the wind and noise shouted, "Move up! Move up!" I locked eyeballs with him, hoping for some kind of reprieve. I didn't move an inch. Cheesey reached out, grasped the left side of my QAC harness, and yanked, *hard!* I jerked forward, not willingly. Ettenborough's hand became more alive, pushing, prodding with greater force. I started to perspire in spite of the cold. I glanced down again and saw that the pushing and yanking had placed my feet close to the lip of the door sill. I looked down and outside the aircraft. We were coming up on the runways again. Another push from the rear, another pull from the left, and the upper portion of my body catapulted through the door opening. The slipstream from the port-side engine slammed against my head and torso, tearing the breath from me. My cheeks fluttered violently and uncontrollably. My eyes watered. As I hung suspended in the opening I noticed that the pressure at the small of my back had disappeared. I felt instead the left hand of Ettenborough locked tightly to the right side of my harness, equalizing the pressure that Cheesey was exerting from the left. I turned my eyes toward Ettenborough, not daring to look at Cheesey, straight into the prop blast, which tore my mouth wide open. In my distorted vision I could see Ettenborough grin and felt a short, encouraging tug on his side of the harness. I reversed the direction of my head, mustering the courage to look at Cheesey. He did not smile, but curtly nodded his head in condescension. His benediction filled me with power. My fear of him gave me added strength. I faced front, took a deep breath, placed both feet on the very edge of the sill, and hung out as far as the jumpmasters would allow. I looked down, confidence building. I knew surely now that I would not fall, that the safety line would hold, that the jumpmasters would not turn me loose. The old saying about rape flashed through my mind—when it is inevitable, relax and enjoy it. At 1,200 feet, hanging out of the aircraft at thirty degrees, I did just that.

The equipment in tower training for Army and Marine Corps parachutists had been born of a common mother—the New York World's Fair of 1939. The same equipment that gave civilians their kick at the fair—the captive towers and the flyaways—were utilized with certain modifications to give student parachutists the sensation of height, a feel for controlled and uncontrolled falls from a height, and to teach parachute canopy control during descent. The Army, which entertained no doubts about the continuance of parachute training, went full tilt into the program and at Fort Benning erected towers 250 feet high. The Marine Corps, unsure of the duration of its own program and operating as usual on a shoestring, leased two of the World's Fair towers, one captive, one flyaway, which had been moved to Hightstown, New Jersey, by an enterprising civilian parachute rigger. The towers were 125 feet high. Better than no towers at all, one might comment, but try a couple of descents from such a short drop and you might change your mind!

Tower training at Hightstown was broken down into two major phases, captive tower drills and flyaway tower exercises. On the captive tower there was no real canopy. We were first raised into the heavens on a buddy seat—two of us strapped together into a swaying swing seat very similar to the old-fashioned porch swings of our childhood—and dropped earthward without warning. This was called orientation, a word very popular in parachute parlance. Then we went on to individual drills, during which we were strapped into a parachute harness for training which stressed landing attitudes. We were lifted 125 feet and dropped, sliding down control cables which allowed us to rush towards the earth. We knew that the buddy seats would be snubbed off inches above the ground just before our backs were certain to be broken, knew that on the individual descents we would be stopped just as our toes hit the landing pad; but the sickening, elevator-drop sensation of falling, of speeding downwards towards certain doom, was hard to shake, even after repeated drops.

On the flyaway it was quite another set of circumstances. Here a canopy was used, attached by releasable rings to a wide circular frame of steel. In the initial drills, the student was raised and was allowed to hang on, receiving instructions from the ground before being tripped off. Later he was tripped off without warning, with instructions shouted up to him as he fell. With only 125 feet of air space in which to execute the orders given, there were many mistakes, many demerits.

Sandwiched in between captive and flyaway tower training was a device of pure deviltry. It separated the men from the boys, the courageous from the faint of heart, sent a lot of people down the Seaboard Line to New River. The beauty of this device was the fact that by failing to complete the drill the student gave himself the demerits. It was that simple. Either he did or he didn't. Not one of the instructors was about to coax him, to try to get him through.

I hung suspended about six feet off the ground, my legs trussed together with harness webbing, my head down, my arms crossed over my chest, my right hand next to the pull-ring pocket. The early afternoon sun beat down on my back, my buttocks, and my legs as I hung like a dead game bird on a hook.

Few animals, man included, like to be tied up so that movement is impossible. Few humans really enjoy being hung in the air, head down, at twenty degrees from the horizontal. Even fewer humans enjoy a combination of the two, and at the same time find themselves attached to a wire cable, ready to be lifted fifty feet above the ground. No, none of this is in the nature of man, yet this is the circumstance in which I now found myself.

The reason for all this? It had more than psychological ramifications. The parachute then in service for Marine trainees was designated a dual-purpose parachute. Its canopy was twenty-eight feet in diameter. It opened by means of a pilot chute pulling it out of the container once the rip cord had been activated. It was called dual purpose because it could be used for either static line or free-fall jumps. The parachute could be activated by either of two parallel rip cord systems, and was routinely packed utilizing both rip cords. The pull ring for the manual rip cord was secured in a pocket on the harness, just down from the jumper's left shoulder. In case of a static line rip cord failure, we were taught that our first immediate corrective action was to yank this pull ring in an effort to activate the main canopy before resorting to the reserve parachute.

This whole drill centered around that manual rip cord pull ring. The student must locate it, pull it, drop the roughly thirteen feet of the length of a standard static line, and recover. During the fall, the student's body attitude quickly would change from a head down, nearly horizontal one to a position approximating that of a live jump after the parachute had deployed—feet down, nearly vertical. Introduction to the feel of opening shock was made doubly interesting, for when the end of the static line was reached, the fall would be terminated abruptly, with much of the sudden jolt hitting the student where the tightly snapped leg straps ran between his legs. The remainder of the jarring shock would be taken up across the chest and shoulders, forcing the student into at least one good, solid uncontrolled swing fore and aft before the movement stopped. This drill was well calculated to pop a testicle or snap a neck, or both, if a student was not careful about where and how he had stowed the family jewels or just how he held his head.

There was one other noninstructional requirement to complete this drill satisfactorily. One had to be sure to retain the pull ring after it had been yanked. If the student came to the ground without it, he was required to buy beer for the instructor staff—a light sentence indeed, for Cheesey well might have chosen the assessment of demerits instead.

Cheesey stood in front of me, silent. Because of the angle of suspension and the fact that he was very tall, I could not see his face, just his chest and lower torso. Two out of the ten students that had preceded me into the straight jacket had failed to pull and had to be brought down. Cheesey was fuming. He wanted no more refusals of any kind. This would be the final class instructed at Lakehurst, and he didn't want to close it out with a bunch of losers to his credit. He grabbed me by the chin and forced my head up until he could look into my bulging, straining eyes. "And what about *you,* Yankee? Are you going up there and freeze? When you hear me yell 'PULL' you *pull!* You hear me, lad?" He removed his hand and my head flopped down again.

Cheesey spun away from me and shouted, "Take him up! Take him up!"

The cable drum motor started to hum, the slack in the wire cable straightened, and my upward movement commenced. Nothing to do now except breathe as deeply as possible, remain as calm as the situation would permit, continue to exist until I reached drop altitude. As the height increased, so did my angle of view. I could see the other members of the platoon, faces upturned. I felt that every one of them was judging me now, even more critically than the instructors. The cable now had lifted me high enough that I could see out over the countryside. I had entertained this view previously, but never from this altitude. I could observe the ubiquitous tourists, who habitually stopped along the highway to watch our training.

I came back to reality with a start! There was no noise. The drum cable had stopped. I was not moving, except for a slight sway. Deadly, deathly silence crowded in on me. Then it hit me! My time had come. My heart changed from an almost imperceptible flutter to a rapid hammering. My chest seemed about to explode. Then, over the magnified heartbeats, an even more fearful sound. "Are you ready, lad? Are you *ready?*" The voice of Cheesey came up at me, beat against my ears like the crash of cymbals.

My throat was dry, constricted. My right hand pawed frantically for the pull ring. In my excitement I passed right over it. I fumbled again, this time found it. I forced my fingers to slide down over the handle, forced my thumb to overlap, to complete the grip. Everything about previous tower training had been automatic, under the control of another person. But *this!* The tower would make no decision for me. No instructor would make it. *I* would control *this* drop. No backing off. No escape!

I looked down at Cheesey, gulped, swallowed hard, and croaked out "Ready, Sir!"

About that time the instructors began their taunts. "A case of beer for us, sand blower? A case of Bud for the troopers?"

Cheesey joined in the laughter. "Yeah, we have got us one for sure! *If* we can get him down at all!"

The jeers of the instructors, echoed by Cheesey, had been enough to spark me into action, to drive out fear with anger, to hunger for self-respect. When I heard the command to pull, I closed both eyes and pulled directly across my chest from left to right. I had that damned pull ring clutched securely, and when I brought my right arm back across my chest, I shoved it inside my dungaree jacket, up against my rib cage. There was no feeling as the line payed out, no sense of falling. Nothing. I opened my eyes in time to see the open mouths of the students, the smiles of the instructors. I felt the metal of the chest strap bite hard against bone, yanking me out of the head-down attitude, slamming me upright. Almost simultaneously I felt both leg straps cutting into my crotch, tearing at the inner tendons of my upper thighs, the hardware digging into the tender skin of my belly. With downward movement terminated, my body weight threw me forward and then back, with neck-snapping acceleration. Then all movement stopped. I hung like a beef carcass, slowly swaying, beaten for the moment by the violence of the opening shock, the overpowering fatigue brought about by the extreme psychological pressures I had borne.

I heard a familiar sound. The engine in the drum house had started up again. I felt downward movement, reached inside my jacket to be positive, found the smooth metal pull ring. I withdrew my hand and reached high on the risers with both hands to simulate a landing position. My toes touched the ground. The instructors moved into unstrap the wide webbing that had secured my legs, their eyes probing for the sight of the pull ring. I bent over to unsnap my leg straps. Seeing no pull ring, the instructors became animated again, convinced that I had dropped it.

"All right, recruit! Show us the pull ring or show us the color of your money! We need a few more cases if we are going to have a blast! Stand clear! Let's get another one in the air!"

I stepped clear, the weightless fall, the opening shock

still vivid in my mind. Suddenly I felt very good. I turned back to the instructors, reached inside my jacket with my right hand, withdrew the pull ring, and held it aloft for all to see. I felt no triumph, just a sense of deliverance. I would not have to go back up there again, would not have to face myself in the narrow alleys of fear again, would receive no demerits. These people, by insult, innuendo, derision, and scorn had saved me from myself, had driven me to perform successfully, my desire for their approbation stronger, more forceful than the terror that had assailed me.

Breakfast at 0500. Dungarees, jump boots, cloth helmets. Very little small talk at the tables. Each of us lost in our own private thoughts. Very little food consumed. No room for it in stomachs already filled with the flopping and fluttering of a thousand butterfly wings. Jump week. The first day. The first long step out into the unknown.

At 0545 we lined up to be inspected and draw parachutes. The main was a parachute that we had packed personally. The reserve, rigger-packed. If our main should fail, we must depend upon a reserve packed by an unknown. A man's life is of some import to him. It was not that we did not trust the riggers, it just was better all around if one's own main activated. *Complete* confidence in our equipment and in the ability of another to prepare it correctly had not been firmly established yet in our minds, an attitude destined to change very rapidly when we reached one of the parachute battalions, where *all* parachutes were rigger-packed.

The second stick was chuted up and standing by. We stood with our backs to the rising sun, its warmth lapping along our legs, buttocks, and arms. Far out, just as a speck in the sky, the jump aircraft was making its approach. No sound at first, then a whine, a hum, a steady drone as it closed on the drop zone. A roar of engines as it passed over the runways at one thousand feet. Out of the port door a black speck, closely followed by ten others. An interval as the eleven main canopies filled, the twenty-eight-foot canopies popping and snapping in the cool morning air. Then three more black dots plunged from the aircraft—the riggers who would aid in the retrieval of equipment and students, their parachutes opening almost simultaneously. Not a malfunction in the equipment of the fourteen jumpers. Every man hanging safely below the mains. We craned our necks to watch the jumpers.

When the aircraft had landed we were called to attention. With arms raised overhead, palms behind our necks, we were given our final rigger check. Inspection was signified complete by the rigger unhooking the static line snap and passing it forward over the right shoulder of the student. Upon completion of the rigger check we were marched up the ladder leading into the aircraft in inverse order. Seat straps were fastened and checked.

The jumpmaster for our stick would be Ettenborough, a very demanding individual to be sure, but not as tough as Cheesey. We all breathed a little easier with him aboard and in command.

At the far end of the runway the pilot held the aircraft braked up tight, engines howling, straining. He slacked off momentarily, rammed the throttle home, and started rolling. Minutes later we felt the upward leap, the aircraft staggered into the air, and we were on our way. We climbed in a long ellipse around the airfield, gaining altitude, coming on course for the final run. Ettenborough dropped to his knees, took a long look, and came back to his feet. He motioned to us, held up a thumb and four fingers. Five. Five minutes out from the drop zone. The aircraft swung lazily around to the right again, still climbing, just about set to go in across the drop zone.

I was number four in the stick. Two lieutenants would lead our stick out the door. Jumping just ahead of me was a broad-shouldered, deep-chested platoon sergeant of Spanish extraction.

The Marine Corps had adopted a jumper exit attitude quite unlike its sister service, the Army, whose trainees sort of hopped out of the door feet first. Marine jumpers were closed up tight on the man ahead all the way down the stick, so that there was physical contact front to rear. Upon the signal to jump, the parachutist pivoted slightly to the right in the door and left the aircraft in a flat dive, with his eyes—if they were open—fixed on the horizon. The exit of a stick of Marine jumpers strongly resembled a string of dominoes falling over. Timewise there was a decided advantage to this method of exit, for the troop compartment was cleared in one mad rush, the last few men in the stick almost double-timing to stay closed up. If one hesitated at the door he might be knocked down and run over and then picked up and thrown out of the aircraft. It was better to remain an integral part of the stampede until one passed under the horizontal tail surfaces of the aircraft.

Ettenborough moved to the door again, looked out, and then motioned to the aircraft crew chief. A nod of understanding and the crew chief slipped forward into the pilot's compartment. In a few minutes he emerged, holding up three fingers and then five. Eight knots of wind on the drop zone. Ettenborough dropped to the deck for a final check, came to his feet, checked his watch, and stepped toward us. *"Coming on the range! Coming on the range!"* he shouted and gestured for us to get ready.

We tugged at the seat straps, loosened them, and stood clear of the seats, trying to compensate, to balance against the constant shifting of the aircraft deck. There were six of us on the port side, five to starboard.

"Stand up and hook up!"

The two sides formed a single line and snapped static line snaps onto the anchor cable. The assistant jumpmaster moved back down the line of students, checking out static line snaps, tracing our static lines back to the container, checking to see if we each held a one-foot bight of static line folded into our hands, just below the static line connector snap. All eleven of us now were hooked up, closed up belly to back, left hands pulling hard on the static line snaps for additional stabilization.

Ettenborough peered out the door once again and without rising turned his head and ordered, *"Check your equipment!"*

We each made a detailed inspection of the parachute pack of the man ahead of us—as detailed as we could jammed together the way we were. The assistant jumpmaster moved alongside, double-checking. When he had finished he nodded to Ettenborough, who stood up, grasped the anchor line cable, looked down the line, and yelled, *"Sound off for equipment check!"*

Starting with number eleven we called off, each man shouting his number and adding "OK" to it. It didn't really prove anything. Just a device to keep our minds off that port-side door!

The warning light flashed red over the door. Etten-borough tapped the lead lieutenant on the shoulder, mo-tioned him into the door opening. Shuffling ahead, we closed up behind him until there was not an inch between us. *"Stand by!"* rang out in the troop compartment. We moved even closer, eleven minds with but a single thought. Get to that door opening and *through* it! Ettenborough knelt at the door, right at the lieutenant's feet, for one last check, came upright almost immediately. He looked at the warning light. *We* looked at it. It winked, turned from red to green. *"GO! GO! GO!"* Ettenborough blasted into the ear of the lead lieuten-ant, and slapped him hard on the left buttock.

When the stick had hooked up, I, being lighter and shorter than the man ahead of me, had been squeezed in so tightly that I could hardly breathe, could not move at all. My reserve was jammed solidly against the main pack of the Spanish sergeant, not an ounce of give. The man behind me was tall enough so that his reserve was pressing on the top of my main. I was locked in, believe it! When the light turned green, the sergeant had taken three short steps, pivoted right, and leaped, not in a flat dive but more up than out. Following much too closely in track, I glimpsed horizon and dived towards it, narrowly avoiding collision with the sergeant, who was falling back and down in an almost feet-down attitude. I felt the prop blast hit me, twist me, turn me over on my back. I felt, rather than saw, the horizontal stabilizer flash by. Then I felt the tug of the static line ties breaking.

The opening shock struck me as I tumbled through the air and over onto a face-down position. The chest strap hardware bit into my breastbone, the leg straps slammed into my crotch, the snaps into my hipbones. I glanced up quickly to check the canopy. As I did so my feet and legs became enmeshed in a smooth, flowing substance. My main was fully deployed. I had no worries there. I transferred my gaze downward. Spread out around my legs, knee-deep, was the sergeant's main canopy. I could see his face through the vent of his parachute, a look of anguish, of disbelief, etched sharply upon it, staring up at me, shouting, "Get *off!* Get *off!* My chute will collapse! GET OFF!"

The situation was no more palatable to me than it was to him. We were falling, losing altitude, losing the opportunity to savor fully the ride down. I called down, "Sergeant, slip to your left. I will slip right. We can make it!"

He felt for the risers and pulled himself up to the connectors on the left side as I did the same on the right. I felt my feet slide along the top of his canopy as it slid down and away from me. In a few seconds we were apart, alone with our own thoughts, our own actions.

All that slipping had built up strong oscillation. Working as quickly as possible I checked it, dampened it out, and then slid my thumbs under the seat of the harness and hitched my buttocks back for a more comfortable ride. I looked forward and back along the line of jumpers. Surprisingly, some of those who left the aircraft after me were below, almost ready to impact. Why was this? Fourth man in the stick still airborne, sixth and seventh man on the ground? I never had given weight any serious consideration before. In subsequent jumps I would become very much aware of it. One hundred and forty-five pounds does not go to earth as quickly as 180.

As I floated towards the ground I was amazed at the stillness that seemed to enfold the drop zone, the clarity of the shouts of the students, the commands given by the ground crew. A hundred feet off the deck I slid out of the seat and sagged into the leg straps. I turned fully into the wind and checked oscillation once again. Eight knots of wind on the ground. About that amount built into the forward speed of the parachute. If I held properly there should be little trouble encountered during landing. My visual acuity increased with my proximity to the ground. Suddenly I was very conscious of forward movement. My animal instinct prompted me to pull my feet up, to protect my lower extremities, but my training told me that I must hang toes-down, knees slightly bent in preparation for the touchdown. The ground became a blur. I couldn't be moving at the velocity being transmitted from eye to brain! I felt the earth reach up for me, felt my toes touch. I reached high, pulled down hard on the risers, and rolled into a forward right tumble. There was a swift, hard blow on the calf, thigh, and buttock; a wrenching of the shoulder; and the tumble was complete without striking my head or neck. I rolled over onto my belly and hand over hand pulled in the shroud lines until the canopy lay flat and inert, the air spilled from its folds. I got up, ran around the peak, grasped it in both hands, and pulled the canopy around until the peak was into the wind. I unsnapped the reserve, laid it on the ground, chained up my main, placed them both in my kit bag, and waited for the rigger truck to pick me up.

When it reached me there was madhouse aboard. I handed up my kit bag and climbed in. Everyone on that vehicle had a jump story to tell. They were ecstatic! What a *feeling!* Every man a superman! Draw another parachute. Go up again. Jump again, *TODAY!* Why wait for tomorrow?

In a state of delightful numbness I went back over the details of this jump, from the time the stick had boarded the aircraft until the instant of landing. Nothing in my life, up to that time, ever had affected me so profoundly. I was sweating copiously from nervous tension, from the airborne manipulation of the parachute during the encounter with the sergeant, from the physical effort exacted during the landing and the subsequent retrieval of my gear, yet I felt a wild exaltation, a resurrection of mind and body, celestial in its origin. Everything in me clamored for instant repetition. To know again that tiny flicker of fear; to endure those moments of utter solitude, of introspection to the maximum degree; to experience the sense of forgiveness, of Divine assurance bestowed upon one by the vision of a fully blossomed canopy; the incredible sensation of lightness, of the buoyancy felt during descent; the devastating, *human* panic at the moment of landing; the fantastic feeling of power, of invincibility, engendered by the total experience.

I looked around me. *They* were all the same! As crazy as I was! Hooked solidly on a high that no drug ever could equal.

We received our silver parachute devices, our certificates of achievement, at a brief, quiet ceremony in the conference room of the Parachute Materiel School. The detachment executive officer called us forward one at a time and the commanding officer pinned on the wings. A gentle smile, the certificate passed to the left hand, a firm grip with the right by the major, and the ritual was complete. We were qualified parachutists in the Marine Corps.

After the major and the captain left the room, we shook hands, congratulated each other. Those new wings never had been polished, were a dull, blackish gray. One of the detachment riggers owned a small buffing wheel. We had seen what wings looked like after he had worked on them. We wanted ours to look like that, polished to a high luster, the canopy worked down a little to achieve that salty, well-worn look. It was illegal, but well worth the four bits that he charged. We came in on the rigger en masse. He made a small fortune that morning.

For some of us it was a waste of time and money to rush over there. We did not know it that morning, but we would have more than ample time to get wings buffed!

During the second week of training we had been given a written examination on the history, nomenclature, and functioning of parachutes. None of us had wanted to take a chance on receiving demerits for failing *anything* during the course of instruction; therefore, we had tried very hard to attain a high percentage of correct answers on this exam. We never were told how well we had done nor how badly we had fared. In fact, the exam never was mentioned again. There were reasons for this.

Directly following noon chow we mustered in the parachute loft. Cheesey was there, and Ettenborough. The executive officer held a sheaf of travel orders in his hand. He commenced calling them out, officers first. Every Marine officer was slated for the 1st Parachute Battalion at New River. Doc Lawrence was scheduled for duty on the West Coast.

The bulk of the enlisted men drew orders to the 1st Battalion. Six names were not called off, mine among them. There was a long pause and then the executive officer read off those six names. Transferred to the Navy Parachute Materiel School for duty under instruction. Why us? We had scored the highest on the parachute examination—*that* was the reason we must remain! Shades of Parris Island! I was hot and angry at the same time. My hand shot up to gain attention. I wanted somehow to be rid of this mess right *now!*

"Yes, Corporal." The executive officer, his whole manner exuding contempt, motioned for me to stand.

"Sir! I would like to request that my orders be changed

to report to the 1st Parachute Battalion. I don't *want* to be a rigger!"

He stared at me a long minute, full of contemplation. "Oh, yes. I *can* send you to New River, Corporal. But one question first. Do you *want* to retain your parachutist designation—your jump status?"

I was baffled by such a stupid question. "Yes, Sir! Surely I do. That is what I came to Lakehurst for!"

"Well, then, go to Materiel School and retain your designation, or go to New River without it. I can do it either way. I *have* that authority. Your choice, Corporal. Give me your decision before the close of working hours!"

He had shot me down in flames, with but a single burst. I was full of holes, hurting, pride gone, deflated as a gasless barrage balloon. I had to have that designation, that continued jump pay. "Sir, there is no need to wait. I will attend the Materiel School. I *want* that designation!" I sat down, burning with rage and disappointment. We would meet again, the captain and I. It already was written in the stars.

The months spent under instruction at Lakehurst were to have a permanent effect on me. It was here that I learned, among other things, the meaning of the word *ambivalent,* for the events of that time and place both attracted and repelled me, took me to a high and dropped me low. The breathtaking excitement of the live jumps; the chagrin, the disillusionment of the orders to Materiel School. The warmth, the camaraderie of my platoon mates in contrast with the machinelike coldness of the detachment executive officer. The pros and cons swirled ceaselessly within my head, belief in one thing torn by doubts about another. I learned, too, that I was introverted, a fact that I had been certain of since early childhood; but I learned also that I was capable of the strongest extroversion. Two segments of the same personality, tugging one against the other, equilibrium maintained only by self-discipline of the highest degree. An ambivert, destined to remain so forever. Not a simple, carefree way to live, but with its own special compensations.

Lakehurst also was an experience in exposure. Exposure to new training subjects, different training schedules. Exposure to more officers and senior NCOs than I ever had been in contact with before. Exposure to a type of discipline that demanded perfection, that brooked no margin for error. Exposure to Marines from every facet of military endeavor—from young, inexperienced boots like myself, to those who already had known a dozen years of service. Exposed to a phenomenon that never would appear again—the hash-mark privates who had come back into the Corps to enjoy the festivities once the war had started. Exposure to a standard of training excellence so superior in caliber that it left its mark upon me for all time. Lakehurst made a believer out of me. Made me believe that *all* Marines could be and should be trained mentally and physically as I had been at Lakehurst—a belief that never has been dispelled from my mind.

And last, but surely not least in importance. While at Lakehurst I got spliced!

Before my enlistment I had met, courted, and secured the permission of the father of a black-haired Maine lass named Helen to marry her. I had left for Parris Island wondering if we would weather the separation, would in fact ever go through with the ceremony of marriage. Boot leave did much to dispel these doubts. The ardor was still there, perhaps in even greater intensity, and the pleasure her company brought to me remained. When, after jump school, I learned of my banishment to Materiel School, the thought occurred to me that now was the time, if there ever was to be one. I telephoned, spoke of my intentions, reminded her that the Corps always must come first, and awaited her decision. Quite surprisingly, she agreed.

Nothing had changed in the mind of the commandant about lower ranks marrying. It still was taboo. Using more guts than brains I asked to see the security detachment sergeant major, who now held my service record. The sergeant major, of Polish extraction, with many years in the Corps and well-versed in the contents of the Marine Corps Manual and Letters of Instruction, immediately went hostile on me. Vot vas I doink, boddering *him?* I explained that since I was between classes and had not been on leave or liberty during the course of instruction, I desired a seventy-two hour pass. Vere vas I goink? To Maine. For vot? I let it slip—to get married. "MARRIED! DONN YOU KNOW COMMANDANT DONN LAK FOR CORPORALS TO GET MARRIED? GOTT DAMN! NO! YOU DONN GET NO

SEVENTY-TWO! GET TO HELL OUT OF DIS OFFICE!"

Nothing ventured, nothing gained. I took a regular weekend liberty, rode a bus to New York and a train through from there to Portland, Maine, on Saturday. I reached home on Sunday morning, was married in a home ceremony before noon, slipped off to consummate the marriage in a field of sunlit Maytime flowers, and was back on the train with my bride by two in the afternoon. We made it to New York by seven in the evening, checked into the Hotel New Yorker, stayed until midnight, and then it was back to Maine by train for her, back to Lakehurst by bus for me. Reveille roll call at 0500. No room for the slightest slippage!

Materiel School was not difficult once one learned that there was to be no doubt about who was in charge—the United States Navy! Things were about as tight as they had been at jump school. Any infraction of the rules, any basic disagreement with the chief parachute rigger, was an automatic drop. For the parachutists, New River without jump pay was still held as a deterrent to any provocative action.

We learned in that course everything that could be taught about parachutes in theory, then we learned nomenclature by heart. We learned to sew with small hand needles, with sail needles, and with sewing machines. We learned how to patch, how to mend invisibly, how to repair heavy webbing, how to make harness repairs. We learned how to pack every type of parachute in the Navy inventory, the cargo chutes, the seat packs used by aviators, the reserve parachutes. We learned to make up cargo rolls for weapons and equipment drops. We were required to pack a total of one hundred parachutes prior to graduation. With repetition we grew very proficient at the packing business. Everyone had packed a hundred plus by the time certificates of graduation were issued. It was sixteen weeks of realistic training, extremely comprehensive in scope.

About two-thirds of the way through the course I was hit by a high fever, which riddled me and necessitated my transfer to the Philadelphia Naval Hospital for treatment. The fever ran its course in two weeks, and I was discharged to duty with a diagnosis of undulant fever—a sometimes lethal disease—normally contracted by cattle, not by Marines.

It was August by the time I resumed instruction. By then

I had lost all interest in rigging. I made an effort to finish the course in style, but in my heart all I wanted was to join a parachute battalion and get with the game. After eight months of hostilities, I had yet to get a taste of warfare. I was spinning my wheels, hating myself and my predicament. It was then that the exigencies of the service interceded and bailed me out.

A Letter of Instruction had come down to the security detachment from Headquarters, dealing with a new program for officer candidate training at Quantico. The requirements were simple. Be an NCO. Be a high school graduate. Be recommended by one's commanding officer. Submit to the commandant, in one's own handwriting, reasons for thinking oneself officer material. I knew that it might be years before I made sergeant in a rank-frozen outfit like the parachutists, so why not give it a go?

I requested an audience with the commanding officer. The sergeant major remembered me and was loathe to admit me to the inner sanctum, but legally could not forestall me. The commanding officer, a rotund, jovial, fatherly retread major, who had been called to duty from the retired list, remembered me also, for after my marriage I had visited him to announce my nuptials and to change my dependency status. Would he recommend me? He sent for my service record, brought in by the glowering sergeant major, and looked at it carefully, turning the pages slowly, one by one. "Surely, Corporal, surely!" A kindly eye, a nod of the head in the affirmative as he spoke. "Get your other paperwork together. I will look it over and then write my recommendation for you."

Others in the Materiel School were interested in the program. Others applied. By sheer luck, my paperwork came together and was submitted ahead of any of the others. In October my orders came up from Washington. My instruction was not complete, but the officer in charge permitted me to receive my certificate ahead of time. On 19 October 1942, I reported to the Marine barracks, Quantico, Virginia, and was assigned to officer candidate training in a class already in its fourth week. I was to be the first enlisted Marine Corps parachutist to go through officer candidate class at Quantico.

3

The Launching

By the time I had joined the fourteenth officer candidate class, the Corps had grown, doubled and tripled itself. General Holcomb was now a lieutenant general, called just plain commandant. I missed the title major general commandant. It had a special ring to it, quite different from the other services.

Like most enlisted men of my time, I stood in awe of the commissioned rank structure, never quite certain about the alchemy that allowed mortal man to reach such a zenith. When accepted for training I was hung up on this, sure that I would be found wanting. It was a happy surprise to discover that the candidate class was little more than a rehash of boot camp on a slightly higher plane. I found that I had lost nothing by reporting late to class—a heavy burden removed from my shoulders, a definite lift to my faltering ego. The training was no snap, but it was no real problem either.

The majority of the students in the class were college graduates. The Regular Marine Corps representatives were few; corporals, sergeants, with a sprinkling of staff NCOs. We came to know the college men, made good friends with some, but there was always a tendency to draw together, for mutual protection as much as any other factor. We might not always have *liked* each other, for competition between us was very high, but we understood each other's motivations much better than we did those of our civilian-background counterparts.

In those days, the class gave five points, to be applied to one's final graduation total, for every weapon in which one qualified as an expert. I was lucky enough to pick up a full quota. A good thing, too, for I was not too swift with the books.

We received our commissions on 16 December 1942. Our guest speaker was Douglas Southall Freeman, chief chronicler of the Confederacy. Not one of us ever would forget him. Slight, stooped, a shock of white hair, standing in the middle of the stage he held us enthralled, his voice, even in advancing age, majestic. Nor would we forget the things he told us. The greatness of our country, of his belief in it, of his faith in it. Of patriotism, love and loyalty, his words tightly woven into a bright tapestry, a banner of glory for all of us to see.

There remained Reserve officers' class, but in truth it was not all that new and different, with one singular exception—we now were allowed single deck bunks. Officers and gentlemen, you know! There was a lot of paper drill during the course of instruction and, while I did not shine, I managed to place thirty-third in a class of three hundred. Had I pushed a bit harder I might have placed thirtieth, which would have entitled me to a temporary Regular commission instead of a Reserve. My company commander, a former platoon sergeant, had told me to dig in, make the effort, but, clever one that I always was, I chose to ignore him. Oh, well, same money, same responsibilities. But I hated that *Reserve* designation after having been a Regular in the ranks, hoped that one day somehow I could shed it.

When our change of station orders were published I found that I had been posted to the Parachute Training Center recently completed at New River. I requested immediate assignment to an overseas battalion. I was quite unaware of it, but once again the information contained in my enlisted service record book and carefully and accurately transcribed into my officer's qualification jacket was, in just a few weeks, to trip me up hard.

My duty would not be of long duration. It was a chance to move about the center, about the post, as an officer and not as a *student!* A chance for a few more jumps, one in winter service greens, because that happened to be the uniform I was in, and the jumpmaster was not picky. Hardly took the spit shine off my low-quarters cordovans! Another, a night jump, in which I fell through my risers upon opening and remained entangled until the very last moment before impact, and so close to a macadam runway at Peterfield Point that I could reach over and touch it. *Both* kinds of luck were riding with me that night!

The officers' mess at Hadnot Point was everything that a mess should be. As you entered through the main doors into the lobby, your eyes instantly were drawn to paintings of two more-than-life-size Marine staff NCOs in dress blues, rifles at present arms, saluting from either side of the entrance to the bar. Passing by these colorful sentries, you came into the main barroom, dominated by a huge, leather-padded, horse-shoe-shaped bar in its center. On the bulkheads of this room were painted murals depicting scenes of battle. Infantry charging out of the ramps of landing craft, leaping down from amphibious tractors, artillery firing in support. Looking overhead you saw Marine parachutists floating earthward in yet another type of attack, another means of troop delivery. Every painting in that room signified one thing, the ultimate destination, the ultimate goal of every Marine, of every Marine officer—*combat!* Of all the other messes that I would visit during my time in the Corps, no other ever would impress me as being so precisely right for Marines as that one.

In the mess, during those early days of the war in the winter of 1942–43, there was an atmosphere of great pride, an air of elan, a certain nobility. We would gather there with our ladies whenever we could, to eat, to drink, to encourage and strengthen each other for the days that lay ahead. Guadalcanal had been fought for and won. North Africa had been invaded. Three Marine divisions had been formed and sent to the Pacific, two of them already blooded at Guadalcanal. A fourth, one which would see four major engagements within fourteen months of its inception, was being formed, its nucleus at New River. Everything was transitory for those of us who met at the mess. No permanence lay before us. Only the certainty that soon we would depart for the combat zone, to return only with the end of the war.

It was a time of closeness, of comradeship, of love and great affection for each other, openly displayed, the poignancy of it all magnified, reflected by the color, the pageantry, and the heraldry of that unique mess. Like Camelot it would appear to us like this only once. Like Camelot its enchantment would fade with the years, never to reappear.

Orders came down from Headquarters in about three weeks posting me to "duty beyond the seas," instructing me to report to the 1st Marine Parachute Regiment, "wherever it might be!" At least I learned that I was to report to San Francisco for transportation; otherwise it might have been a difficult set of orders to execute.

There followed leave in Maine, a trip across country— our first—ten beautiful days and nights at the old Palace Hotel in the City by the Bay, and then the interlude was over. We had been married ten months, had spent a third of that time together on weekends in New York and Baltimore. Now it was time to close that door, to lock up the house of normalcy, to wait for another time to open it.

Time now for movement, my wife to the East Coast by air, me west on the old SS *America*, once a cruise ship, now a troop carrier, heading out alone without convoy on a course south by west from 'Frisco to Noumea, New Caledonia.

Time now, too, after nineteen months as a boot Marine, boot parachutist, and boot lieutenant, to wipe myself dry behind the ears, to stand up and be counted, to learn the lonely game of leadership, to get my feet wet out where the water was deep.

Part Two

THE SLOT

4

The Battalion

Place names changed as the strategy changed during the first year of the war in the Pacific. New Georgia, Rendova, Vella Lavella superceded Tulagi, Tanambogo-Gavutu, Florida, and Guadalcanal in the Solomons. Some names remained, were always there, not erased, never diminishing in operational importance right up to the close of hostilities. Far out on the western horizon, just off the China coast, Formosa—unknown, foreboding, containing the heartbeat, the lifeblood of the Japanese Navy, harboring every secret of its strength. It seemed a foregone conclusion that one day Formosa must be taken, assaulted at great cost. Truk, spoken of more often by the members of the joint planning staffs, was nearly as awe-inspiring as Formosa. The name set up a wild clamor in the heart, set imaginations aflame with visions of countless air and surface craft ringing the island, induced a spirit of heavy mystery, a sense of persistent apprehension. Finally, another name—Rabaul—the third one that consistently nagged at the minds of the planners, one that was much closer to them geographically. A name that conjured up illusions of military power without peer, of an unassailable fortress protected by swarms of fighter and attack aircraft, kept inviolate by the presence of the strongest of naval patrols. Rabaul, located at the eastern tip of New Britain, which, in conjunction with the Japanese air units based at Kavieng airfield on neighboring New Ireland, effectively guarded the southern approaches to the bastion of Truk and provided a strong base for Japanese operations against New

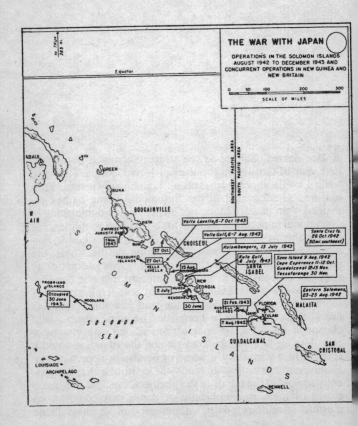

THE WAR WITH JAPAN

OPERATIONS IN THE SOLOMON ISLANDS
AUGUST 1942 TO DECEMBER 1943 AND
CONCURRENT OPERATIONS IN NEW GUINEA AND
NEW BRITAIN

SCALE OF MILES

Zealand, Australia, and portions of New Guinea. Rabaul, like Truk which it guarded so well, took on a shadowy magic. A preconceived yet totally believable legend of invulnerability.

Neither Formosa, Truk, Rabaul, or Kavieng ever would be assaulted by ground forces of the Allies, but the threat that they posed to Allied operations, real or imagined, never could be ignored. The very existence of these bases colored the weaponry, the strategy and tactics of those early years of the war.

Because Rabaul was the primary remaining threat to the Allied lifeline in the South and Southwest Pacific areas, it somehow must be destroyed or neutralized, the sting taken from the scorpion's tail. After considerable discussion and deliberation, it was decided by the warlords that Rabaul would be neutralized through the extensive use of air power alone.

To the south and east of Rabaul, at a distance of more than 250 miles, lay Bougainville, the largest of the British Solomon Islands. The Japanese held an airfield at Buka, off the island's northern tip, and another just south of Buka passage at Bonis, the combination commonly referred to as Buka/Bonis. To the south the Japanese launched air attacks against Allied forces in the Central Solomons from the largest of the Bougainville airfields—Kahili. The Shortland Islands, south of Bougainville, included a first-class airfield at Ballale. The location of these well-dispersed airfields, and the combat strength of the air units operating from them, precluded successful Allied bombing operations against Rabaul from airfields in the Central Solomons. If Kavieng and Rabaul were to be put out of action, Bougainville had to be secured.

It was against that background that we now found ourselves, loaded into the LCP(R)s, hanging from the ship's davits, bottoms skimming the water, engines running, waiting for the signal to go in. The APDs *Kilty, Ward, Crosby,* and *McKean* had brought us across The Slot, the destroyer *Conway* running interference. It had been a busy day for the APDs. In the morning they had landed elements of the 8th New Zealand Brigade Group on the Treasury Islands, south and west of the Shortlands, and then late that evening had

taken us aboard off the JUNO beaches at Vella Lavella for
the run to Choiseul. It was now nearly midnight.

Somewhere on the beach, 2,000 yards across the black
seas from us, Rea Duncan and his platoon already had
landed. If the landing site near the village of Voza was secure,
he would signal the old Churchillian "V" for victory signal,
dit-dit-dit-da, by shaded light. If things were not good at
Voza we would land a mile south. H Hour was 0100, 28
October 1943. We waited, eyes straining, trying to pick up the
flash from that tiny light.

We had been waiting for this night for a long time. I had
joined the 2d Parachute Battalion at Tontouta, New Caledonia, in April 1943. From then on it had been a steady, six-
day-a-week training schedule, performed under the watchful
eyes of one of the most demanding, perfectionist taskmasters
that the Corps ever would see.

Upon my arrival, almost before I could introduce myself, I had been kicked hard and skillfully in the genital area.
My paperwork had come out ahead of me—bits and pieces of
damaging evidence, including my rigger school certificate.
The battalion parachute officer eagerly had awaited my arrival. He had been chosen to serve as regimental parachute
officer, wanted to be on his way. I grunted, groaned, rolled my
eyes back up into my skull, all to no avail. I was stuck, would
remain stuck until fate would intervene. My humping of the
autumn and winter hills of Quantico, my field exercises
"astride Chopawomsic Creek," my desire to become "platoon leader, 1st Platoon"—all for naught.

I had arrived at the battalion just a few days before a
change of command, the new colonel coming aboard with a
fresh broom, its straws strong and supple, its owner itching
for a clean sweep-down, fore and aft. Being a newcomer, I
would see the cleanup through different eyes, would suffer
less in the process of change, since I had no established
habits to break.

In the battalion, which was a West Coast outfit, were
hundreds of new faces, but among them some recognized
from Lakehurst. Rea Duncan who had left Lakehurst as a
corporal was now a first lieutenant leading a platoon in "G"

Company. Red Harper, now a platoon sergeant, was also in "G" Company. Tucker Gougelmann, a sort of jack-of-all-trades on the Lakehurst staff, was now a captain. Doc Lawrence, who consistently had driven Cheesey up the wall at Lakehurst by appearing at formations without headgear, was battalion surgeon, still casual about his uniform, bareheaded more times than not. So there were old friendships, something upon which to build new ones.

The rigger section that I inherited was a potential time bomb. Within it were certain personnel I had trained with at Materiel School, personnel I now must supervise—always a sticky situation, a continual test of wills. I must come down hard on them, reeducate them, show them their proper place within the command. Good basic training for young officers, pleasant or otherwise. As for the rest of the section, they were longtime riggers, efficient, proficient, far more help than hindrance.

We all had met the new colonel at the mess. In physical stature, very short. Small bones and light frame. Diminutive is as good a word as any. Unnerving mannerisms. Head cocked to one side, looking up, for there were few in the battalion he could look *down* upon. Eyes alert, glittering, inquisitive, boring into those of the person with whom he was conversing, giving that person the uneasy impression that in some way he had been found wanting, placing him instantly upon the defensive, in a position of weakness, of retreat, even before the colonel voiced an opinion. A most disconcerting experience. A chronic sniff, fired off in bursts of two, punctuated his conversation. Most distracting, especially during the course of official business, when it behooved one to catch the colonel's instructions the first time around. The colonel did not like to repeat himself.

The officers' billeting area was located adjacent to the billeting area of the rifle companies, but set slightly apart and at a somewhat higher elevation. Pyramidal tents housed all hands, including the colonel. The officers' mess was located on the high ground to the north of the main billeting area, as was the general mess. It was constructed of tent flys and white target cloth, strong-backed and wooden-decked. It consisted of a bar and social area and a galley and messing area. Nothing fancy. Utilitarian. It was called the shake-out room.

Messing was conducted informally at breakfast and lunch. At dinner one might imagine himself aboard a ship of the line. Seating arrangements at the evening meal were in accordance with the combined lineal list, just as in the wardroom mess aboard ship. Junior officers did not sit until the senior officers sauntered in from the bar; then everybody sat. No one left the table until the senior officer had risen to depart for the evening. Permission had to be granted for any call of duty or nature after one was seated. These procedures were not followed in the other messes in the regiment, but in the small colonel's battalion they were enforced. You were taught to do things correctly at the academy. You had to properly instruct your subordinates, regardless of circumstance or environment. Especially important when you were saddled with such a high percentage of mustangs in your command.

We learned many things about the colonel very quickly. He had been taught as a company officer of the old school to match up faces with service record book photos; to know the names, the home towns, the family background of the men in his platoons and companies. Now he carried it all one step further, to the battalion level, a prodigious task even for one so talented as he. He astounded the men with his detailed knowledge of their past and made the officers acutely aware of their own lack of factual information concerning their troops. He tightened us all up, brought the battalion together. His thirst for facts and figures encompassed everything— questioning, challenging existing techniques and practices in the art of parachuting, of aerial resupply, discarding that which he found nonproductive, absorbing that of positive value. Lack of technical information never would be a fault of his.

I was treated to a personal interview with the colonel soon after his assumption of command. I had no cause for complaint, since I asked for what I received.

Both company and battalion did an average of two night exercises out of the six training days of the week. Jump aircraft were very scarce, so more often that not our "jumps" were made from the tailgate of a slow-moving truck, with the exercise usually oriented towards a return to the camp by foot. On one such exercise of battalion level, my riggers were "dropped" in to simulate retrieval of parachutes and equipment. Before the night was over my section had been scoffed up by the battalion logistics officer to help bring in supplies that had been used in the exercise—water cans, equipment rolls, boxes, and mock ammunition loads. I got hot, insulted, embarrassed because control of my section had been usurped arbitrarily. The next day, still consumed by false pride, I requested office hours with the colonel.

At 1000 I stood outside the colonel's tent, waiting to be admitted. I had been advised by the Headquarters Company commander to back off, but I *had* to play out my hand. Young and foolish? No. Young and stupid!

A call from inside the tent and I was led hastily inside the throne room. Behind a huge combination desk-table the colonel sat. He did not look up until I was in position, three paces in front of his barricade, centered on it and at attention. Then he looked up, cocked his head, and drilled holes through my soul with those cold eyes. "You wanted to see me, *Mr.* Averill? Your company commander can't help you? What *is* your problem?"

I took a long breath, spilled my guts, and terminated my outburst with a request to be transferred to the 1st Raider Battalion. Instinctively, I said all of the wrong things, but by the time I realized it, there was no way out.

Those eyes came at me again. Pure steel. The head not cocked anymore, fixed straight on me, both hands resting on the table, palms down, as if in preparation for a leap that would smash me to the deck. Voice quiet, penetrating.

"*Mr.* Averill! In the first place, officers are *not* transferred! *Officers* receive change of station orders. In the second place, I don't believe that the 1st Raider Battalion would *have* you! Now—as to your problem—I don't think that you have one, but I will send the executive officer to the parachute loft to talk with you and your people about what you *think* is wrong! Anything else?"

Have you ever had a dream of being caught naked in the middle of a city at midday? Of being without part of your uniform at a formal inspection? Of searching unsuccessfully for a way to cover those mistakes? That kind of feeling enveloped me. I wanted to disappear, to evaporate, to be anywhere except in front of those burning, accusing eyes. I choked out a barely audible, "No, *Sir!* Thank you, *Sir!*" spun on my heel, and bolted outside without waiting for dismissal.

I had been caught short in boot camp, at Lakehurst, at Quantico, had been chewed out by some fairly well-qualified people, but never with the finesse, the expertise that the colonel had shown. He had sliced chunks off my posterior, destroyed my crusading self-esteem, stripped me of my pride, sent me into a quivering state of shock with just those few words. In the years that followed, I never would find another who could equal him.

The executive officer did come to the loft. The section never again was used as a glorified working party during exercises, and every once in a while the colonel would smile at me in a knowing way at the mess. Like a cat already caught messing in the corner of the living room, I hastily would avert my eyes, never daring to smile in return.

The months of spring and summer had moved on by, days and nights devoted to little but training. We hit the road on thirty-mile forced marches; jumped whenever aircraft were available, not often; and learned, as thoroughly as live-fire exercises would permit, the art of jungle warfare and the special techniques required for the reduction of mutually supporting fortified positions. These techniques were practiced so often that during assaults on such positions, the assault team could almost point to where the demolition man was able to hurl a satchel charge through the embrasure of the pillbox or bunker without any slackening of protective fire by the machine guns. Tap-tap-tap-tap-tap—single shots, moving neither right nor left, up nor down—a steady stream of lead streaking into the opening, the rounds often seeming to be plucking at the sleeve of the demolition man as he threw, giving the occupants of the bunker no chance to retaliate, to drive off the assault teams. The Browning light machine gun sections and the Johnson light machine gun teams, proud of their skill, kept a hail of fire going in until the charge exploded, the rocket man moved up to fire, and the flamethrower man enveloped the pillbox with napalm and black smoke. Then once again they lay down their blanket of fire until it was called off by the assaulting rifle platoon leader. Such teamwork, such trust between team members awed all of us, awed the visitors who had come up from Noumea to observe the training. I had watched combat films taken by the Germans as they moved into the Low Countries, and by the Japanese in China during the opening phases of the war. By late summer the battalion matched the professionalism that had been so apparent in those films. The little colonel had his act together. Another few months of such training and we might pass from perfection to the staleness brought on by overtraining. We never had that chance.

In June, the march northwards up The Slot began. The Raiders moving against the New Georgia Group, at Segi Point, Rendova, Viru, and Wickman Anchorage, in July seized Rice Anchorage, and, by the first week in August, secured Munda airfield. Observers from the parachute regiment went on these operations for an update on current Japanese battle tactics and weaponry. Some gained this information the hard way. Tucker Gougelmann was seriously wounded, would lose the use of a leg from that wound.

At the close of summer the parachute regiment was ordered north to be prepared for operations in the Northern Solomons against targets as yet not disclosed.

The 2d Battalion was the vanguard. With my usual luck, accepted now by me as something that physically had grown on me, had become a visible appendage, I was informed that *all* parachute officers would remain with the regiment to supervise the crating and storing of cargo and personnel parachutes and parachute supplies. It was evident from this that there was to be no parachute assault, no matter what the target or where it might be. I again asked to see the colonel, was treated with exceptional kindness and consideration, and received assurances that I would rejoin the battalion in the forward area once my duties with regiment were completed. I was told that Colonel Williams, the regimental commander, had concurred in this, that I should remind him, that he would not forget. Then I was left alone, the battalion gone, even most of the riggers assimilated into the ranks of the line companies.

The day came when the regiment was ordered up. That night I gingerly approached Colonel Williams after dinner and told him that I had been instructed to remind him of my return to the battalion. Yes. He remembered quite well what the little man had said. There would be no problem, but first we must load out the regiment from Noumea and get it to Guadalcanal. Once that was done I would be free.

It had been a matter of close timing and sheer luck. The afternoon that the *American Legion* had anchored off Tassafaronga, the 2d Battalion was preparing to move still farther north. I had just enough time to get my gear together, slide down the canvas cargo chute into a boat, get ashore, and report for duty. After that I turned over to supply my sea chest and all other extraneous gear, received an assignment to one of the APDs that would carry elements of the battalion, and at dusk embarked.

The feeling of security, of belonging, of returning to my own people warmed my insides. As the ships moved away from Guadalcanal I was briefed on the movement. The battalion was to establish a forward base on Vella Lavella and await orders for future operations. The remainder of the regiment would follow at a later date. Vella had been declared officially secure the first week of September, with a Marine defense battalion, a battalion of Seabees, New Zealand anti-aircraft units, PT boat squadrons, and Marine aviation units deployed ashore. With the exception of small bands of Japanese who had not yet escaped from the island, there were no ground forces to contest our landing.

5

Vella Lavella

At dawn we had arrived off the JUNO beaches at Vella
Lavella, the sun outlining the volcanoes of Kolombangara.
We had railloaded the boats and hung suspended just off the
water, screws turning, waiting to be dropped; the APDs slic-
ing towards the shoreline; the LSTs, which had left Tassafaronga much earlier because of their slow speed,
lumbering along behind. Looking inland we could see palms
fringing the beach area; see the moisture on the giant banyans; the mahogany trees behind the beach shimmering; and
in the background the misty mountains, wreathed in clouds.
"Land the Landing Force!" came over the loudspeakers. The
boats dropped from the davits; the APDs pulled away to the
north and south, circled, and joined the destroyers to screen
the landing.

We had moved towards the beach without challenge,
except for the snorting, belching bulldozers of the Seabees,
who at this early hour already had started their clearing,
grading, and rolling operations on the roads and hardstands
behind the beaches. The first elements of the battalion
landed, formed up, and moved out up the muddy, slippery

access road that led to the assigned bivouac area when the Japanese struck.

The attack had not come from the sea or the land, but from the sky. Camouflaged by the glorious sunrise streaking the heavens behind Kolombangara, the Japanese aircraft had formed up for their run in the shadow of the mountains and aircraft bellies riding just off the sea, had launched the attack without detection by the destroyer screen or by the P-38s of the combat air patrol, circling at an altitude so great that one hardly could discern them.

Two bombing runs, followed by the strafing. Ordnance expended in a highly profitable manner. Both LSTs hit, one very badly, hit hard enough that it had to be towed seaward and sunk. Columns of black smoke reached high into the morning sky as the petroleum products of the battalion fed the hungry flames. Special camouflage suits, issued to the men of the battalion, turned to ashes. Those bombs had been well placed by people who knew what they were doing.

On the last strafing run, as the Japanese aircraft whipped by at treetop level, the flight leader pushed his canopy to the rear, leaned out and grinned, saluted those of us on the road with thumb to nose, four fingers extended. He knew the American insult, probably had graduated from a West Coast university, class of '39!

At the beach there were human casualties also, two of them platoon leaders. Before the sun went down that day, I was designated "platoon leader, 1st Platoon" assigned to "E" Company. My actions and orders would be monitored at some distance from Chopawomsic Creek.

Vella had been an excellent teaching vehicle for all of us. That air attack on the first morning demonstrated with exceptional clarity just how nakedly exposed man could be made to feel. After their success on the beach, the Japanese concentrated on the column of troops moving towards the palm grove where the bivouac was staked out. No one was hit by the aircraft cannon or machine gun rounds, but all of us were pinned in place, humiliated beyond description as we grovelled in the slime; the whining, snapping slugs tearing up the palms, throwing chunks of them through the air, blowing holes in the mud and coral, forcing us deeper into the mire, causing us to cling to the bases of the trees in an effort to escape that wicked, demoralizing fire.

Enemy bombing had become a routine thing those first weeks on Vella. No deliberate attacks on specific targets. Nightly runs, coming down from the Shortlands or Kahili. Usually a single bomber, unescorted, determined to keep us awake, determined to hit the airstrip at Barakoma with a couple of bombs each night. To my knowledge the airfield never was neutralized, but I can verify the fact that we lost some sleep, if not from the bombs at least from the side effects of the raids.

We had landed on Vella carrying a U.S. Army jungle kit, a jungle pack that resembled a small seabag with shoulder straps, into which had been stuffed various and sundry items purportedly invented just for jungle use. One of these items was the jungle hammock. It was basically a fine idea, if you were allowed adequate time to mount and dismount it. It was constructed with a sort of tent top that extended out from the sides and from the front and rear when the hammock was hung. The distance between the tent top and the hammock bottom was about two feet. This distance was filled on all sides by mosquito netting. Access to the hammock was accomplished by the manipulation of two zippers—one vertical, one horizontal. With care and practice, and under ideal conditions, you could get up into the hammock, zip the zippers, and stay reasonably comfortable. You had to learn not to turn suddenly to the right or left, however. If you made that mistake you might find yourself twirling like a pig on a spit, often ending the twirl facedown in the tent section of the hammock. Brahman steers were tame compared to riding this hammock!

Foxholes were dug close by the hammocks, in many cases directly under them. It rained on an average of four times a day. The foxholes were always knee-deep in water. When the enemy bombers came down The Slot at night and sentinels called out "Air Raid!," the sirens started to wail— the signal for all manner of strange noises to erupt. Zippers worked. Zip! Zip! Plop! as a trooper manipulated his zippers successfully and slid down into his hole. Zippers did *not* work. Hammock upside down, occupant swearing, the sound of net tearing, loud and obscene phrases, then plop! Overhead the enemy aircraft bored steadily in. Down came the bombs—WHOOSH! WHOOSH! WHOOSH!—and coinciding with the fall of the bombs the New Zealand antiaircraft batteries threw the projectiles from their weapons almost vertically into the air, the sound of the guns sometimes obliterating the explosion of the bombs. The fallout from the exploding 90mm shell fragments was a downpour of broken steel more deadly than the Japanese ordnance.

No one in our battalion was hit by the Japanese bombs, but no one ever dared to be too casual about them. After the 1st Battalion moved up, one of my Lakehurst classmates took a bomb from a floatplane right *into* his foxhole. Bad luck plays no favorites.

Vella had put us in touch, too, with the ever-present natural enemies. The heat; humidity; the rainfall of early morning, midday, midafternoon, and sundown. The constant wetness, steaming hot when the sun was upon you, cold enough to cause a teeth-rattling chill after dark. Wet clothing—crotch rot. Wet footgear—immersion foot, the skin peeling off along with the sock on those rare occasions when your boots might be removed. Dysentery, malaria, a general apathy toward everything. Drinking water fouled with dirt and minute animal life, doped up with Halazone tablets so that it might pass down your gullet, be used to rinse your mouth; water so bad that dogs would not touch it, but somehow we survived. Atabrine tablets, because there was no quinine. Atabrine that turned your urine a rich orange color, that triggered urination to a point where it seemed that fluid was forever passing, that turned your skin a hue as yellow as the men that we opposed in The Slot. The malaria bug did not die from Atabrine, but it became sleepy and inactive, so your body could continue to function as the bug slept.

The combination of terrain and vegetation, biting, tearing, scratching, sucking, holding you in place, dogging you from all sides, slowly, insidiously, wearing you down. Muck everywhere except on the slopes and ridges of the mountains. Muck so deep, so constrictive that it tore the heels from combat footgear as you withdrew your foot from it. The chemicals within the muck so strong that the leather uppers of boots and shoes would stink and rot after exposure to them. The coral, a scratch from which heralded a painful, festering, inflamed wound, difficult to heal. The jungle gloom, its dimness caused by the interlacing of vines and the heavy foliage of the giant banyans and the mahoganies forming a canopy, sometimes one hundred feet in the air; the banyans reaching down as well as up, their huge root formations fascinatingly grotesque. The mangroves that edged every low spot along the rim of the island, swamp dwellers, swamp creators, treacherous, slippery, odoriferous, hell to penetrate, hell to navigate, costing hours in time, immeasurable cost in physical exertion.

All this Vella taught us, in addition to the air raids, the patrols into the north country where the Japanese stragglers still roamed, and where their sign, if not person, was everywhere—sign enough to keep the patrol leaders alert, to keep the heartbeat accelerated. New Caledonia had been our trade school, Vella our finishing school, a chance to blend the techniques of jungle warfare with the weather and terrain of the Solomons.

In late October the colonel had disappeared from the island. Upon his return we learned that the battalion was to execute a special mission, a combination raid and diversion, in support of a larger landing elsewhere, to operate alone, to create the appearance of a much stronger force. Its code name was BLISSFUL. It was the kind of operation that everyone wanted to be in on, the kind that movies sometimes were based on. The news set the battalion afire with anticipation.

A couple of mornings later at a battalion briefing, we were introduced to a massive figure of a man, black bearded, intense, a sub-lieutenant of the Royal Australian Navy. His name was Seton. With him were his two dusky native bodyguards from the island of Choiseul, where Seton and his partner Waddell had been stationed as coast watchers since October 1942. In the year that almost had passed they had organized the natives, led Marine reconnaissance patrols, and learned the island's secrets as no two other Occidentals had done before. We would get to know Seton well. Waddell in his mountain fastness, sending out his coast-watcher reports by radio to the Allied forces in the Solomons, we never would see.

If rehearsals can make an operation, BLISSFUL had been made prior to our leaving Vella Lavella. The colonel was exacting, demanding, every day filled with training and preparation. Intelligence briefings, night and morning; school on code names; inspections. Boating drills with no boats, boats outlined on the floor of the coconut grove the exact size and configuration of the LCP(R)s that we would use; troops embarked, troops disembarked, practiced in darkness as well as daylight. Inspections of weapons, equipment, and personal gear. The colonel was adamant about two things—every man would shave on the operation and there would be no rank referred to in conversation; once ashore, nicknames would suffice. No sense in getting all your rank blown away just for the sake of military courtesy. John Richards, leader of the 3d Platoon of "E" Company, and myself, both mustangs, caught hell regularly. We forever were sir-ing the colonel, a hard thing *not* to do after being instructed so well along the way to do *just* that. As for the shaving, it was not for cosmetic reasons but to help prevent infection brought about by long hairs being blown into the facial tissues by bullets or shell fragments. Quite understandable. I had laughed to myself the morning the colonel inspected the company, all gear laid out on the ground, for the captain turned out to be the only member of the organization without shaving gear displayed. The colonel immediately turned toward him, fostered that inimical, quizzical expression, head cocked to one side, just the shadow of a smile appearing as he looked down at the display again, the voice coming out low but sharp as a well-stropped razor. "You understood my order to mean *everyone* would shave, did you not, Bobbie?"

. . . . The sound of boat engines snarling into full throat brought me back to the present. The signal had been seen. Duncan was calling the battalion to land at Voza. "F" and "G" Companies would land first. "E" would follow on call.

In solid blackness "E" Company unloaded boatload after boatload of cargo and carried it inland from the beach.

On an island just off Voza, called Zinoa, John Richards and his platoon found concealment for the LCP(R)s that had been furnished the battalion for operations. Before dawn, the battalion, reinforced with nearly a hundred native bearers of Seton's coast-watcher group, carrying heavy-duty radio equipment, ammunition, and rations, struggled up the narrow, single-track trail toward the base camp location. It was high ground covered with forest growth, well-concealed from the ground and air, a stream of clear, rushing water sliding around one side of the bluff.

On the beach, other natives using palm fronds and their hands carefully brushed away footprints and other telltale marks left on the beach by the heavy-footed Americans. The Japanese knew that we had landed on Choiseul, for we had been bombed twice during the approach and landing phase, and Allied forces in the Solomons had broadcast by radio that a large combat element of Marines had gone ashore. But for the immediate future at least, the Japanese would not know how many troops had gone ashore, nor at what specific location.

6

BLISSFUL

The second day ashore would be a busy one. We moved both north and south on patrol operations. The colonel, the S-3, and a small war party went south toward Sangigai, a Japanese barge-staging area. I was sent north with the mission of determining the feasibility of bringing landing craft into the vicinity of Moli Island for future operations against enemy forces known to be in the Choiseul Bay area. Also included in the mission was the selection of tentative radar equipment locations and a search for possible PT boat bases in the Moli Island area. My patrol consisted of eight Marines, one sergeant, one corporal, and a radar specialist from the Army. We carried individual weapons, ammunition, and one "D" ration—an oversized, dried-out slab of milk chocolate. That delicacy was supposed to bring you through a day of hard patrolling in high spirits.

The maps issued for BLISSFUL were unbelievable, next to useless. A gridded overprint of aerial photographs of our area of operations, which supplemented these maps, left much to be desired. The jungle growth was so dense that the camera's eye had no more success in penetrating it than did the eye of a human. Trails were inked in and overprinted, pure guesswork, for beneath the umbrella of the rain forest no trails actually could be observed. Native villages and known Japanese installations likewise were overprinted, these locations the most accurate of any on the map. The larger streams and rivers were portrayed with some accuracy also. What were *not* shown, perhaps not known about at all by the planners of BLISSFUL, were the rocky spurs that extended from the central mountain mass, east and west, projecting into the sea at places. In following the northwest trail along the beach, there was no way to circumvent these spurs except to seaward, so it was up and over, up and over— the slow, tedious, exhausting method of maintaining headway. The colonel had not known of these spurs, nor had the intelligence officer. They expected an easy passage, expected the patrol to return before nightfall. The map indicated a wide, easy trail, the distance not more than ten miles.

The previous night, after being briefed by the intelligence officer, I had stopped by the colonel's hole for a few minutes as darkness closed down on the hilltop. Were there any special instructions from the colonel? No, but if you come across a sick Jap, bring him in. Would love to have a prisoner for more intelligence of the area, but don't get into a wrestling match. Reconnaissance patrol, not a combat patrol. Again—*don't* get into a wrestling match! I got the message. I really had no illusions about a squad snatching a prisoner away from the Japanese force that had been reported just north of my target.

We left the bivouac before daybreak; slipped, tripped, and slid down the greasy, wet trail that led to the beach; and turned north up the beach trail. We were supposed to pick up one of Seton's natives as a guide just as we hit the beach, but it was not until we had moved roughly a mile up the trail, across streams, through swampy areas, and up and over our first spur that he appeared. Maybe he was just sitting back on his haunches, watching us thrash around in the heat that was building up just after dawn. Maybe he wasn't too keen about going with us. In any event, he finally let us see him.

Ebony. About five foot eight. Straight, erect carriage. Well-muscled body, covered only by a loincloth. Hair black, kinky, curly. Feet planted firmly, long toes splayed out like the webbed feet of a duck. Wide smile. A spurt of blood-red saliva off to the side as he chewed on and spit his cud of betel nut. He bowed slightly, turned, and, carrying no weapon but a six-foot-long pole, took up his guide position in the lead. There would be no oral communications. We did not know his language, did not even do well in the pidgin that the Australian coast watchers had taught him. Sign language, grunts, exclamations, mutual trust, and confidence would have to get the job done. That, and just plain luck. That jet-black guide would turn out to be the finest talisman we could have carried.

We moved out, a point man behind the scout, then me, the rest of the patrol in trace at a three-pace interval. Seven degrees south of the equator, the morning cool does not linger. The heat and humidity bore down on us immediately. Even with the guide leading, the movement was slow, tortuous. There were occasional stretches of white beach, the sand packed hard, which we might have traversed with speed and comfort. These we had to skirt, under cover of the forest's edge, but never openly, for the Japanese air patrols already were alert and aloft, searching the beaches on either side of the island. As the day wore on, as our strength depleted, we were tempted more than once to gamble on detection. In the beginning we had been determined not to be observed.

About midmorning we lost our first man to terrain and heat. One of the gunners carrying a Johnson light suddenly keeled over and dropped to the ground, face gone pale, his breathing spasmodic, eyes wide in fright. A sorry exchange of pidgin and pantomime with the scout. We must go on. Must leave this man here. Can another guide return this man to Voza? The smile again, a squirt of red fluid. Yes. Yes. Can do. The light machine gun swapped for a rifle, an extra canteen for the disabled trooper. We propped him up in the roots of a giant banyan, assured him that he would be brought back to the main bivouac, and shoved off up the trail. It is hard to leave one of your own like that, even harder to be the one left behind.

The march seemed to affect the scout not at all. He just kept picking up those great feet and planting them on coral, sand, or rock. The bottoms of those feet must have had the toughness of elephant hide.

We reached Moli Point at 1400 after walking, climbing, struggling for more than eight hours. Just in time, too, for the other light machine gunner was about to fade after having twisted his ankle coming up over a spur. What the map had shown on that carefully white-inked overprint as six miles of good trail had cost us twice that distance in effort. Anxiety had taken us down, too. When you have two light machine guns as your heaviest armament and eight men to keep them in action and protect them, you do wonder constantly just *where* the nearest of some of the several thousand Japanese troops reported to be in your patrol area might be! Every time we slipped up on an evacuated enemy supply dump or an empty barge-staging area along the way, every time I saw the scout's black hand motion us down to the ground, I could feel my hackles rise, feel my machinery shift into high gear. The combination of forest terrain, heat, high humidity, and unfettered solicitude can render one powerful weary.

There was no place to base landing craft at Moli Point or on the island. A sluggish stream met the sea just at the point. The beach gradient was so shallow that boats would have grounded far out from the beach. Neither were there locations for the installation of radar equipment. All of this was duly noted by the experts concerned. Now something of equal importance—where to spend the night? We never could make it back to Voza during daylight. It was already midafternoon. Movement during darkness was not considered. We had seen sign of recent enemy activity at Moli. Ration cans, ammo and ration cases, discarded web equipment, gas masks, and worn-out, split-toed sneakers. We had sighted a fully loaded sixty-man *daihatsu*, a big Japanese landing barge, moving off to the north, just off Kuku, as we made our approach to Moli. I was convinced that we were in a potentially sticky situation. Just then a late-afternoon rain squall hit us. I made up my mind. We would move south to Kuku village where there still was some shelter, spend the night there, and attempt to reach Voza the following day.

The clouds blew away, the sun scorched us once again, steam rising from our saturated clothing as we cuddled up and moved on down the trail towards the village, long since abandoned by the natives. Upon arrival there, we outposted the trail north and south of the village; the remainder of the patrol searched the huts. One, judged the most likely to survive the night without collapsing around us, was picked for our shelter. As the sun halved itself on the western edge of the world, we prepared for the coming of the night.

In better days, Kuku might have typified the native villages of the Solomon Islands. A small, fast-moving stream tumbled down from the rocky bluffs behind the village and gurgled through its center. The huts, built on stilts, constructed of bamboo and thatch, were high enough to be cooled by the sea breezes and to keep the inhabitants dry during the heavy rains. The village sat just inland at the inner curve of a small cove, the beach lined with palms which circled the cove from landward to seaward. Wet, beaten, disgusted, the place still had natural charm which penetrated, still made its impression on all of us. Idyllic. Not readily defensible, but definitely idyllic.

Darkness came down like a well-greased sliding garage door, bringing with it an immediate chill to the sodden garments, an ache and a growl to the stomachs now empty, the "D" rations long gone. The cold, clear awareness of our situation—a reinforced squad, on the second night of the battalion's operation, roughly ten miles from home, with no communications equipment, camping on the periphery of the largest concentration of Japanese on the island—invoked a shudder, a shiver, a shake of another sort.

The native scout had vanished almost as soon as we had closed on the village, had moved off into the bush behind it. I had no reason to believe that he had deserted us. He did his thing, we did ours. As we sat in the hut in our skivvy drawers, our outer clothing wrung out and hung to dry on projections of the hut, wiping down our weapons and oiling them in the gloom, a most tantalizing odor assailed our nostrils. A huge grin on his face, the scout, his arms laden with banana leaf trays, entered the hut, squatted in our midst, and, like a hot dog hawker, passed each of us a hot, baked banana, wrapped tightly in a smaller leaf in order to retain the heat. During the time he had been absent he had dug a pit, fired it, manufactured coals, picked and wrapped the bananas, and baked them in the ground for us. It was my first try at baked banana. A new taste experience as well as much needed sustenance. Nothing could have tasted better.

While there was still light enough to see, I changed outposts. By the time the off-coming sentries downed the roasted bananas that I brought them and we returned to the hut, the curtain of night had dropped, nothing less than Stygian, leaving nothing to guide on. Just shadows and shades of shadows. Dark, light, medium, clear, and out of focus. It is better to be in a fighting hole at night. Everything outside of the hole is enemy. There are no doubts.

The sound must have hit us all at the same time, for within the hut the shadows swayed and bobbed, changed in attitude. South of us and approaching the cove, sound that we recognized. YAMMER-YAMMER-YAMMER-YAMMER-YAMMER-YAMMER-YAM! The engine noise, the off-center beat of a daihatsu! The engine noise closer now and much louder. Eyeballs straining, popping open wide, we slipped into suspenders, hooked up cartridge belts, slipped helmets on, readied weapons. Maybe they would slide on by us and go up the coast, follow the route of the barge we had seen in the afternoon. Sit tight.

As the daihatsu came even with the cove entrance, the coxswain cut his engines, turned shoreward, and eased in, barely maintaining headway. Hell! Better get into position to dump a load on the barge just at landing. Better to take a bunch of them into paradise with us than to try to crash the gates alone. I passed the word in quick whispers—hook on in single file, grasp the cartridge belt of the man ahead. We would get to the beach, position ourselves just at the fringe of the palms, and wait for a chance. No one fire until I did, then pour it on strong. With two Johnson lights, two Springfields with grenade launchers, Johnson rifles, and individual grenades, coupled with the element of surprise, we stood to make a good dent in the Japanese force, whatever its size.

Someone—Buddha, the Divine Wind, Tengoku, the Spirits of the Samurai, the Knights of Bushido—must have guided the hands of that Japanese coxswain during his maneuvers in the cove that night. My prayers already had been said. I was committed to the beach, no turning back from destiny. I would go down in Corps history as the leader of the

first Marine combat element ordered into combat in their
skivvy drawers. To make it worse, some, like myself, were
not addicted to drawers. What a way to go! I was positive that
the Japanese survivors would photograph us, expose us to
the eyes of the world. Japanese prisoners had stated on
numerous occasions that they had been taught to believe that
patricide, or matricide, or both, was one of the primary
qualifications for acceptance in the Corps. I wondered what
special significance these Japanese would read into the sight
of our nearly naked bodies, strung with combat gear.

The coxswain gunned the engines suddenly, the daihatsu
moving in, dead center on our position. Then he shut down
the throttles again, the craft drifting ever closer, its dark
shape visible against the night sky, the 13mm guns on either
side of the bow standing out in sharp relief. In just moments
more, the hull would hit bottom, grind to a stop, the ramp
would be lowered, and a load of Japanese soldiers, quite
unaware of our existence, would come sloshing through the
shallows towards us. I took a long breath, held it, and aimed
my carbine into the center of the blackness that was the bow
of the barge.

Another roar of the engines, a loud clank as the screws
were reversed, and the barge went full astern, backing out
and away from us. Then it moved forward again, slowly, very
slowly, creeping around the curve of the cove to its entrance,
through it, and on into the open sea. YAMMER-YAMMER-
YAMMER-YAMMER-YAM! Pulling strongly and steadily,
heading north. We waited quietly on the beach as the sound
receded. We were hardly breathing. Just as quietly we returned to the hut, each with his own thoughts, his own
questions. As fate would have it, the quietness of self-examination probably saved our lives that night, for quite unknown to us, even more peril would move closer as the hours
of darkness passed.

Close to the equator everything opens up without fanfare, abruptly. Dawn arrived, the sun leaped into the sky.
There had been moments of sleep, perhaps, nothing more.
There would be no breakfast, no coffee. We were dull, stupid,
preoccupied with the simple task of donning our now nearly
dry clothing, fighting with the laces of our boots, slipping
into our web equipment. Again the guide was missing. I was

about to do something very gross, about to shout in an effort
to gain his attention, to bring him to me, to get some kind of a
movement plan made for Voza. Thank God he saw my movement before I sounded off. He stood up in the bush near the
beach, beckoning me down. I crawled to his position at the
edge of the cove. He pointed north, held up both hands,
flashed his fingers in the air four times. "Jap! Jap! Many-
many!" in a soft whisper. Switching on his haunches he
pointed south of the cove. "Same-same! Many-many!"

Damn! We had heard more barges all night long, but had
heard none changing course, making a landing near us. Ob-
viously we had missed at least two parties. There would be
no return to Voza by the trail that had brought us to Moli, for
it was blocked by a force I did not *want* to wrestle with.
Maybe we already had closed out our books and didn't know
it, but no, again that spurt of crimson, that big smile. Still
hunkered down he pointed to the high ground behind Kuku,
to the ridge line leading up to it. The slopes were covered
with brush and trees. Plenty of concealment and some cover,
if we worked it right. *My* turn to smile.

We might have been walking on eggshells so deliberate
was the process of pick 'em up and lay 'em down. Each
careful step took us onto higher ground where we could fight
if we had to. Each step took us closer to the mountain range
that ran down the western side of the island, a spur of which
broke off just behind the main bivouac at Voza. That guide
was good! He had an imprint of that hill country in his head.
It was evident that he knew quite well the fallacy of frequent-
ing the coast trails. The Japanese would delight in gunning
him down. Waddell and Seton ran their operations from the
high ground, so it was natural for the natives to follow suit.

Just for a moment the guide paused, turned, and pointed
through the foliage at the now clearly visible beaches on
either side of Kuku cove. A daihatsu on both, and close by
each craft a platoon of Japanese soldiers cooking rice, eating
breakfast. Many-many! For sure!

We made it up to the mountain range without discovery.
Just as we left the upward spur and turned south along the
range toward Voza, a Zero came flipping up over the ridge
line, those red meatballs on the lower surface of the wings so
close that it seemed that we could reach up and touch them.

The hatch cover was back, the pilot swinging his head from one side to the other, intently eyeballing the terrain below him. Long periods of training in passive air defense kept our white faces downcast. We stopped in our tracks, did not move again until he had passed twice over our location. Just after the second pass we picked up the sound of heavy explosions to the south, bombs and the almost inaudible stuttering of aircraft cannons and machine guns. The Zero pilot must have seen or heard it also, for he swung his aircraft away from the mountains and zoomed straight up, as only a Zero could, fast disappearing into the cloud cover high above.

About 1000, after coming down off the high ground and picking up the beach trail about two miles out from the main bivouac, we met a twenty-one-man patrol that had been sent out to search for us. Someone at battalion level cared about us, although I never found out who it was.

Just short of Voza, at the Barogasonga River, our guide left us. He had his own rendezvous to make. We were deeply in his debt, but had nothing with which to reward him except our thanks, and no language common enough to express even that. We all shook hands with him, locked eyes for a long moment, and smiled. So very much can be conveyed by such simple actions. Kipling was right, you know—"there is neither East nor West, Border, nor Breed, nor Birth, when two strong men stand face to face, though they come from the ends of the earth!"

I had learned to recite those lines at my father's knee as a child. I began to learn the true meaning of those words that morning when the guide slipped silently away from us and melted into the jungle.

Back at the bivouac things were jumping, a raid on Sangigai the chief topic of conversation. About 0600 that morning, following the air strikes we had heard on our way back, "E" and "F" Companies, reinforced with machine guns and rockets and led by the colonel, had launched an overland attack, hoping by such brazenness to convince the Japanese that Marine units of far greater size than a battalion had landed on Choiseul. "F" Company was to move in a flanking movement from the east of the village, "E" Company was to move south and attack from the north and west.

Right then we were about as welcome in that bivouac as pimples on a coed's face the night of the senior prom. Eventually we were debriefed. Eventually we drew rations. Eventually we went back to the empty company tactical area and flaked out.

There was *one* person in the company area genuinely glad to see us, glad and a little angry, but more glad than angry—the lad we had propped up between the banyan tree roots to look after himself.

"God!" he said. "It was spooky in that jungle after you left, but it was light and I could see, keep track of things pretty well. I must have slept a little, late in the afternoon, for when I awoke the sun was going down. When it got dark it was just plain hell! And then, a couple of hours after nightfall, I got *that* feeling. Something or someone was getting close to me. My eyeballs ached I was staring so hard. Then a hand touched my arm. A voice very soft, very low. 'Me friend—me friend. You come by me.' I had nothing better to do so I went with him."

I gathered that he nearly had succumbed to heart failure at that nocturnal touch. One of Seton's scouts had been contacted sometime during the day by the dark prince who had led us to Moli and back, had given direction to our lad's position. When? How? A mystery without solution, but the scout had come, located the Marine in the darkness, led him to the beach, placed him in a canoe, and paddled him back to the security of the Voza outpost. Astonishing people, those natives of the Solomon Islands.

"E" Company came back to Voza that night about 1830 and shortly thereafter reached the bivouac. My platoon was together once more. "F" Company had taken casualties, would be picked up by boat the following morning.

Vernon Hammons, my platoon sergeant, was more hyped-up than I ever had seen him, his Mississippi drawl advanced from its normal slow crawl to an agitated chatter. It had been a ball, he said, the Japs taking off for the high ground to the east and north of Sangigai as soon as the dust and smoke had settled from the first salvo of rocket and mortar rounds dumped into the village by "E" Company. Then they ran headlong into a platoon from "F" Company moving in from the east flank of the Sangigai position. After that, he grinned, a right smart little firefight developed, leaving "E" Company free to move through the administrative buildings, the field hospital, and the barge-repair and staging areas. According to Hammons it was just one big bang after another. They blew up everything in sight, including bunkers, fighting holes, supply dumps, and a daihatsu that happened to be beached there.

Searching through the buildings for documents, Hammons came across a gold mine. Hydrographic charts of the Bougainville-Shortland-Fauro island group showed the routes used by the barges evacuating troops from the Central Solomons to the staging areas on Choiseul and onto Bougainville. Others contained exact plots of the Japanese mine fields laid to protect the approaches to the Northern Solomons. This information was flown out the following day with some of the "F" Company casualties. Later on we learned that those charts had turned the trick on the Japanese in at least one instance. Coast watchers reported the sinking of two Japanese ships as they proceeded through what they thought to be secure channels, but which in fact had been mined by the Americans, based on the information taken from the charts Hammons had seized.

We shot the breeze until late into the night about the hike up the coast to Moli and the big blowout at Sangigai. We wondered, too, about the situation of "F" Company, still out. We were bone tired, whipped, physically. It had been a long day, but it did not seem to cut us down mentally or psychologically. We were alone in enemy territory, the whole battalion plus reinforcements, just a little more than 700 men sandwiched in between major Japanese forces that we *knew* about, 1,000 at Kakasa, at the southern tip of the island, and another 4,000 at the Choiseul Bay area to the north, but things were breaking fast, going our way. We were getting away with the deception, faking the Japs out of position, creating the impression of a much larger force. If it takes confidence to win, *we* couldn't lose.

Even as we rattled on, charging our batteries, other men of the battalion still fought the jungle night, sweating, straining, hurting, moving the wounded of "F" Company to the boat pickup point. Doc Lawrence and his medical corpsmen, laboring to get the casualties safely out on litters, propped up the walking wounded, Doc carrying one badly torn up Marine across his shoulders up the treacherous, ill-defined trail. The corpsmen struggled to catch up with the company, to make the rendezvous, stopping to establish an interim aid station in the darkness, laying the wounded out in rows in order to find them by the sense of touch, to treat them as a blind man must, with no visibility, saving ten of the twelve that had commenced the straggling movement toward the sea. Doc told me about it much later, humble about his part, making the account more impersonal than it ever should have been, giving credit to his corpsmen, the security men, and the litter bearers for all that went right.

"F" Company and the colonel's party returned the following morning with Doc and the wounded. Both the colonel and the company commander had been hit, painfully but not seriously. The badly wounded were taken out that same morning by seaplane.

Satisfied with the operation just concluded, it was the colonel's desire to strike again at a different location, to keep the enemy guessing, to do as much damage as possible before our true strength was perceived. An operation to the north, in the area south of Choiseul Bay, was his choice, and about 1000 that morning the battalion executive officer, the intelligence officer, an intelligence detachment, and a platoon from "G" Company moved up the coast by boat to reconnoiter the area around the village of Nukiki and the Warrior River. They returned that evening. Negative contact. No enemy troops observed.

That night, plans for a northern operation were discussed. Two platoons from "G" Company, a radio team and an intelligence detachment led by Lieutenant Sam Johnson, would move up the coast by boat and land in the vicinity of Nukiki. Sam, with his detachment, was to recon the Warrior River. If no enemy forces were discovered, the remainder of the force would disembark and strike out to the northeast toward Choiseul Bay. An island called Guppy, just off the coast, had been reported by the coast watchers as a major enemy supply point. The force would endeavor to destroy the supplies by mortar fire. Operations were to be completed, the force reembarked no later than 1730 the evening of 1 November. The colonel's customary cautionary orders were attached to the plan—*avoid engagement with strong Jap forces!*

1 November 1943 would turn out to be one of *those* days! Some typical activities:

At 0550 a thirty-six-man patrol was dispatched toward Sangigai to determine enemy reaction to the raid, to take under fire any survivors found.

At 0630 the Northwest Task Force, as it had been dubbed by its leader, moved up the coast by boat to conduct combat and reconnaissance missions in the Choiseul Bay area.

The Sangigai patrol made contact with the Japanese at midmorning in the vicinity of Vagara village, and after a brief firefight drove the enemy back toward Sangigai. At 1415 the patrol was back in the bivouac area.

At 1600 John Richards, platoon leader of the 3d Platoon of "E" Company, moved his men south to ambush in the Vagara area. An hour and a half later his platoon ran into a force of more than twenty Japanese Imperial Marines moving north toward our outpost at Voza. In the meeting engagement the Japanese were more surprised than the U.S. Marines. As a result they lost eight, and an undetermined number were wounded. The remainder of the Japanese patrol took off south down the trail at a high port. One of Richards' men was killed during the firefight—the first man in "E" Company to go down.

That night just before sundown I took position on the east bank of the Barogasonga River, with my full platoon, to establish the northwest outpost for the battalion. We had crossed the Barogasonga going north on the Moli patrol. We knew that the trail north of the river was good for a distance of a mile, well-traversed, easily defined. The Japanese had used it many times, could use it at night as easily as in the daylight. A simple, well-oriented approach into our position. With the Northwest Task Force operating to the north, I really had no fear of early enemy contact, but it was something to think about, to prepare for.

Our communication to Voza and the bivouac was by sound-power phone, which required a twenty-four-hour phone watch, since the alert signal for an incoming message was a sharp whistle into the transmitting end of the wire. During the hours of darkness we whispered into the mouthpiece. The human voice, like the tiny glow of a lighted cigarette, a dead giveaway in the jungle where an enemy scout always can be expected just beyond the perimeter.

The sound power was good, though, in many ways beyond the security angle. Hooked into the bivouac and to the Voza outpost, we could stay on top of events as they took place. Even though at times I might have felt as guilty as a farmer's housewife listening in on a two-party line, it gave me a feeling of how things were going, sometimes as well not known.

It was quiet that night, the stars so close, so huge in that sky of the southern hemisphere that it seemed entirely reasonable to reach up and snatch one out of the heavens. The outline of the Southern Cross was revealed clearly for all of us to see. I sat in my hole—the sound-power background scratchy, humming slightly along the open line—looking out across the wide expanse of sea that was The Slot, wondering how the "G" Company lads were making out, why they had not returned at sundown.

The following morning the Northwest Task Force still had not returned. Don Justice, platoon leader of the "G" Company platoon that had been left at the bivouac, passed through the Voza outpost about 0800 on his way to test the Sangigai defenses and to block enemy movement toward Voza.

About an hour later, boats from the Northwest Task Force appeared off the position, moving south. A short time later the sound power cut us in on the scoop. Things had not gone well on the Warrior River, in fact damned badly. Rea Duncan had been sent through the jungle to relay that word, had found Japanese everywhere along his route, but had eased on through, found the boats, and come south with his message.

At 1400 Justice had not returned from the south, could not be contacted by radio. The entry in the war diary for that date and time is concise. "No word from Justice. Presume him hit." On the way back from Moli I had been told the same thing when Don Castle and his search patrol had met us—"We had already written you off." You learn about your expendability in short order.

Seton's scouts were dispatched north in an attempt to locate the Northwest Task Force and bring it out overland. A little after 1600, Duncan's boats passed by the outpost, trying to link up from the sea. Not known to us was the fact that the colonel had requested PT boat support from Vella to aid in the evacuation from the Warrior River.

Late that afternoon, Castle and twenty-seven Marines appeared at the outpost to mine the west side of the river. Six mine groups went in, hooked up in three series of two groups, with separate control wires to set them off in sequence. The wires were tagged and led into the outpost command post. Just at dusk the demolitions team packed up its gear and took off for Voza, taking with it the sense of security, of well-being that its additional numbers had brought to us. You don't put in mines unless company is expected.

Later, well after dark, the sound power at Voza informed us that Justice and his platoon just had passed through their position. "Presumed hit" was home safe.

Still later, between 2130 and 2200, we heard the boats from the Northwest Task Force pass by, shepherded by the PTs, heard its commander reporting from the sound-power phone at Voza. He just had finished his greeting to the colonel when the phone was passed to me in time to hear the colonel's reply. A pause, then, in what seemed to me the most expressionless voice I ever had heard, yet packing the sting and cutting power of a cat-o'-nine-tails across a naked back, "Things got a little *confused* up there, did they not?"

I passed the phone back to the phone watch. It was not right for me to hear more than that.

Of course the colonel had been correct in his initial assessment of the operation. It had been confused. I was not there, so I cannot recount accurately the events that took place, but even the official reports were cloudy. Days later, with the experience still fresh in their minds, members of "G" Company and other members of the force could not give a precise account of what or why.

Some positive things did happen. A Japanese outpost

had been overrun the second day of the operation and three of the four enemy soldiers killed. Guppy Island was located and taken under fire by the mortar gunners of Red Morton's weapons platoon of "G" Company, with considerable success, causing huge fires in a fuel dump and detonating ammunition and explosives stored on the island.

From there on confusion mounted. Returning to the Warrior River the force came under enemy fire from the east bank. Sam Johnson and two Marines, Sergeant Muller and Private Pare, started swimming across the river in order to contact Duncan, who was mistakenly thought by the force commander to be on the east bank. Again confusion in the reports. Did this team volunteer to swim the river or were they ordered across? Both stories are told and even now, forty years later, I could not tell you for sure which was correct. In any event, Muller was killed by Japanese fire and Pare was wounded. Sam Johnson made the far bank and vanished, never to be seen again.

Duncan had brought the boats up from Voza late that afternoon, had taken Sergeant Wilson and a communication team from the east bank of the river, and then had attempted to take aboard members of "G" Company. The boats came under fire. With two boats loaded and ready to move to Voza, one of the boats started to sink. Two PT boats from Vella Lavella appeared in the lowering darkness, riding in on a rain squall, and transferred men and weapons from the sinking boat to PT 59. In that group was Doc Stevens, the other battalion surgeon, and a seriously wounded Marine, Corporal Schnell. Schnell was taken below to the PT boat skipper's quarters, where Doc Stevens tried in vain to save his life.

The skipper of PT 59 was a singular man. That afternoon when the emergency call had come in to the PT boat base for help at the Warrior, his boat had been down to one third of its rated fuel capacity, 700 gallons out of 2,200. He wanted to make the run across The Slot, had fuel enough for that and for a short time on station at Choiseul, agreed with the other PT boat skipper to attempt it with the provision that PT 59 be towed back to base by the other boat, which was fueled to capacity, and the two boats zoomed out across The Slot. PT 59 remained operational until 0300 the following morning, and then was taken in tow. The skipper was a man of action, of compassion—a gambler. In later years he would endear himself to us even more than on that precarious November night in 1943, would gamble against higher odds, would die for his country on the streets of Dallas on another November day twenty years later as our commander in chief, John F. Kennedy, thirty-fifth president of the United States.

At dawn the next morning strike aircraft began hitting Bougainville. Wave after wave of B-24s flew high over the outpost. The SBDs, the TBFs came roaring up The Slot on their own special runs. The P-38s roamed the high skies, searching for Japanese interceptors. The bent-wing Corsairs flew like swarms of snarling hornets toward the beaches of Empress Augusta Bay. We stood looking up, ground-bound, open-mouthed, transfixed at the sight of such an air armada.

A short time later word came down that the final hand of our own game was about to be played out. By now the Japanese had doped it out, not off-balance anymore. We had hit hard, torn things up, laid down a lot of fire, but we had never remained on position, had never occupied a tactical locality once we had seized it. We were tapping at the Japanese, not hammering as a strong force would. The native scouts went north and south, into the mountains and along the rivers. The Japanese were patrolling in strength, down from Choiseul Bay toward Moli, up from Kakasa toward Sangigai, reinforcements already in place at that destroyed base. It was time for the curtain to come down on our little one-act play. The battalion would move down off the bluff, would establish a perimeter defense on the Voza beach. My platoon would move about a mile and a half south and east of the Barogasonga River and set up delaying positions. The platoon would fall back to the battalion perimeter on the colonel's personal signal.

About noon I gave up the Barogasonga position, sent Hammons and the platoon back down the trail with instructions to set up on the south bank of a small stream, outpost north and south, and screen the swamp that lay to the east of the new position. I kept one corporal with me and two cases of fragmentation hand grenades. We had a lot of work ahead of us as we moved back.

On the trail, just back from the river's edge, we started pegging down grenades—booby-trapping—tying grenades together with lengths of light, fine communications wire at a distance of about ten feet apart across the trail from one to another. Using small, forked branches cut from the under-growth, we wedged the points of the fork down over the grenade, the spoon left free to fly off. To prepare the grenade for activation, we secured the ends of the communications wire to the pull ring; bent the ends of the pull ring flat to allow for an easy, rapid passage out of the neck of the grenade once the wire was pulled; and then camouflaged the grenades and the wire with debris from the jungle floor. It was touchy work, but we had a lot of distance to cover, a lot of concentration to expend. We had to get that trail booby trapped well before the sun went down. We were two ma-chines, moving, working, moving, completely intent upon the task at hand.

It happened just a few yards out from the new platoon position, in sight of it, as a matter of fact. For some reason the wire between the grenades had kinked up, twisted, or had been cut just a tad short. I just had finished anchoring the grenade and flattening the pull ring ends, was just about to start covering the grenade when I saw the slack go out of the wire abruptly, felt it go tight, heard the pop of the fuse as the pin came out and the spoon flew off, saw a trace of white smoke. I dove for the ground, reaching out with my left hand as I did so. I was lucky. I scooped the grenade up off the ground and flung it seaward. As my head hit the ground the grenade exploded in the sand on the beach. *Close!*

I got up, breathless, brushing my clothing, shaken, safe, but worried sick about just how far the sound had carried, wondering if the Japanese had heard, would be alerted to the booby traps.

I walked across the trail to talk with the corporal. He had been in a far safer position than I, but I could not see him anywhere. Moving carefully past his pegged-down grenade, I found him hunched at the base of a palm tree, attempting to regain his feet, a blank look on his face. It was hard to believe, but when that grenade had popped he had taken off running and had slammed into the trunk of the tree, knocking himself nearly insensible. I had intended to crawl all over him for yanking that wire so hard, but realized that it would have been a wasted effort right then.

At dark we were in position at the mouth of the stream, just to the rear of a long spit of white sand, which gave us excellent visibility and a good shot at the first of the enemy to venture forth onto the spit. The phone had been brought back, tied in. Crazy, but even an inanimate object like that unnerved me, things were getting so tricky out in front of us. I hated to hear any strange noise at all. The colonel had told me that the call would come about midnight. I hoped that the alert whistle on the phone would not be too loud or shrill.

If you watch a certain area long enough at night, things will appear that really do not exist. In those long hours I saw, heard, and felt movement around us for minutes on end, my eyes riveted now on the sand spit, then inland toward the swamp, seaward, and then back to the spit. There was no sound at all from our rear. Had the battalion pulled out already, leaving us behind as a sacrifice?

Just above and to the rear of my head, a stealthy movement in the foliage, a gentle, almost imperceptible scratching sound, as of steel against wood. I went into paralysis, total, my eyes attempting rearward vision, without any movement of the cranium. Then my sense of touch came into play. Something sharp, pointed was against the nape of my neck. I recognized it immediately. The point of one of those overlong Japanese bayonets! How had the enemy gotten behind us, between us and the battalion? I swallowed hard, started a quick break to the right rear, hoping to deflect the point of the bayonet, to bring the enemy to the ground before he stabbed down or pulled the trigger of his rifle.

As I moved, a sharp pain shot through the back of my neck. The skin had been grasped by something that had clamped down viciously in a savage bite, and then had dragged across my neck before release. I heard something fall to the ground. There was no Japanese soldier grinning sadistically at me. A land crab had hung in the brush behind me, had probably smelled rather than seen the rancid skin of my neck, figured it for edible carrion, decided to make out with it before any of his fellows, and had neatly ambushed me!

Timed almost concisely with the ferocious attack of the

crab came the first of the booby-trap explosions. Two. A long silence, then another two. We had the distance out to every one of those booby traps cranked into our memory banks. We snuggled a little bit deeper into the fighting holes, propped our eyelids a little farther open. They would stop now, the Japanese out on the trail, move forces out onto the beach, move into the approaches to the swamp, and try to flank us from the east. Some would remain on the trail, testing, hoping it would become free of grenades. Ten minutes, and two more explosions, still a good distance out. But what of the enemy flankers? Where were they? What progress had *they* made?

I checked my watch. A few minutes from the magic hour of midnight. Had the battalion actually gone and left us? In answer to my question a low whistle whipped along the line and into the handset. I raised it to my ear. "Outpost. Ave."

A silence, then quietly, "This is Vic. Take a powder!"

They *hadn't* written us off! They were waiting on us! Time to go. "Ave here. WILL DO!"

In whispers, the order to pull out went down the line. We formed silently into single file, each man hooking onto the belt of the man ahead. Roll call. All present, and down the trail toward Voza we went as more explosions rocked the night air behind us.

Coming into an opening where once had stood a native village, I heard a bolt go back and forward, chambering a round. I threw my own piece against my hip, ready to fire. In a low voice I called out. "Outpost! Outpost coming in!"

A laugh, quite Occidental, then, "God, Ave, you looked just like a damned Jap coming into that clearing! I almost drilled you!" The muzzle of the M1A1 carbine dropped, a hand clasped my shoulder. Johnny Young, the company executive officer, out to guide us in, to take us to our gear, the jungle packs and gas masks that we had come ashore with laid out in neat rows by other members of the company. No need now to establish proper ownership. Pick up a pack and a gas mask and keep moving. The colonel had stated that we would leave the island with all the gear that we came with. He intended to be a man of his word.

Between 0130 and 0150 we filed up the steep, narrow ladders of the LCIs that had arrived while we were still on

outpost. Just at the top of the ladder, Hammons lost control
of his weapon and it dropped over the side. Immediate disgrace in the eyes of the company commander. The old numbers game, the let's-look-good-to-the-colonel game, the
battle for political survival beginning all over again, once
more of paramount importance now that combat operations
were over. Forgotten were the maps, the charts, the documents that Hammons had brought out of Sangigai. Forgotten
too, their admitted importance to the Cape Torokina-Em-
press Augusta Bay landings. We were the only platoon to
lose a weapon openly. We would hear about *that* for weeks to
come!

And so we came back across The Slot, the sunrise behind us, on a beautiful November morning, to the JUNO
beaches of Vella Lavella. The colonel, his face wound freshly
bandaged, rode in on the LCI like a baron returning from the
Crusades. The regimental commander, his staff, the battalion
commanders of the other two parachute battalions, and selected members of the I Marine Amphibious Corps staff were
on the beach to greet him. Incongruous against the jungle
setting, a section of the Amphibious Corps band played
marches and martial airs.

It turned out that we had done much better than we had
realized. Small-unit leaders and their men rarely know what
has been accomplished during an operation. Evidently the
battalion had performed well, for soon after we returned, a
letter came down to us commending the colonel and the
battalion. The colonel also received the Navy Cross and the
Purple Heart.

UNITED STATES MARINE CORPS
HEADQUARTERS, FIRST MARINE
AMPHIBIOUS CORPS IN THE FIELD

5 November, 1943

From: The Commanding General.
To: The Commanding Officer, Second Parachute
           Battalion (Reinforced).
Via: The Commanding Officer, First Marine
           Parachute Regiment.

Subject: Commendatory action of Second Parachute
Battalion (Reinforced) on CHOISEUL
Island, British Solomon Islands, from 27
October, 1943, to 5 November, 1943.

1. On the night of 27 October, 1943, the Second Marine Parachute Battalion (Reinforced) landed at VOZA on CHOISEUL Island, British Solomon Islands, and for a period of seven days conducted vigorous attacks against the Japanese forces on that island. They were withdrawn from CHOISEUL on the night of 4–5 November, 1943, after having successfully carried out their mission against great odds.

2. A series of raids by your Marine Parachute Battalion resulted in the destruction of several hundred tons of Japanese supplies, the capture of Japanese documents of great value to our nation, and the devastation of an enemy barge and staging area at SANGIGAI. During the period on CHOISEUL one hundred and forty-three Japanese were killed and an undeterminable number wounded with a loss of only eight killed and thirteen wounded in your battalion.

3. These highly commendable and aggressive actions on the part of the Second Parachute Battalion (Reinforced) contributed greatly to the success of the current operations in the South Pacific Area and were carried out in conformity with the highest traditions of the Marine Corps.

A. A. VANDERGRIFT.

Quite without warning the little colonel was ordered away from us. He had won his battle honors, had proven that he could lead as well as plan. Time now to move onward and upward. Excelsior, and all that good stuff!

Before he departed, the colonel set aside time for those of us who wanted a chance for a personal farewell. I had thought that a few might take advantage of the opportunity, but nearly the whole battalion filed by his tent as the day wore on. In the short time that he had been with us, he had instilled a genuine admiration in our hearts for him and a great respect for his professional abilities. He was a master showman, a manipulator par excellence, but also a man of integrity, a man one could believe in, a man who demanded maximum effort from himself as well as from others, a man one could ask a reasonable favor of and expect it to be granted. You either loved him or you hated him. There was no middle ground. In *that* battalion I think that I can state without fear of denial that love far exceeded hate. Over the years I would never change my mind about him.

When I went into his tent I was tongue-tied, as I always was in his presence. I faltered, but made it clear that I considered it an honor to have served with him, especially during the Choiseul operation.

We were both so short that there was no looking up or down, just eyeball to eyeball. He smiled that curious little smile. "Gerald," he said. "You have been a good soldier," and shook my hand.

There was no need for anything else. From him that was enough. I would not see him again in that war, but I would remember for its duration the high state of combat readiness he had driven us to, the cool professionalism displayed by him during BLISSFUL.

Victor H. Krulak. The Brute, as he was called by his Annapolis classmates and his contemporaries in the Corps. One of a kind. They made him and broke the mold. A sad thing. The Corps could have used a lot more exactly like him.

7

The Waiting Game

Vella was dead, literally, after we came back. The parachute regiment, minus our battalion, had moved up into the Empress Augusta Bay area for operations with the 3d Marine Division. After a solid week of almost constant wakefulness on Choiseul, we still could not sleep. We were in pyramidal tents, in the same area where before we had hung our jungle hammocks, but now we were high on the hog—camp cots and mosquito bars and nets. Across The Slot, we had watched the sea, the sky, the edge of the jungle with such fixed intensity that this peaceful existence was just too much. The Japs no longer could bomb us as they used to. There was not even that left over from the old days.

At night we would crawl into the camp cots, tie down the nets, and wait for the floor show to commence. In just a few minutes, rats the size of small dogs would scamper across the hard-packed earthen decks of the tents. If you shone the beam of a flashlight on them, they would sit up on their haunches and glare at you. They were not the least bit afraid of us, not nearly as nervous as we were about them. The doctors had told us that they carried typhus, and we did not

fancy being nicked by a dirty rat. To further amuse themselves and us, some of the rats would race up the trunks of
palm trees and fight it out with the fruit bats to see who was
going to control the heights. There would be hellish scream-
ing from the bats, the rats, or whoever was winning, and a
few coconuts would come crashing down. Not conducive to a
good night's sleep, even if our screwed up nervous systems
would have allowed it.

We visited a lot when training was not scheduled. We
went south to Barakoma, to the airstrip, its length so white
that it sometimes hurt your eyes to gaze upon it in the
sunlight. It was built by the Seabees mostly of coral crushed,
wetted down, rolled, and rolled again. Better than concrete
and much more available. On occasion we were invited to the
mess, to the quarters of the fly-boys. We found that their
living accommodations far exceeded ours in terms of comfort
and plushness. But after watching the aircraft limp in from
operations over Kahili, Buka/Bonis, the airspace over Empress Augusta Bay; after seeing the bent propeller blades,
the torn skin of the wings and fuselage, the tail surfaces shot
away, the holes in the Plexiglas canopies; seeing the SBDs
come sliding in on their bellies, wheels locked up, gunners
dead or wounded, draped over the gun rings, we didn't be-
grudge those people anything extra that they could get. They
lived high, fought like fanatics, died hard, often far from the
Barakoma strip, far from their own kind, in the glittering sea,
over the Japanese airfields, often outnumbered by the
swarms of enemy aircraft that rose to meet them, but always
pressing home their attack.

And sometimes in the solitary hours between taps and
midnight, we kept the vigil with them as they tried to transmit
a radio message through the dense night fogs of The Slot to
one of their team members long overdue at the strip—calling,
calling, often with no reply. Discouraging, but not so heart-
rending as finally to pick up a signal, a call sign, repeated
once or twice and then lost forever. Somewhere out over the
lonely sea an aircraft down, a brother lost. Somber nights.
Somber thoughts.

They thought us crazy to do the things we did—to fight it
out toe-to-toe with the Japanese on the ground. We thought
their approach to combat just as wild. We drank their coffee,

took a shot of booze from them now and then, listened to their war stories, the narrative illustrated by the use of both hands, each representing an aircraft maneuvering in the sign language of flyers everywhere. A very special breed, those eagles and hawks of the Solomon Islands skies—the pilots, gunners, night-fighter crewmen who rode the upwinds of The Slot, in Corsairs, F-4s, F-6s, SBDs, TBFs, and PV-1s.

Then there was Lambu Lambu, the PT boat base. We went north, into the mangrove swamp that provided concealment for the boats, to visit the crews. On my first patrol on Vella we had passed by the base early in the morning, been shattered to see the officers eating from china plates, drinking coffee from crockery mugs. *Navy,* we said, *Navy*—mess boys to shine your shoes aboard ship, clean sheets, a good bunk, and three hot meals a day—a fine way to fight a war! But after what those boat crews did for us at the Warrior River, they could have messed on gold and silver.

The boat skippers liked to have a squad or so of Marines make the run with them across The Slot. The boats had plenty of their own firepower, but the addition of three or four Johnson lights and some Johnson rifles often helped in a tight spot. The battalion now was commanded by the former executive officer, who usually was amenable to the dispatch of a few Marine volunteers to give the PT boats a hand.

About two weeks after our return to Vella, a group of us went up to Lambu Lambu for an all-night patrol. Two boats would cross; land a coast watcher, his men, and equipment on the northwest coast; and then run in close to the enemy installations at Choiseul Bay for shore bombardment. We drank coffee with the crew at sundown; were shown over the boat, its armament, its control spaces, including the radar scope, which was at that time a thing of wonder; and then the boats cast off, commencing the passage of The Slot on a run into Choiseul.

It was a totally new experience, riding those boats into the darkness. Out there in the waters that separated the western chain of the Solomons from the eastern, there were more real dangers than imagined ones. The boats were very vulnerable to attack, constructed of light materials, extremely flammable, with little armor. The Japanese were still trying to evacuate the Central Solomons, trying to move barges each night from as far south as Kolombangara, staging along the Choiseul coast during the northward movement. Direct fire from the 13mm guns of the daihatsus could splinter the hull of a PT boat, turn it into match sticks. Then, too, there was always the danger from aircraft, our own as well as the enemy's. With so much action taking place in such a restricted area, some of our own pilots were prone to dump an ordnance load on anything that moved, unless an immediate recognition signal was flashed. Within the last few nights, the crewman told us, one boat had been attacked by unidentified aircraft and one had gone dead in the water from engine failure. We had a run of more than fifty miles into Choiseul, another fifty back. Anything could happen.

Time did not drag on the crossing. The boat's executive officer let me watch the radar scan, pointed out its salient points, told me what we might see on the screen as we approached the Choiseul coast. It was my first instruction in modern magic. I was glad that we, and not the Japanese, had it aboard.

Then the boats were slowing. We were off the beach, somewhere between Moli and the Warrior River, the rendezvous point established earlier by radio with the coast watcher ashore. The boats were barely underway, moving smoothly toward the landing spot. A slight shudder as the boat touched down. With the big engines muttering, murmuring, we watched the coast watcher and his men shoulder their gear, move across the bow, and slide off into the shallows.

My heart, my mind went with them. It seemed inconceivable to be back on the Choiseul shore. My skin started to crawl, the ghosts of the troopers who remained here came flooding in around me—Harbert, Kosma, Biggs, Augustine, Gruidl, and Slivkoff at Sangigai; Andrews missing in the same action. Prevost at Vagara. Of Muller, wounded and drowning in the Warrior; of Gallaher at Nukiki; of Schnell on PT 59. Of Sam Johnson, gone, never accurately accounted for after he swam the Warrior that fateful afternoon. Was he dead, murdered by the Japanese as one report had it, or did he live on as their captive?

The engines growled, the boat shivered as we backed down into open water, bringing my thoughts back to reality with a jolt. The bow swung seaward; we lined up behind the other boat, still moving slowly, the twin-six, twelve-cylinder Packard engines humming, longing to burst into full throat as we stole out of the landing area and into the channel. Fifteen minutes of lazy, almost soundless running and it was time to get on with the game.

A turn to the west, a long swooping circle from the north to the southeast, with the engines kicking into flank speed, the sterns dug in, the bows almost clear of the water. We roared in port side to the beach, the Marines at the port rail, weapons ready, the 40mms and the 20mms swinging toward the shore. The lead boat erupted into a long sheaf of tracers arcing inland, the 40mm shells looking for all the world like molten footballs. Chunk-chunk-chunk, kicking those footballs out in a steady stream. Then we heard our own boat's skipper yell "FIRE!" and everything that could throw a projectile vomited flame. The sound of the firing beat us into the deck, the smell of gunpowder crisping our nostrils.

We reversed directions, coming up from the south, firing from starboard, each boat hammering hard at the Japanese installations as we ran on past. Another turn, and the final run from the west and north, this time close in, *very* close in, muzzles depressed, pumping the rounds straight in, hoping for a hit on a critical portion of the installation. A flash of light, the crash of an explosion, a ripple of flashes, of sympathetic detonations in the area just behind the beach. Pay dirt!

As we turned away and headed west and south toward Vella, I thought again of the lads left behind on Choiseul. I looked back at the flaming beach, the palms stark against the firelight, heard the explosions continue. It seemed a fitting requiem. There are many ways to light a candle for the dead, a variety of altars upon which to place it.

November fled. The Christmas season arrived. On Christmas Eve day I was promoted to first lieutenant, to rank from 30 November 1943. A surprise package, much appreciated.

On Christmas Day afternoon John Richards and I walked along the beach, just down from the bivouac, throwing bits of coral into the water, feeling less than festive, looking out over the sea toward Munda. Probably just to harass the Marines stationed there, on an American holiday, a single Zero fighter commenced making repeated runs on the airfield. Two Corsairs rose to contest it, to drive it off. That Zero pilot had been in the area a long time and knew his business. The Corsairs could not touch him. Running out of fuel or tiring of the contest, he stood the Zero on its tail and blasted off into the high blue, leaving his would-be attackers far behind, becoming a speck in the sky as he leveled off, streaking for home. A good show all around and no one killed on that Christmas afternoon.

The battalion received two bottles of beer per man to celebrate the Nativity. Never much for beer, I hastened to pass my ration on to Hammons. That night I hunkered down on my haunches alongside Red Harper and Doc Lawrence at the Doc's tent and watched them belt down a few of those special small bottles of medicinal brandy that somehow had escaped consumption during prior celebrations, chasing the fiery brandy with fetid water from a five-gallon expeditionary can, kidding each other about the 14th Platoon, the foul-ups at Lakehurst. In the coconut grove that Christmas of 1943, there was little to be bright and cheerful about, but we made do with what we had at hand, and did not succumb to the maudlin. We had neither the means nor the desire.

Rumor time. The parachute regiment was coming out of the Torokina beaches along with the Raiders. An operation against New Ireland was to be launched. The entire parachute regiment would be dropped on Kavieng airfield. The Raiders would spearhead the landing of a Marine division and one from the Army, and would link up with us on the airfield. We locked onto that piece of misinformation like a bunch of starving moray eels. Not a thread of truth in it!

Oh, there was to be a move, the regiment clearly involved, but it had nothing to do with a combat jump on Kavieng. In mid-January the regiment came together once again on Guadalcanal at Tassafaronga. There it received official word that it would proceed to the United States for the disbandment of the regiment and for assignment of its personnel to the 5th Marine Division (Reinforced), then forming at Camp Pendleton. It appeared that we had not earned our jump pay throughout those long months without aircraft or the ground facilities necessary to execute training jumps. The Raiders, too, faced extinction, a few returning to the States with us, the majority to become the reconstituted 4th Marine Regiment. The experiment in division and corps special troops evidently had not proven a profitable experience Corps-wide. We had our own opinions about *that!*

On a Sunday, in the midst of a torrential rain, we loaded our gear into boats on the beach and off-loaded it tied up alongside merchant shipping that was to carry us to the States. The merchant seamen decided against laboring on the Sabbath, so we had to man the equipment, bring up the gear, and stow it in the holds. We worked nearly the whole day in the downpour while the civilians of our great country slouched just inside the hatchways, jeering and jibing at our efforts, counting mentally the extra pay they would draw for being on duty in the *combat* zone. Finally, just before dark, we finished, closed the hatch covers, and went below.

The next day, the civilian crew having voted almost unanimously to go to work, the anchor came up and the ship sailed from Guadalcanal, bound for San Diego.

Part Three

SAND AND
BLOOD

To you, who lie within this coral sand,
We, who remain, pay tribute to a pledge
That dying, thou surely shalt not
have died in vain . . .

****

When we with loving hands laid back the earth
That was for moments short to couch thy form
We did not bid a last and sad farewell,
But only "Rest ye well."
Then with this humble, heartfelt epitaph
We marked this spot, and murmuring requiem,
Moved on to Westward.

Lines taken from a plaque in the cemetery at Tarawa, composed by an unknown Marine, used by Robert Sherrod in his book entitled *On to Westward.*

8

The Cadres

We pulled into San Diego after dark, the dock lights illuminating the ships and the unloading area with a clear, cold brightness.

Under the glare of the dock lights we would catch our first glimpse of women—bus and cargo truck drivers assigned to transport us and our gear to Camp Elliott. The commanding officer of troops had been forewarned that females would be carrying out the transport duties, and had promulgated an order prohibiting catcalls, profanity, or obscenities from being directed at the women Marines. First Sergeant Mieure of the 1st Battalion had been even more emphatic, had promised to break his Reising gun over the head of any violator of the published order.

You never can be sure of absolute control, no matter what the deterrent. As the ship warped into the dock, two hefty females in dungarees stepped down from the door of one of the buses, into full view of the troops massed on the forward well deck. Loud and clear came a rebel yell—"Ahhhhhhhh-Haaaaaa!" from the throat of a trooper just in front of Mieure. WHAP! Down came the Reising gun on the trooper's steel helmet with force enough to break its wooden stock, dropping the malefactor to the deck. Mieure never lied to his men. There were no further outbursts during the unloading.

For ten frustrating days, we were locked into the confines of Camp Elliott. Ten days of quarantine, waiting to determine how well the malaria bug and all the other little bugs that we had been exposed to in the Solomons were doing. Ten days, and then thirty days leave, the troops spinning away to every state in the Union, me to Maine in midwinter, after months spent at seven degrees off the equator.

During the final days of our leave period the officers of the parachute regiment came together for nearly a week in Los Angeles. We knew not what lay in store for us in the infantry division at Camp Pendleton, hating the thought of it, our loyalties still strong for the parachute battalions, refusing to give up what once had been. We played hard, carefree, happy, enjoying old friends, learning to enjoy new ones from the other battalions and those from the Raiders who had come back with us. We made love late at night, at midmorning, relishing the easy life, trying to stretch it to the limit, in an environment when the military uniform was not anathema and more than one civilian was glad to buy a round of drinks for the crew. Good days and nights, never to come again in our lifetime.

Then the fun ended. Time to move south to Pendleton, to report for duty with the 5th Marine Division. Duncan and I found ourselves assigned to the 3d Battalion, 26th Marines, where Duncan was given command of the 81mm Mortar Platoon and I was sent to "H" Company as second in command.

The company was commanded by a noncombatant captain, fresh out of the battles of Quantico and Washington, D.C. He knew nothing about a Fleet Marine Force rifle company and did not want the knowledge. He owned a Packard roadster and his only real concern was how many trips he could make, driving it up and down the coast road to Los Angeles and back—weekends and working days included. Once a qualified infantry officer had been assigned him as executive officer, he felt more free to fly than ever.

The company itself was in good hands. First Sergeant

Mieure from 1st Parachute Battalion was the first sergeant. Charlie Cona, who had gone through officer training with me and had joined the 2d Parachute Battalion on Vella, now commanded 1st Platoon. His NCOs, including the guide, Sergeant Buziuk, were from 1st Parachute Battalion. Tex Bechtold, another parachutist, who had fought at Bougainville, had 2d Platoon. Ernie DeFazio, a corporal with whom I had become good friends at Lakehurst, had been wounded on Guadalcanal and joined the 2d Parachute Battalion on Vella a year later. Now a sergeant, he was Bechtold's guide. Ernie would do thirty years, would fight in three wars, would be promoted through every rank from corporal to lieutenant colonel. Johnny Phelps, an old-timer, a mustang in for the duration, had 3d Platoon, backed up by the most experienced NCOs in the company. The machine gun platoon—six heavies and six lights—was run by a mustang from 1st Parachute Battalion named Rudy Moffler. The 60mm mortars were under the care of an inexperienced young lieutenant named Clark from the Confederate aristocracy. The weapons NCOs, both in mortars and machine guns, were combat-tried, experienced professionals. A quirk of fate had given each of the rifle platoons noncombatant platoon sergeants fresh out of Posts and Stations—not a good way to win a war, but we were stuck with them.

As a part of my duties as executive officer, I was responsible for the assault platoon, flamethrowers, rocket launchers, and demolitions. Three teams each of such specialists.

When the company reached authorized strength, it included five out of seven company officers with prior combat experience and 70 percent of the enlisted ranks having gone through at least one campaign.

With four Marine divisions overseas and a sixth being formed out there, Headquarters probably did the best it could to fill the command billets. Headquarters, Marine Corps, the schools at Quantico, and the Marine barracks security detachments all over the country had to be stripped to provide the rank and the numbers. The mix could be nothing but a poor one, the bottom of the barrel, providing less than the optimum in efficiency. Our battalion was to have five commanders before I left it. Only one of those commanders had prior combat experience. In many battalions, ours included, the executive officers were drawn from the ship's detachments, had gone aboard a cruiser or a battleship as second lieutenants and had remained there until they were promoted to major. No two environments could be further apart than life in the jungles of the South Pacific and that of a clean bunk, wardroom messing, and teakwood decks. No two environments could produce more intransigence when pitted one against the other.

Enough said about general background. We had been spoiled by the light-infantry aspects of the parachute battalions; spoiled by the Johnson weapons with which the 2d Parachute Battalion had been armed—the rifles and the light machine guns, machine guns that weighed just over twelve pounds; spoiled by the rather free-wheeling atmosphere of duty in The Slot, by the phenomenal esprit de corps exhibited by the Raiders and the parachutists. We were guilty of snobbery toward the new officers that we were to serve with and under. We were spoiling for trouble, ready to make it at the flick of an eyelash.

Young warriors tend to be very parochial in their views, tend to identify only with their own war, the one then being fought. Gross ignorance to be sure, but we were eaten up with it at that point in time. Most troopers who have been exposed to combat hold in contempt those who have not been so blessed. It would take me years of learning, with special instruction from some of my most battle-hardened seniors, before I would change that view. In the 5th Division there were many who thought as I did.

A few weeks after my assignment to "H" Company, I met General Rockey, the division commander; his chief of staff, Colonel Worton; and the general's aide-de-camp. I met them out in the training area. They came upon me at the wrong time.

The company commander had left mid-week for a Los Angeles liberty run, leaving me to conduct the training and administration of the company—a practice fast becoming routine. Added to that irritation was the fact that the Browning automatic rifles we were attempting to fire were malfunctioning so consistently that it was quite impossible to conduct the surprise-firing exercises shown in the division training schedule.

The general accepted my salute and asked me how I liked duty in the 5th Marine Division. My reply came tumbling out of my mouth in a blur of words, in proper third person, with "Sir" used in proper context, but the message all negative—my dislike of the huge, 200-man companies; the undependable weapons; and my special dislike for a company commander who never was present for duty.

"Oh! You are not the commanding officer? Who *is* the commanding officer? *Where* is the commanding officer?" The commanding officer's name was supplied. Instant recognition by both the general and the colonel. A knowing look passed between them, a smile touching the general's lips.

Were there other complaints from the lieutenant about the division? Where had the lieutenant served prior to 5th Division? I was out of complaints, caution squeezing itself back into my skull, but I did answer his query on prior service. Parachutist? 2d Battalion? Colonel Krulak? The general, still smiling, returned my salute, walked to his sedan, and left the range.

That afternoon the "H" Company officers were called to battalion headquarters, where we were interrogated about the events of the morning by the commanding officer and the executive officer. Since I was the one who had sounded off, it was I who took the abuse, which I did, gladly. We had upset the general, who had upset the regimental commander, who had upset the battalion commander. What more did we have to say?

I reiterated my complaints concerning the organization of the division, the faulty weapons with which we were supplied, and the sorry company commander who never was aboard for duty, and then we were dismissed.

The next morning we received a new battalion commander, and Don Castle, who had been in Headquarters Company of 2d Parachute Battalion, appeared at the barracks to take command of "H" Company.

The general had read my complaints as valid. There was nothing to be done about the weapons except to report them faulty by serial number. He could take immediate corrective action in the personnel field, and he did, in a more agreeable manner than I would have dreamed possible.

Everything was not slanted toward training for combat during those early months of 1944. There were other things to make life worthwhile. Most of the staff NCOs and officers had brought their families into the Camp Pendleton area—to Oceanside, Carlsbad, Vista, Fallbrook, and San Clemente. Commuting was the order of the day.

For the first time since our marriage, Helen and I lived together for more than a weekend at a time. We occupied a single room, shared shower and toilet facilities, and had to usher our guests out of the building prior to 2200 in the evening. Our place of abode was a Rosicrucian monastery perched high on a hillside overlooking the Santa Margarita Valley, a most peaceful and scenic location, tightly controlled by our hosts, who served only vegetarian meals in the dining facility. If we were to satisfy our longing for the flesh of a beef critter, we must walk to Oceanside—perhaps a couple of miles—where, with some frequency, we would come across the monastery supervisor and his wife savaging a hamburger or a cheeseburger.

On 6 June we basked in the sun on the beach at Oceanside, bodysurfed in the cold water, ate from our picnic basket, and snuggled close on the blanket, the radio turned on for music. During a break in the melody came the announcement of The Longest Day; the Normandy landings had begun. Our thoughts changed quickly, wondering how much longer we had to know each other as we had in the past few months, dreading the inevitable loss of it all.

The Normandy landing was a portent. The war was far from over. During the remainder of June the Pacific war erupted into a series of violent actions in the Marianas. A little more than a month later, as our regiment crossed over Highway 101 during a routine amphibious landing exercise, a message came down from higher echelon halting the maneuver. Our time in the States was nearly over. With Saipan secured there would be an attack on Guam. Somehow in the troop list shuffle, we had been tagged as floating reserve for the operation. We had ten days in which to get our gear together and mount out.

The wives and sweethearts of the regiment took this turn of events as stoically as their men, found new temporary or permanent quarters in anticipation of the final breakaway— the evaporation of the rosy mists through which we all had moved during that spring and summer of 1944. My wife took up residence at a rooming house in Los Angeles, heavily pregnant in the July heat, a trip back to Maine by air to be made subsequent to the sailing of the regiment. By their determination, resiliency, and acceptance of the reality of the moment, the sisters of the Corps set a shining example for all to see, to emulate. Their men took from them a transfusion of their quiet courage, making the closing of the door less difficult.

The regiment did not go to Guam. An Army unit located much closer to the scene of action had been utilized. War is like that, a lot of abortive lunges, a lot of energy expended and wasted, a lot of wear and tear on the nervous system. Hurry up and wait, an adage oft-repeated, calculated to build within one's soul an infinite patience, an acceptance of the futility of expecting reason to prevail.

In lieu of the contested beaches of Guam, we landed on the Big Island of Hawaii, rode up the narrow road from Hilo to Kamuela, and there in the shadow of Mauna Kea, in the dry, red dust of the high plateau, occupied a section of the old 2d Marine Division's Camp Tarawa. It was hot in the daytime, cold at night, sometimes three- or four-blankets cold, even in July; the wind was never still, moving across the flatland at the base of the ancient volcano, moving the dust with it, to cover us night and day. We trained hard, slept hard, waited for the rest of the division to join us, and pondered what the future held as the war moved steadily toward the Japanese homeland.

9

X-RAY

The remainder of the division arrived and came up the hill to join us, bringing rumors of our next deployment. The Marianas, Saipan, Tinian, and Guam had been secured by the summer's end. In September, the 1st Marine Division had been hurled at Peleliu in the Carolines to secure an airfield from which MacArthur could support his attack on the Philippines. With more than 1,200 Marines of the 1st Division dead and more than 5,000 wounded, MacArthur, in his usual cavalier manner, had seen fit to change his attack plan, to land at Leyte, without need for the airfield secured for him at Peleliu with so much Marine blood.

By mid-November we had a target. By that time the war had moved west so far that one of the old names, Formosa, that old planner's nightmare, now could be deleted, set aside for consideration only in conjunction with operations against mainland China. A direct attack on Japan through the Volcano-Bonin Island chain was considered far more feasible than the time-consuming, manpower-depleting Formosan campaign. A move into the Volcano-Bonins would negate enemy air operations in the area, would allow the establish-

ment of forward air bases from which American fighter aircraft could be launched to cover the long-range bombers
operating from Guam and Saipan on strikes against the Japanese home islands, and would provide emergency landing
facilities for bombers crippled over the target area. A critical
survey of all the islands in the Volcano-Bonin group revealed
only one that could fulfill effectively those multiple requirements. Its code name was X-RAY.

It lay halfway between Saipan and Tokyo, south of Japan
by some six hundred nautical miles and along the axis of the
long-range bomber routes of approach. Viewed from seaward
it took on the appearance of a sleeping sea monster, its tail a
worn-out volcano rising five hundred feet above the surface
of the water on the island's southern tip. To the north its head
was formed by a plateau of jagged high points reaching nearly
four hundred feet, broken in many places by deep serrations.
The surface of the plateau was sandy, rocky, heavily laced
with huge boulders, sharply rising cliffs like spines upon a
monster's head and neck. Where the head entered the sea on
the northern tip, other cliffs plunged vertically into the foam.
The island was two-and-a-half miles wide at the shoulders,
dwindling to half a mile across the junction of the tail and
back, the surface here formed by layer upon layer of fine,
black volcanic ash that once had poured down from the
mouth of the now-extinct volcano. Almost five miles in length
from the northern plateau to the mountain. Seven-and-a-half
square miles of unadulterated hell.

Security about the operation was tight. Planning behind
closed and locked doors. Slowly, very slowly, we were fed
bits of information—order of battle, troop lists. It would be a
big one, two maybe three Marine divisions committed, the
target very close to the Japanese home islands. Training
accelerated, became more sophisticated. Live-fire exercises
with overhead mortar and artillery fire—fire coming down
with almost too much realism, losing men and weapons to
short rounds, to less-than-perfect fire-support coordination,
lessons better learned on the Big Island than on X-RAY.
Tank-infantry exercises, with infantry leading, guiding, pro-
tecting the armor. Close air support with live rockets,
bombs, cannon and machine gun fire. Total team effort, getting more professional as the training days passed. Always

dirty, always sweaty, coming in from the field after four or five days of continuous joint training to sluice down in the tiny trickle of water that reached our battalion area—the one at the end of the pipeline—the one with the smallest diameter of pipe to deliver the water.

The 28th Marines ran all their operations against a special hill out in the training area. Every battalion of that regiment took turns assaulting that hill from every direction, in every tactical formation, with artillery and air support always on call. It didn't take a military genius to figure out that somewhere on X-RAY there was a difficult piece of high ground and that the 28th would be pitted against it.

On the sixth day of December my first son was born. Word came staggering down through Red Cross channels some time later, but even the delay in communications could not spoil the joy of knowing that the bloodline would be perpetuated, that there was a son to carry on the family name.

When Christmas rolled around the operation was locked on. On Christmas Day we started loading out. Fifteen days later we were aboard transport shipping and would remain aboard about the same time as the people of Noah, forty days and forty nights. Looking back on it, Noah's troops might have had it a bit better than we did. At least they were not blacked out every night, and the animals could not have smelled worse than the troop compartments of our ship, both officer and enlisted, after continuous nights of blackout, hatches dogged, hold covers firmly in place, the blower systems hardly moving the hot, thick, humid air below decks.

For two days, the ships of the Expeditionary Force had swung at anchor off the coast of Saipan. For two days the holds had been uncovered, fresh air allowed to penetrate, to circulate, to cleanse the foulness of the living spaces. For two days the underway slap, the surge, the rise and fall, the rolling of the ships had been stilled, a gentle rocking the only noticeable movement. One almost could feel human again after the long voyage from Hawaii.

The latest intelligence information concerning X-RAY was dispensed to us; the most recent photographs displayed; the newest vectographs examined minutely through infrared viewers; the numbers of defensive installations, by type, cross-checked; the order of battle updated. On the port side of the forward well deck, Charlie Cona and I briefed our units at the same time.

In our spare time we found sunlit spots on the open decks; cleaned our individual weapons and ammunition; checked crew-served weapons, ammunition boxes, communications equipment; catnapped in the sun; wrote letters; and stared at the Saipan shoreline. Two days out of X-RAY we rested, preparing ourselves physically and psychologically for the ordeal of the beaches.

And then on 16 February the moment of respite was over, the movement to the objective began. The clouds lowered, obscuring the skies. Scud overhead. Scud across the gray seas. The landing ships, the flatbottoms, had gone ahead, their slow speed dictating an earlier departure time. Outbound now from Saipan on a course directly to X-RAY was the largest convoy yet to be assembled in the Pacific— more than 450 ships—combatant, transport, and supply, and in them six regiments of Marine infantry and their combat support units.

When we left Saipan we gave up the sham of referring to the target as X-RAY. Instead we called it Iwo Jima.

10

The Assault

The planners thought that for Iwo they would be very clever. This time they would subject the target area to a prelanding bombardment such as the world never had before observed. From the Marianas and from fields on Saipan and Guam, they would send continuous flights of Seventh Air Force B-24s. Fighter-bombers from the carriers would add volume to the ordnance dropped. There would be no emplacements left; the two main airfields would become rubble and craters. A toy airplane would not find useable space to land safely. The defenders would be driven deep into the ground, those not killed or wounded made mad by the countless, endless explosions surrounding them. After the aircraft had mutilated the island and everything on it, then the battleships, the cruisers, and destroyers would come alongside at close range to destroy selected troop unit and weaponry targets. When the assault troops came ashore it would be a walk-in, standing upright, with nothing left but mopping-up operations to be accomplished.

For seventy-four consecutive days the B-24s struck at the island. At specified intervals naval air joined in the attack.

The photographs brought back by the returning pilots were most impressive. We saw them within hours of processing. They showed towering columns of smoke rising over the island, almost obliterating it from view. They showed hundreds of bomb craters on and around the runways. The photographs indicated complete neutralization of the airfield facilities in Iwo.

We saw all this on the photographs; the admirals and generals saw it too, and believed what they saw. But photography and reality are sometimes at variance.

Each night, long after the pilots and crewmen of the B-24s slept securely in their pads in the Marianas, a Japanese engineer battalion equipped with but eleven trucks, three rollers, and two bulldozers would work steadily, without a break for the twelve hours allowed them, and upon the rising of the sun at least one main runway once again would be operational. Such determination, such obstinacy had not been included in the estimate of the situation drawn up by the planners.

Well, they had slipped a little, these planners, but they still had the naval gun. The work would be completed properly yet. There would be no looseness of fire, no near misses. The sixteen-inch guns of the battleships, the fourteen-inch—the lesser calibers of the cruisers and destroyers, the rockets, and the 40mms of the LCI gunboats would rake the island. Every foot of the island was covered by some sort of naval gunfire on the fire-support charts. All the voices of naval gunfire would chorus together—the sibilance of the rockets, the crack of the high-velocity rounds, the drumming of the 40mms, the thunder of the heavy calibers. The naval guns would speak, would be heard, would induce fear and respect.

Smoke rose, clouds of dust filled the air, flame flashed along the length of the island. But through the pall, through the rain of shrapnel, through the shattering concussions, Iwo fought back, belching fire and steel. Like the aircraft before them, the ship's guns would pummel the island, would rend it, but they would not totally subdue it or its garrison.

At dusk on the evening of D-1, as the convoy ran in on Iwo, a courier ship moved down the length of the column, dropping off last-minute top-secret dispatches. We lined the rail to watch the trim, agile destroyer-escort thread her way through the line of ships, marvelling at the superb ship-handling, the sureness and grace of movement. We watched, too, far out on the horizon, the destroyer screen zigzagging, twisting, turning, doubling back, securing the flanks of the force. Closer inboard were the battleships, the cruisers, the carriers looming hugely astern. Darkness fell; the troops were sent below before we could relay to them the information brought to us by the courier. News of the *Pensacola,* hit solidly by six rounds from the casemated guns at the base of the mountain—hit hard—lifeless now in the rise and fall of the offshore swell. News of the courage, the gallantry of the men of LCI Gunboat Flotilla 3, wiped out as a functional combat element by fire from those same Japanese guns, as they tried to support the operations of the underwater demolition teams. Nine of the twelve gunboats hit and put out of action. Disquieting.

After midnight I ducked through the blackout curtains, slipped quietly through the hatch, moved to the rail, and stared out into the darkness at the island. I had written my last letters to my wife and to my parents late that evening, had made my peace with this world, secure in the faith that whatever might happen on the morrow and all the days and nights thereafter lay in the hands of God.

The cruisers and the battleships were pounding away at the mountain—Suribachi—and at the cliffs bordering the high ground above the 4th Marine Division landing beaches, tearing up the narrow neck of land that joined Suribachi to the bulk of the island, working over the airfields, laying down a cordon of steel, searching for the vitals of Iwo Jima. I watched the strike of the projectiles, wondering how long any human could stand up to such a beastly beating. Salvo after salvo, deliberate in execution, the flashes of the exploding shells illuminating the mountain and the beaches. It seemed impossible that the Japanese could endure long under such pulverizing fire.

But they could and did. As I watched, the casemated guns at the base of the mountain came alive, slamming their projectiles seaward, shredding the air with the power of their passage, tearing the water and the steel of the ships. Iwo's defenders might be deafened by our gunfire, torn by its shards, but they were very much alive, quite capable of strongly contesting our landing.

I breathed deeply of the clean night air and went back into the sweaty, acrid stench of the junior officers' bunk room, convinced more than ever that I never would leave the island alive.

Dawn. The sun peered over the eastern horizon, completed its reconnaissance and heaved itself out of the sea. The scud had disappeared, the clouds had blown away. D Day would be one of beauty, the sea calm, almost no wind to ruffle its surface.

Before sunrise the ritual of steak and eggs, the traditional sacrament of D day. For some, a waste of good food and preparation time. For others, a gorging. For all, the last full hot meal for weeks to come.

It was time for a variety of final rites. The pre-H hour softening up of the landing beaches by fire-support ships; the air strikes behind the beaches by planes from the fast-carrier task force; Navy and Marine pilots delivering napalm, rocket and machine gun fire. The launching of the amphibious tractors from the landing ships, the lowering of landing craft from assault transports, the assembly of boat teams, the emptying of cargo holds. The whole process of transferring men and equipment from long-range transport into craft capable of beach assault must be carried out before any phase of actual ground combat on Iwo could materialize. One must see, hear, feel, smell all of these components, must participate in a major amphibious operation to even begin to fathom its awesome complexities, its nearly machine-like requirements of timing.

The magic moment established for that morning was 0900. The combat-loaded tractors churned slowly through the water, circling, waiting to be called, bobbing about like a line of corks in a swimming pool. The routine messages—flag and radio—were dispatched; the pattern was set. The tractors formed for landing, wave upon wave, and at 0830 reached the line of departure, the point of no return. Four thousand yards to touchdown, a little more than two miles to travel through the unknown. It took the first wave just two minutes longer than planned to ground in the sand and ash. One hour and twenty-eight minutes later the beaches were a clutter of tractors, broached landing craft, bogged-down vehicles, and troops, but elements of all eight assault battalions were ashore. Knee-deep in the black volcanic ash, trying desperately to keep the beaches clear, to climb up and over the first beach terrace—in some places twice the height of a man and masking the supporting fires of the tractor howitzers—the men of those battalions came first under carefully registered mortar and artillery barrages of the enemy and, once over the terrace, found themselves exposed to heavy and accurate machine gun and small-arms fire delivered from enemy pill-boxes concealed in the sand.

No one walked straight in, standing up.

Our regiment's mission on D day was to act as V Amphibious Corps reserve, with the 1st Battalion of the regiment assigned as 5th Division reserve. We were to boat early, prepared to land on any beach, to reinforce any regiment of the two assault divisions.

We went over the side, down the nets, and into the landing craft at 1100. We had watched the H-hour landings through field glasses and the more powerful pedestal-mounted glasses of the ship, had seen the tractors hang up in the sand and ash, had seen the tanks creep slowly over the terraces, had listened to the radio messages coming in from the units ashore. Shortly after 1100 our boats started to circle, waiting for the signal to move up to the line of departure, to be given a beach upon which to land.

We did not go in all day, just stayed in those damned boats, inhaling exhaust fumes, getting seasick, vomiting over the side, urinating over the side, crapping over the side. Around and around until we were so exhausted by the idiocy of it all, so worn down, so uncomfortable, so *irritated* that we did not care where we landed, just as long as we could escape another minute in those boats!

At 1600, with half a day of circling in our systems, V Amphibious Corps released the regiment to the 5th Division. We stopped circling, formed up in waves, and headed in.

Even that late in the day the fire-support ships still stood close in, the heavy calibers booming. It was a breathtaking sight, the sound equally so, as we slid on past one of the battleships, the muzzle blast of the sixteen-inch guns threatening to lift us clear of the water as we came abreast on our way in to the Red Beaches of our parent division.

As we left the line of departure we struggled into our equipment. Can you believe that we had been ordered to wear the heaviest pack of the Marine Corps pack combinations, the field transport pack, for an *assault* landing? Haversack, knapsack, long blanket roll, shelter half, a gas mask, a unit of fire, two filled canteens, fragmentation grenades, smoke grenades, and two rounds of 60mm mortar ammunition per man as an average, plus his weapon.

My basic weapon was the service .45 pistol. In addition to that I carried ten pounds of Thompson submachine gun; two thirty-round magazines taped end to end in the piece, and four more in canvas carriers on my pistol belt. One hardly could discern my five-foot-six-and-three-quarters human form under all that equipment and weaponry.

The company commanders and the operations officer, Bill Day, had pled for the light marching pack, but the battalion commander was adamant. We would take everything ashore that could be carried.

Our wave hit the beach; the ramps went down. We slogged through the surf and on up into the black sand, sinking in to the calf of the leg with each step. No small-arms fire on this beach, but mortar fire rained down steadily as we staggered forward, falling, regaining our feet, lurching onward once again.

The last man out of our boat caught a mortar fragment in the calf of his leg before he reached the ramp. He tumbled backwards into the boat, the ramp came up and was secured, the boat backed off and headed seaward. A Purple Heart, a battle star on the Asiatic-Pacific ribbon, and a free ride to the hospital ship without ever setting foot on Iwo. We called them million dollar wounds in those days.

That first night ashore was a sleepless one. The Japanese had us locked on from the mountain to the south and from the northern defense line. They kept hitting us with 90mm mortar and artillery fire throughout the night, with considerable success. Small wonder. At daybreak we discovered that the battalion executive officer had given the company an assembly area centered on a Japanese aiming stake—which was taken down with some haste, I might add.

It was surprisingly cold. After training in Hawaii, and the trip out from Saipan, we were not ready for the damp chill. I thought at first that it was nerves that were causing me to shake and shiver, but I found that once I had donned the issue M1943 jacket, my quivering subsided almost immediately.

Among the rounds that came whizzing in that night, one struck dead center in the V of a chevron-type foxhole just south of mine, blowing both occupants out of their sides of the V, but miraculously injuring neither.

Another round bit at the battalion executive officer—another million dollar wound, but requiring evacuation. Some of us gladly would have paid that Japanese gunner for the delivery of that shell.

The fire-support ships pulled out to sea that night to avoid attack by enemy aircraft, but left enough shipping within range to keep star shells dropping without cessation until morning. The falling flares kept the terrain as bright as daylight, their smoking trails twisting and turning, adding to the icy unreality of it all.

At midmorning the following day we shifted to the west to back up the 27th Marines, our mission division reserve, along with the 2d Battalion. Dan Pollock's 1st Battalion was attached to the 27th Marines and held down the west beach, the left flank of the division. For the two battalions in reserve the day passed without incident except for the constant artillery and mortar shelling.

That night, in the rain and the fog, the Japanese came down from the north with aircraft from their special attack units, found our ships, and tore them up, before being destroyed or driven away by defensive fire. A good bag by anyone's reckoning. *Saratoga,* damaged so fearfully that she must return to Pearl for repairs. *Bismarck Sea* sent to the bottom. *Lunga Point* damaged, but able to continue operations. We heard the aircraft passing overhead that night, wondering whose they were, learning that they were enemy when we heard the explosions echo from the eastern sea areas.

On the third day, the 1st Battalion, still holding down the division left flank, attacked with the 27th Marines to uncover the ground west of the second airfield. By nightfall, after heavy casualties, a thousand yards of terrain had been wrested from the enemy.

Rea Duncan, leading "B" Company, was knocked down twice by enemy fire striking his helmet, once by shrapnel, once by a bullet. Not a scratch, no blood on either occasion, but before the day ended Rea was down for the count. Wounded by explosive bullets in his left leg and groin, he was evacuated to the beach, where he lay from midmorning until 2200, full of brandy and morphine. The last ship in the anchorage finally took him on board and placed him in the morgue. The doctor looked at him, judged him not repairable, and returned to the operating room. At this juncture someone in the morgue attempted to strip Duncan of his wristwatch. Wrong move. Rea raised so much hell that he was overheard by the doctor who had just judged him too far gone to repair. Learning the source of the hell raising, the doctor changed his mind and went to work on Duncan, furnishing him a half-pint of Old Forester in lieu of an anesthetic to steady his nerves. As Duncan was finishing off the Old Forester, a deep bass voice floated up from somewhere below him—"Well if it isn't old drunken Duncan." The owner of the voice, another old trooper—Bob Ettenborough, the jumpmaster at Lakehurst—in pretty rotten shape himself, but still with a sense of humor.

For his exemplary leadership, his dogged persistence, his boundless courage in the midst of the bloody maelstrom that had swept the island's western shores, Duncan was awarded the Navy Cross and the Purple Heart.

On the fourth morning it was still raining. It was to be my worst day on the island, possibly the worst day in my life as far as personal loss was concerned.

On that sodden morning the planners had been busy. All along the V Amphibious Corps line there were to be changes in front-line units. In the 5th Division zone of action our regiment was to relieve two battalions of the 27th Marines on the line, with Pollock's battalion reverting to parent control. There was much talk about relief of the lines, but what was actually intended by the planners was a passage of lines, the battalions of our regiment attacking through the static positions held by the 27th Marines. Passage of lines—one of the most difficult of infantry maneuvers to execute, even when well-coordinated. On that morning, coordination was one of many missing ingredients necessary for success.

In their haste to ram us through the front-line positions on the right flank of the 5th Division, no proper reconnaissance of terrain or enemy positions was made. Boundary lines were drawn through terrain not physically held by the 27th Marines, lines which extended into the adjacent division's zone of responsibility, terrain held in strength by the enemy. On the eastern or right flank rose a long, sloping bluff commanding the approaches to the second airfield. Upon it, in bunkers, pillboxes, and fire-communication trenches, the Japanese waited for us to make our move.

At first light we started moving up. The company commanders had gone forward to meet with the battalion commander and representatives of the battalion of the 27th Marines through which we were to pass. "I" Company moved up on our right, along a ridge line leading into the southern end of the airfield. I brought "H" Company up along the left side of a taxiway connecting the two airfields, with instructions to cross over and gain the high ground at a spot to be designated by Castle.

We marched in a long column in clear view of the enemy mortar and artillery observers located on the high ground. There was no other way to go and still reach the assembly area in time for the attack. The Japanese were excellent with the mortars, kept the shells walking up and down the column, slowing, but not stopping our movement. Long before we reached the crossing site, there were many casualties, among them Lieutenant Moffler, the first of the company officers to be hit.

Along the eastern side of the taxiway, Japanese bulldozers had carved aircraft revetments out of the side of the ridge line, half-circles large enough to accept an aircraft, high enough to afford protection from strafing and bombing attacks. Our crossing site to reach the ridge line was between two such revetments.

Charlie Cona's 1st Platoon already had crossed, was

easing into position along the ridge line. Tex Bechtold of the 2d Platoon, with his runner and his guide, Ernie DeFazio, also had crossed. His platoon sergeant was to bring the remainder of the platoon across while Tex was being briefed by Castle. Enemy forward observers caught sight of the movement across the taxiway and laid down a barrage of 90mm and medium artillery fire in an effort to deny us the crossing site. The artillery was being fired from short range, with minimum trajectory, which saved a lot of us, the shells falling over or short of the target area.

I was in the center of the company when forward movement ceased. Working my way to the head of the column I saw the platoon sergeant of Bechtold's platoon face down in the sand, prostrate. Several other members of the platoon lay in similar attitudes. Had they all been hit by a single round?

Reaching down I grasped the sergeant's pack, heaved, and rolled him over faceup. He *wasn't* hit! Had not a visible scratch upon him. Fear of that steady pounding of artillery and mortar shells had gotten into his head, his gut, self-preservation wiping out any sense of duty or responsibility to the platoon or the company. Looking down on that expressionless face I knew that someone else must get that platoon across.

Opposite from me, on the eastern side of the taxiway, DeFazio was standing, unaware of the situation within his platoon, waiting to guide them into attack positions. I hailed him, gestured for him to return to the platoon. No hesitation from *that* one! Back across the fire-swept taxiway he sprinted, dodging the strike of the shells, breathing hard from excitement and exertion. Staring down at the platoon sergeant he saw what I had seen. Not only was a staff NCO caving in, but an *Italian* NCO to boot! But that was incidental. The real problem was to get the platoon across and into position to attack. DeFazio was more than adequate for that little chore. When his deep-chested bellow hit the ears of the platoon members, they snapped out of their temporary trance, reacted as Marines always react to positive leadership, and raced over the taxiway to the protection of the revetment. And yes, with a little sweet talk, and some more with considerable sting to it, DeFazio got the platoon sergeant up and across.

Out of that episode came DeFazio's first Silver Star for gallantry. Out of it also came a platoon sergeant who never would fail us again.

With incredibly good luck I got the company across without another man being hit. Castle's command post was just up from the revetment. I reported the company present, told him of Moffler's wound and of the incident at the crossing site, and then went forward to reconnoiter the front.

Heavy fighting was in progress in "I" Company area, on the right flank. In some places the Marines were so close to the Japanese positions that the principal weapons were grenades. With the rainfall, the low cloud cover, the high saw grass, and the dwarfed but very thick scrub brush that covered the ridge line, visibility was extremely restricted. If there were enemy troops to the front, it was difficult to determine where, for in addition to the problems of terrain and weather, we faced line upon successive line of Japanese fire-communication trenches running all across our front. We were in bad trouble with no place to go except forward and without sufficient troop strength and coordinated firepower to do so.

I turned to the left, slid down the side of a revetment forward of our lines, checked out the taxiway for enemy troops, and then climbed up the northern cut of the revetment. No sooner had I gained the crest, catching a fleeting glimpse of the second airfield, than I was blasted off the lip by shells from an enemy light mortar. Not in the least deterred by this, I crawled back to the crest again, this time noting the existence of one final revetment along the taxiway before it joined the southern junction of the service runways on the south. Bam! Bam! Bam! This time my back and shoulders stung hotly, the concussion throwing me to the bottom of the revetment. As I picked myself up, brushing debris from my clothing, Charlie Cona appeared at the southern side of the revetment lip and slid down to me, laughing at my appearance.

There was no reason to climb again, to tempt fate further. I told Charlie what I had seen in those two fast observations, and we slipped out around the northern rim of the revetment and onto the taxiway for a quiet check of the low ground.

Tat! Tat-tat! Tat-tat-tat-tat-tat! Tiny spurts of dust and sand just ahead of us, ricochets from the hard-packed taxiway whining off in all directions. Tat-tat-tat! This time closer to our feet. Then we saw the gun and its crew, a Hotchkiss heavy, its gunner and assistant gunner plainly visible through the wide embrasure of a concrete pillbox not fifty yards north of us. The gunner cut down on us once more, just as we hightailed it for the safety of the revetment.

There was nothing either of us could do about neutralizing that Hotchkiss gun and crew, so Charlie took off to bring up the light-machine gun section attached to his platoon, .30 caliber A-4s. I started back along the ridge line to report conditions to Castle.

Standing in the center of the trail was one of the company field cooks. We called him Slug, short for "Slugger." Slug Csanadi. An ex-boxer, he was tough, solid, a large head carried inboard toward his left shoulder as though he was always ready to deliver a left jab. He could have read about Iwo in the local papers, but he would take no chances with an exemption slip-up, of induction into the ranks of the Dog Faces. In July 1943 he had enlisted in the Marine Corps for the second time.

Now, on this bleak ridge line, amidst the din of machine gun fire, the explosions of grenades and mortar shells, he turned slowly toward me, his eyes set, almost glazed, the right side of his head a bloody mass of red, purple, and black. He tried to smile.

"Mr. Averill," he croaked. "What kind of war is this? When I was a young lad in the Corps they taught me to knock the ass off of a fly at one thousand yards with the '03. On this island I don't see any Japs at long range or short—and if I get close to a bunker the son of a bitch blows up in my face!"

I knew now the cause of that battered head. Ever since we had landed, the Japanese had fought from inside the pillboxes and bunkers until the positions had been overrun, then with preplaced charges they had blown themselves into paradise, blowing away numerous Marines at the same time. Slug had just stumbled away from such an explosion, had taken a foot and a half of concrete slab against the side of his head. It might have completely done in a lesser man, but Slug had shaken his head and staggered to his feet. I pointed south

toward the aid station, patted him on the shoulder, and
started him on his way.

Weeks later Slug would get his wish. He would see the
Japs up close—would blow a goodly number of them away,
get more than even for the concrete slab that had nailed
him—during one of the furious grenade duels that marked
the closing days of battle on Iwo's northern tip. He would be
awarded the Bronze Star and the Purple Heart for his actions.
Emeric J. Csanadi. Old Corps. Hard-core.

A few seconds later DeFazio materialized out of the
mist, his face solemn. "Did you hear about Charlie?"

Charlie? I had left him just minutes ago. I shook my
head in the negative.

"He's dead, Ave. Caught one right between the eyes. A
Jap heavy. Buziuk got killed by a mortar round at the same
time!"

"Did he get the A-4 section up? What in hell was he
doing? He *knew* where that heavy was located!" I just
couldn't get it through my head, couldn't see how it could
have happened.

"Yeah, he got the section up, but couldn't wait for it to
get into firing position. Tried to take that Hotchkiss out with
an M-1 rifle. The A-4 section got the Hotchkiss right after he
was killed!"

I felt hollow, completely empty. I couldn't say anything. I
was hurting too much. It had all happened too damned
fast . . .

Cona, Angelo Mario. First lieutenant, U.S. Marine
Corps Reserve. I always had known him as Charlie. No one
ever said why. Perhaps the closest friend I had known in the
Corps, our personalities fusing, complementing each other,
the quick fiery temper of his Italian heritage often held in
check by my dour Scots-Irish ancestry, his good humor and
deep understanding lifting me more than once out of my
Gaelic despondencies. Brothers, without a common drop of
blood between us.

We stood there in the drizzle, the rain seeping down our
spines, our thoughts in the past. Just across the bluff from
where Charlie and Buziuk had died, another Marine had
gone down. Tied to his pack had been two smoke grenades,
one white, one red, which had exploded when he was hit. A

curious mixture of whitish pink smoke now curled upwards into the mist. The Japanese, always alert for signals, started dropping 90mm mortar rounds where the smoke rose. The overs came in on us, blowing bits of grass, scrub, and rock into and around us. We just didn't give a damn, until two rounds came spitefully close. It was time to get off the skyline. We broke it up, Ernie heading back to his platoon, I toward the command post.

My mind was churning. Moffler gone. Charlie dead. Buziuk dead, Duncan hit and gone the day before. Bobby Dunlap of the old 3d Parachute Battalion hit on the same day. The parachutists were taking it on this show, being systematically wiped out.

Ten minutes later DeFazio was hit, and hit yet again before he could reach the aid station. The artillery that had searched so diligently for us on the taxiway had found itself a worthwhile target. Shifting its fire to the ridge line, with its first fire mission it had knocked out the battalion command post, killing the battalion commander, Bill Day, and Sergeant Major Mieure, who had left "H" Company to become the leading staff NCO of the battalion. All this before 1000 in the morning. All this and a steady stream of casualties being carried to the rear from both "H" and "I" Companies, by members of "G" Company, battalion reserve. All this and not a single yard of ground gained, not a single Japanese position breached.

For a couple of hours, Dick Cook of "G" Company acted as battalion commander. Then, about noontime, Maj. Richard Fagan, division inspector, who previously had commanded the 1st Parachute Battalion, came down from division to take command.

By midafternoon the troops of the 21st Marines, 3d Marine Division, had closed the gap on our right flank and assumed responsibility for the badly drawn boundary line that had so decimated our ranks that morning. We slid to the left, toward the southwest tip of the airfield. In the late afternoon we moved four hundred yards forward, only to be fired upon by tanks supporting the 2d Battalion operating on the low ground to our left, who mistook us for Japanese. Nothing went right that miserable day. *Nothing!*

At dusk, with the rain still falling, we were ordered to

move off the bluff down onto the low ground and establish night positions. The 21st Marines would take over the high ground. The battle for it had raged all day, and at its close we had nothing to show for it but our dead and wounded.

Darkness closed in through the fog and rain as the troopers dug in. I checked the lines and established contact with friendly units on the left and right. Water, rations, and ammunition came up from the rear and were distributed more by the senses of touch and hearing than by sight. The star shells started to pop, their usually dazzling light hardly penetrating the low cloud cover, the perpetual drizzle.

Alone in my foxhole, I started thinking about Charlie, Buziuk, and all the others lying up there on the bluff in the cold rain. It got to me, *bad!* I yelled over to Castle that I was coming to his command post, and moved across the intervening distance in one mad rush.

Overcome by a completely irrational, unreasonable compulsion, I demanded that I be allowed to go back up on the bluff and bring Charlie's body down. "NO! Graves Registration will attend to that in the morning." "*Damn it!* I want to *go!*" "*NO! Go back to your hole.*"

Hate is a terrible thing. It can consume one as no other emotion can. That night I hated Castle with such an intensity that my eyeballs jumped with pain, my heart hammered at an increased rate, my head ached incessantly. Of course he was correct, to be cool, to be without emotion is the ultimate answer. I wasn't that detached, then or ever. For some reason, the human factor was always important to me. I don't think it ever hurt my performance of duty; it even might have helped it.

The next morning I accepted Castle for what he was—a Marine Corps captain, my company commander—and let the rest go by the board. Hate was a luxury I could not afford.

11

Images

Those days on the flatland west of the second airfield were when continuity escaped me, when a smoothly moving film on the screen changed to a series of color slides, some of them painfully acute. Slide on. Slide off. Click. Click. Nothing in between.

After we came down off the bluff there was no forward movement possible in our zone of action. We were pinned in place by artillery and mortar fire and from long-range, small-arms and automatic weapons fire from emplacements and caves along the high ground to our right flank. Units of the 3d Marine Division had not been able to uncover that terrain, leaving the Japanese free to zap us every time one of us made an effort to move. A situation of little glamour and no romance. We could not even leave our foxholes to relieve the needs of our bodies. Keep a tight rectum and hope for the best. Otherwise, dig a little deeper and cover like a cat.

A Japanese stay-behind had been planted in the center of the company area. Periodically he would raise his Nambu light machine gun over his head and, with the selector set on full automatic, would twist the gun in a half-circle over his head and then reverse it, filling the air with lead right at head and neck level as we squatted in the foxholes, keeping us ducking. Then he'd slip through a tunnel into another firing position. He was still putting on his act days later, when we were able to move out of the position. No one ever saw him, just heard that gun whacking away, the rustle of its bullets passing close overhead.

Someone rushed up to the lip of my hole, babbling, sand cascading in on me immediately from the extra weight against the edge of the hole.

"Can I come in for a minute? I need to talk to *some-one!*"

Cona's platoon sergeant. White, trembling, a bad case of the shakes. No prior combat, and Iwo a hell of a place to get snapped in. How could I refuse? Cona dead. Buziuk dead. The two experienced leaders gone; no one but the squad leaders to rely upon. They would cut it OK, those squad leaders, old-timers from the parachute regiment, from the days of Empress Augusta Bay. They would do nothing to hurt the platoon sergeant, but neither would they take over *his* responsibilities. He slid into the hole, jamming me up against the side, and I heard him out. What can you say except that it is bad for everyone, that he must do his duty. Still shaking, he crawled out of the hole, half-burying me as he scurried back to the platoon position.

Two days later he was gone, sent to the rear for evacuation, unable to cope. The squad leaders ran the platoon.

Using the western taxiway that connected the first air-field with the second, the 5th Tank Battalion, supported by the 3d Tank Battalion, was to slam through the Japanese defenses of the southern tip of the second airfield and open the way for its capture. Crouching in our foxholes we watched them trundle up in column, moving like huge bugs toward the top of the airfield. We watched them hit the first of the Japanese antitank mines; watched them survive the mine fields and move on to bigger and better things—Japanese aerial torpedoes standing nose-up just below the surface of the ground; watched them shattered by the explosions, one

Sherman tank rising slowly, lazily into the air, turning on its side as it fell back, coming to rest, turret down. We watched the enemy artillery and mortar shells reaching for the Shermans; watched those wicked 47mm antitank rounds rend the skin of the turrets, penetrating them, death ricocheting within those turrets. They tried hard, those tankers did, but it was just too much. They had to back off, back out, salvage their strength for another try on another day. The gates to the airfield stood fast. It would be yet a little while before they were breached.

I was talking with one of the assault platoon section leaders as we dug our holes a little deeper, about ten feet from each other. There had been a lull in the incoming mortar and artillery fire, a good time to improve the protection afforded by the foxholes. I bent over to fill my shovel and the 90mm rounds started dropping in on us once again. When the explosions ceased, I cautiously raised my head and started to call over to the section leader. A useless gesture. One of the 90mm rounds had blown his head off, right at the shoulder line, his body still standing erect.

Just before noon it seemed that every radio in the three Marine divisions came to life simultaneously, crackling, popping, spitting static, pouring out unintelligible traffic, but after a while, comprehensible. Coming through in the clear, the message was compelling. "The Flag is up on Suribachi! The Flag is up on Suribachi!"

We turned our heads to the south, ready for another disappointment, another piece of misinformation, but there it was, the national colors, not fluttering, but standing out, fully extended, held stiffly squared by the wind across the mountaintop. It looked good, that American flag, good beyond the normal emotion of national pride, good because we knew that now *Marines* were on that mountain peak, good because it gave us the assurance that there would be no more Japanese fire missions directed from its heights, no more artillery and mortar rounds crippling us from the rear.

That flag looked splendid up there on Suribachi. In my lifetime I never again would see it displayed in a more magnificent manner. A feeling of hope started to steal through my consciousness as I took one long, last look before turning my head back to the north.

People have such weird ideas about the dead. You may tell them over and over again in training that the dead need neither water, rations, ammunition, nor weapons, but it takes some doing to make them accept those facts when the time comes. As we came out of the holes to move forward, a youngster appeared with no weapon. On the ground at his feet lay a dead Marine, not pleasant to look upon, his chest cavity neatly cleaned out by the explosion of an artillery round, but holding intact in his right hand a perfectly good M-1 carbine, on his belt two full magazines of ammunition. The youngster's sergeant pointed to the corpse, indicated that the young Marine should take the weapon and the ammunition. Pasty of complexion, gulping, sweat breaking out, head shaking in the negative, he would rather be weaponless than take one from the hand of a dead man. With a swift, smooth movement the sergeant broke the carbine loose from the death grip of the hand, unhooked the belt, pulled it from beneath the body and threw the weapon, ammunition, and equipment at the young Marine's feet.

The gift was taken without hesitation.

Moving up, we passed through an area once held by elements of the 27th Marines. Approaching from the rear, we came up on a heavy machine gun team, the gunner, feet planted firmly in the sand on either side of the tripod, head low against the rear sight, aiming in on an unknown target. To his left the assistant gunner lay alongside the gun, his hand on the half-empty belt, just short of the feedway.

Both of them had been shot exactly between the eyes.

Up on the high plateau, troops of the 3d Division finally had overrun some of the strong points along the escarpment, strong points that had been harassing us for days. After neutralizing a bunker built into the western edge of the escarpment, a 3d Division platoon had halted briefly to reorganize before moving forward again.

It was just at sunset, the sunlight sharply outlining the

figures of the Marines on the high ground. Out of nowhere arose the silhouette of a very tall Japanese, a samurai sword held high overhead in the attack position. One long, swooping chop with both hands and arms behind the swing, and the head fell from the shoulders of the Marine platoon leader who had faced the Japanese. Almost before the severed head struck the ground, the Japanese officer was falling, riddled by countless rounds from BARs and rifles fired by the platoon members.

We had broken loose for the first real gain on the ground since we landed. Broken loose so far and so fast that we had lost contact with elements of the 21st Marines on the bluff to our right. A company from the 1st Battalion was attached to our battalion to gain and maintain contact on the right.

With our battalion's usual luck, higher echelon decreed that we must break contact and move back in order to straighten defense lines. Breaking contact, like a passage of lines, is bad medicine. You ask for everything you get.

The Japanese were so close to the Marines along the line that it was quite impossible to move back during daylight hours without such movement being detected. At nightfall, units attempted to disengage and fall back as ordered. They could not escape detection even in darkness, and the Japanese quickly organized a counterattack force with two companies, driving straight for the center of the defense line. The smell of chaos was in the air.

Destroyers in fire-support stations off the west coast saved the day and the troops along the line. Firing enfilade fire with the main battery 5-in. 38s, the destroyers kept such a hail of steel on the advancing Japanese that the two companies were torn literally to shreds, the survivors charging drunkenly northward to escape the hellfire that had come down on them.

Stragglers from the withdrawing units filtered back through our lines until after 2200 that night. What a gamble—just to straighten out the grease-pencil marks on a situation map in division headquarters!

At dusk that same evening I was getting dug in, sulphur fumes and wisps of steam rising from the superheated ground in which I was digging. A medical corpsman stopped by the hole, pointed at my back, and asked, "What happened to your shoulders and back?"

I was not aware of anything wrong in those areas and told him so.

"Take off your jacket and your dungaree coat and let me have a look. Something is not right!"

I pulled off the zipper jacket, glancing at the back of it as I did so. A heavy brown encrustation covered a good part of the jacket's back. The top of my dungarees seemed even more saturated.

The corpsman squatted down at the lip of the hole and examined my back. "When did *this* happen? You have a hundred small pits and scabs in your shoulder and back—some still bleeding!"

Then it came back! Those light mortar shells on the crest of the aircraft revetment. I had been too upset by the hellish day, too busy since then to even think about that sharp impact, the stinging of those bits of steel and sand, to even notice my soiled clothing. Time does fly when you are having fun! A washdown with alcohol, a clean back and shoulder for a change, a good hard shake of the garments before donning, and a thank you to the corpsman as night came down upon Iwo once again.

After seven days on the flatland, fighting, pausing, fighting again, the regiment was ordered back for a rest, the 27th Marines pressing the attack, the 28th Marines, the Flag Raisers, moving up through the 27th to continue the attack.

As the Flag Raisers moved up the road through our lines, we gave them a hard time. We had been whipped to a standstill, decimated by the bitter fighting at the edge of the second airfield and those long days and nights on the flatland. We catcalled to them, taunted them, asked them where the flags were, where they would plant the next one. We had old friends among the ranks of the Flag Raisers—members of the parachute regiment, Raiders we had known and brawled with in the bars of Noumea, combat people we admired and respected. Our sarcasm was the sarcasm, the bad-mouth that comrades have for one another. The Flag Raisers hurled it back in our teeth and moved on. We knew what they were in for. Another hill lay to the north, close to the uncompleted third airfield. That hill would cost us all dearly. There would be no flag raised on Hill 362-A.

We watched them pass, then picked up our gear and moved back, a chopped-up imitation of a Marine rifle company. We had come across the beach on the afternoon of D day with more than 200 men. We stood now at half-strength.

12

Hit

We were allowed less than twenty-four hours in which to rest after seven straight days of constant enemy artillery and mortar fire—less than a day out of the lines—and then we were saddling up, moving back over ground that we had fought for, back up toward Hill 362-A, where the 27th and 28th Marines still struggled unsuccessfully. By ramming our regiment through the lines, perhaps the hill could be taken.

The terrain around the partially completed airfield was nothing short of moonscape—pitted, serrated, smashed by 16-in. naval gunfire, some of the dud projectiles still where they had fallen. Below the surface were huge caves, improved upon by the Japanese to furnish underground command installations, hospitals, and troop-assembly areas, all connected by tunnels between the caves. The high ground around Hill 362-A was broken by ridge lines emanating from it like the spokes of a cart wheel. We saw no Japanese, heard only the fire of their weapons, for they were buried in the ground and had been for months before we landed. They came to the surface only when lucrative targets were available or when direct pressure was upon them from the attacking Marines.

The boundaries between divisions were being shifted again. Again we would tie in with the 3d Division. I hoped that the results would be more successful than they had been around the entrance to the second airfield.

We went into position with a company of the Flag Raisers on our left flank and orders to make contact with the 3d Battalion, 9th Marines, on our right. Moving into position, I saw two dead Japanese soldiers, blackened and crisped by flamethrowers. They were the only enemy dead I had seen since we landed. The Japanese made it a point always to remove bodies. If you can't see the dead, you can't count them.

Late that afternoon the company established night defensive positions. After a long, lonesome hike over that desolate terrain I had found elements of the 3d Battalion, 9th Marines; established the fact that I was about to hook onto their left flank for the night; and, with far too much frontage for one understrength rifle company to cover, started west again, staking out platoon frontages, as I moved. It was quiet, no mortars or artillery rounds falling, no small-arms fire zipping by. I made the distance across the front and back again without being fired at. Scary!

I moved toward the left of the company to discuss night defenses and to start the platoons setting in along the line to the east. Lieutenant Clark, who had started out as leader of the 60mm mortars, had come ashore that afternoon after serving as Ship's Platoon officer, moving all of our baggage and heavy gear ashore from the transport. Castle had scheduled him to take over Cona's platoon—without an officer since Charlie's death—that evening.

A group of us met some fifty yards out from Johnny Phelp's 3d Platoon position. Clark, three enlisted men, and I pulled in tight over the map to check the platoon areas assigned. The water-cooled Browning heavy machine guns were moving up into the lines, needed to be positioned to support the platoons. The engineers were moving in with demolitions to back us up. Always too much to do, too little time to get it all accomplished correctly. The sun was sliding low over the nightmare landscape, trying to drown itself in the western sea, trying to blot out the sights it had witnessed that day on the island.

Whap! Whap! Whap-whap-whap! Whap-whap-whap-whap-whap! Something that kicked like a raunchy mule hit me in the rear of the right thigh, burning, jolting, tearing through hide and flesh, but miraculously missing bone. My right testicle smarted, seemed on fire, then went numb. Not *that!* I feverishly felt for my symbols of manhood, found all intact, and, for reasons quite unclear to me, shouted "Land mine! Land mine!" Evidently the increasing numbers of casualties from antipersonnel mines were right at the edge of my thought processes.

It was no land mine. To the north and west of where we had gathered, a Japanese Hotchkiss heavy machine gun team, in a carefully staked-out fire position, had waited all day for the beautiful target that we had presented, standing centered in the fire lane of the gun. One long, searching burst had bagged five Marines, and we knew not where the gun was located. Clark was down, badly wounded, hit hard, his ankle and leg shredded, the foot dangling, held in place by skin and sinew. As the burst had climbed and moved to the right, it had penetrated the calf of one of the Marines, gone through my thigh, gut-wounded another marine, and struck the arm of the Marine on the extreme right.

Clark was in extreme pain, going into shock. I broke out my morphine and shot it into his thigh. A corpsman who had moved quickly forward of the lines when I had shouted my meaningless message about land mines shot him up again.

That Hotchkiss gunner evidently had communications with a mortar section, for soon the explosions from 90mms shook the ground around us, making it tough to get the litter teams up to take out Clark and the gut-wounded Marine. The walking wounded already were on their way to the aid station after being treated superficially by 3d Platoon corpsmen. My leg was stiffening fast, the bullet having passed through the thigh muscle. No great pain or loss of blood, just a loss of mobility.

As I lay there alone, a chill creeping over me, dusk closing in, the crump-crump-crump of the mortar shells pounding in my ears, I knew just how precious life is, how

much we value it, want to cling to it no matter what its
disappointments, its frustrations, its pain.

The bravest of the brave, the Navy medical corpsmen,
guiding the litter bearers, came out into the gathering
darkness to bring me in. I had them stop briefly at the 3d
Platoon command post where I contacted Castle by radio,
told him of the front-line situation, and reported the casualties from the Hotchkiss burst. He seemed to resent the fact
that we had been hit—as if it had been done deliberately by
all of us and by me in particular. You just can't please some
people. At the battalion aid station, Doc Root, a young,
proficient, tough-minded Navy lieutenant, junior grade, who
would end up carrying the full medical load before the island
was secured, looked at my thigh, ruled it not serious, but
requiring evacuation.

As the jeep ambulance bobbed, bounced, and jolted its
way to the beach, I looked toward the cone of Suribachi and
thought that I saw the elongated shadow of a B-29 coming in
for a landing. Pure fantasy. The official record states that the
first B-29 came in on 4 March, three days after I had been hit
and evacuated. I suppose I wanted somehow to make it all
worthwhile, to compensate for the losses in our company, in
all the other companies across that stretch of hell. The mind
plays cruel tricks with us, our innermost thoughts mirroring
vividly, realistically, those things we want so much to see.

On the transport, designated an auxiliary hospital ship,
wizards with knives, saws, pins, needles, and thread put
Clark's ankle back together, kept him alive, gave him back
the use of his foot and leg. Wounded in the kneecap, one of
the assault platoon men lay in an upper bunk across from me,
laughing at first, sobering as life ran out of him in a stream of
blood that would not coagulate. He was not blessed with
Clark's luck. Toward midnight, with the overhead lights of the
sick bay blazing down on him, a pool of blood widening
against the sheets, he died.

Casualties ran so high in numbers that there was no
room for me on a regular hospital ship or in a Navy hospital
in the Marianas. One of the Army hospitals on Guam took
me in for repairs. The care was good, the nurses were pleasant and competent, the general atmosphere bordered on the
bizarre, for the ailments of the patients ran all the way from

the common cold and dysentery of the Air Force and Army
personnel stationed on the island to wounds of a mortal
nature suffered on Iwo. In the bed next to mine, an Air Force
sergeant with mild pneumonia cavorted playfully with any
nurse who would stand for it, while across the passageway
from me a youngster from the 3d Marine Division kept bleeding through plaster casts and bandages on his right knee,
bleeding so steadily they flew him on to the States for a better
chance at survival.

Vaseline gauze, inserted through both openings of my
wound, got the healing process done quickly and with little
pain. I was detached from the Army hospital as cured and
sent to the Fleet Marine Force Pacific, Transient Center, for
further disposition.

It was here that I came to know Craig Leman, a young
replacement officer who had taken over what was left of
Charlie Cona's old platoon two days after I had been evacuated. Leman had led the platoon through six days of heavy
fighting before sustaining a gunshot wound along the right
side of his head, which put him out of action. We returned to
Pearl Harbor together on HMS *Reaper,* a British carrier of
American vintage, and served together in "H" Company
upon its return to Hawaii.

13

Aftermath

Talk about ghost towns, the old camp on the Kameula flat was like one of those seen in western movies only more so. Red dust had covered everything, had sifted into every structure. The tentage was ripped and torn by the wind, a wind that soughed and simpered through the encampment, carrying on its wings the whispers of those taken from us on Iwo, specters riding on its gusty sighs.

A number of the old battalion had preceded us to this place of lonely seclusion from hospitals in the Marianas and on Oahu, had established their own living spaces, set up their own rituals. The first night we were back, they treated us to a concert, a beer ration fueling their efforts. Across the flat, dismal, nearly empty regimental area, the sound of the music rose and fell, echoing hollowly—a chant, punctuated by the striking of empty, fifty-five-gallon fuel drums. "Iwo-Iwo-Iwo-Jima!" *Bang! Bang! Bang!* "*Iwo-Iwo-Iwo-Jima!*" *Bang! Bang!* The chanting at first gentle, then rising to a crescendo. Pagan, phantasmal, eerie, the nights and days on Sulphur Island creeping to the fore in minds made more receptive by the solitude and the effects of the 3.2% beer; primitive warriors paying homage to the gods of their own destruction.

And then the heroes returned. What was left of the battalion came up from Hilo and once again the area was full of the sight, the sound, the smell of life, the spirits of the dead pushed back out into the prairie, to the periphery of the camp. They were out there, though, you may be sure of that, not quite believing what they saw and heard anymore than some of the living did.

The Purple Heart parades went on forever. The infantry regiments of the division had suffered more than 5,000 wounded, our own regiment close to 2,000, the battalion more than 500. In the company, out of 242 that went across the Red Beaches on D day, 80 returned. Cona and Phelps had been killed. Every officer except Castle and including replacements had been hit hard enough for evacuation. P. J. Carpenter, the first sergeant, had been killed. Tex Bechtold, Leman, and I were the only officers who returned to duty with the company.

Shortly after the company returned to the Big Island, Castle granted me another of his special favors, the task of writing letters of condolence to the families of those Marines who were killed in action or died from wounds. Until you have had *that* cross to bear, you know little of the weight of sorrow and despair. My mind was flooded with the way they went, the purity and the selflessness of their courage, the simplicity and grace with which they gave their lives for their comrades and the Corps. You can set down trite phrases from the manuals that deal with such things, perhaps breathe a little life into the deeds, if you had seen them or heard about them first hand. But what do you say when the wife or mother of one of the fallen insists on knowing in precise detail the manner of his passing, what it was that whisked his life away? How do you tell a mother that you watched her son's head disappear from his shoulders as if by magic? How do you tell a wife her husband was cremated, turned to a lump of blackened ash when his flamethrower was hit by incendiaries?

It all got to be too much, the posturing of the heroes, the influx of green replacements, the maddening indecision of the command structure. Leman and I put in for a long week-end, a seventy-two-hour pass, just to escape the whole damned mess. Our friends in the mess hall provided us with eggs, bacon, bread, and enough meat to last the three days. We put the high plateau behind us, found a camping spot on a tiny bit of headland overlooking the sea, and started to live. I still have snapshots of that beach, the thorn trees behind it, blue waters that foamed at its edges. No other humans for miles. No sound except for the seabirds, the rustle and the ripple of the wind through the thorn trees, the gentle slap and crash of the ocean. A place in which to forget the world; to swim, to battle the waves until exhausted; lie in the sun, letting it soak into the skin, burning into the skull, building new life, new attitudes in the mind. Food cooked over an open fire, the coals twinkling, sparkling, snapping, long after night had enveloped us. A time for talk, for questions, for self-examination; a chance to be released temporarily from those enemies of reason and logic—anger, spite, resentment, and intolerance; a time for a cleansing of the heart and spirit.

But not for long, not even for the seventy-two hours that had been promised to us.

A jeep chugged up behind our campsite. The driver jumped out, walked over to us. "Sir, the colonel wants you to return to base camp immediately. Why? Don't know, sir. Colonel just said to find you. Get you back to camp!"

Paradise gained and lost in less than forty-eight hours. Back up the 2,500-foot grade we went in answer to the summons, bitching all the way to the commander's hut. "Sir, Lieutenant Averill reports as ordered, Sir!"

I could tell by the flicker of the eyes, the shadow of a smirk on his lips that something devious was going down. He rode back on his chair until the front legs were clear of the deck, balancing precariously on the rear legs, plucking at his moustache.

"Mr. Averill, we have a problem. Captain Mack has had an accident. Fell off his horse while riding this afternoon. Broke his leg. Might be back to duty in a month, maybe longer. Want you to take over "I" Company, train it, get it ready for combat, have it *right* for Mack when he returns!"

I heard and comprehended every word as it came out past that moustache. Mack was one of the Inner Circle, a good drinking buddy of the colonel. The relaxation, the intro-spection, the sorting out of things while at the beach had sharpened my awareness, made things crystal clear. I was being set up—used!

"Sir! I would like very much to train "I" Company, but not to then turn it over to Captain Mack or anyone else! If I am considered proficient enough to train the company for combat, then I am proficient enough to command it in com-bat. Sir! I have never refused duty before, but unless the company will be mine, I do not wish to train it!"

The chair slammed down hard on all four legs. The colonel came upright in his seat, his mind apparently blown by such blatant effrontery. "Well, sir, if you can't be reason-able, if *I* can't convince you to do your duty, then maybe the regimental commander can! Do you want that to happen?"

I knew that the colonel was not held in the highest esteem by the regimental commander. I was already in it clear to my nose. Why not try submerging completely and see how it would all turn out?

"My pleasure, Sir! I believe that the regimental com-mander will be able to discern that the proposal is manifestly unfair. When does the colonel wish me to report to regi-ment?"

Impasse. That florid face assumed a dark red, beetlike hue. Heavy breathing, rapid plucking at the moustache, then expostulation. "Will you take the chance that Mack does not come back? Will you take the company on those grounds? It is wide open, as much one way as the other!" The colonel was lawyer-trained, could change direction in a heartbeat if he thought it would win for him.

It *was* a straight gamble. No one knew when the division would be committed again, or where. No one could tell how long a fractured leg would take to heal, or *how* it would heal. I wanted that company, wanted to command it as a lieutenant, wanted to try my luck. There were some good people left in "I" Company. I needed them. They needed me. If the colonel could back off a notch, so could I. I repressed a smile, my decision made. He saw that smile glimmer in my eyes. The hard breathing ceased, the angry turndown of the mouth straightened.

"Sir! May I have a few hours to think about it?"

"By the close of working hours, lieutenant. No later. Understand?"

Ten minutes prior to the close of working hours I was back. In that ten minutes, by fast talk and some kind of miracle, I got the company with no strings attached. It would be mine regardless of Mack's recovery.

Two weeks later Mack was flown to the States, never to return to the battalion. The colonel no doubt had known about Mack's final disposition late that evening when he gave me the company.

By the time the division was back to strength and into a heavy training schedule, Okinawa had been secured, the Philippines had been won, and the planners were selecting targets on the home islands of Japan. We entertained no thought of a quick, easy fight, for we knew that the homeland would be defended by every man, woman, and child, knew that for many of us luck was about to run out, the law of averages about to catch up with us. By midsummer the rumors started to build. Two landings, one on Kyushu, the southern island in the chain, the other on Honshu—the main effort, with the Tokyo area as its target. Each landing, it was said, was to be spearheaded by three Marine divisions. The Army had long wanted to do away with the Corps. On this soiree it might well achieve that goal.

We would be going south to Kyushu, to a place called Kagoshima. There were no maps issued, no terrain studies. One thing did leak out. The area behind the landing beaches was flat, afforded a thousand yards of grazing fire for the defenders, fire that never would rise more than three feet off the ground, fire that could cut us down by the hundreds before we could close with the enemy. The thought kept me awake more than one night.

The certainty of our final destination was a spur that could not be ignored by the unit leaders who held any sense of responsibility. There were days and nights in the field—continuous training—of companies with more than half their strength made up from raw recruits from the States. I had two platoon leaders with prior combat experience. The rest were fresh-caught, not even ready for the training on Hawaii let alone an assault on the home islands. One hell of a lot of training to accomplish, teamwork and leadership to instill, that thousand yards of flat terrain behind the Kagoshima beaches constantly before my eyes.

The bearing down, the long hours, the concentration on realistic training paid off throughout the division. I always had thought that nothing could equal the state of training excellence reached by members of the 2d Parachute Battalion prior to Choiseul, but the troops of the 5th Division reached a point in individual and team training which never again might be seen in the Corps. Platoon leaders, platoon sergeants, squad and fire team leaders, assault squad leaders from strange units could be superimposed with no prior warning, their skill so consummate that the troops would react to these strangers, take their direction as they would from their own officers and NCOs. We saw it happen in demonstration after demonstration, not just muddling through, but confidence and proficiency—the Marine Corps way—each man trained and ready to take over the next job up at any time required, the old "Fall Out One!" drill of prewar days set to a different pace, a different pattern. Incredible to watch, every performance near perfection. If we had to die on the tableland at Kagoshima, we would die well. The Japanese would admire our way of *hari-kari*.

We came down off the hill after a ten-mile forced march. No water allowed on that march. Chewing gum, pebbles, grass, any saliva-producing element quite proper, but no water. No canteens on the belts. The jeep ambulance crawled up and down the column periodically with water aboard for emergencies. No need for it to be there. No one had fallen, had passed out. No one had even complained, beyond the routine bitching that always can be expected. The company was shaping up, about as ready for Kagoshima as it was possible to make them. I pushed them hard, pushed them beyond their own self-imposed limitations, knowing full well that I never could push them as hard as the deadly realities of combat would.

The battalion area was in complete disorder as we entered it. Troopers lounging about as if on holiday schedule, talking loudly, laughing, sitting in little groups along the company streets. They jeered at the company as we went on by—hot, sweating, mouths and throats dry, heading for water in which to sluice down, to let trickle into our mouths as we showered. What *was* all this? What had taken place after we had left camp that morning?

"Didn't you know? We have just dropped some hellacious bombs on the Japanese homeland. Yesterday at a place called Hiroshima. Today on Nagasaki. Must be bad stuff. Radio says the Japs are wanting to quit. No one really knows."

Astounding information. I couldn't believe that the Japanese ever would quit, surely never would quit just because of bombing. We had firebombed the Japanese cities for weeks, with no sign of weakness. It was not in me to think that any new type of explosive would change the enemy mentality that much. But then, I never had heard of a place called Alamogordo, never heard of the explosion that had taken place there a month before, an explosion that equalled 17,000 tons of TNT. It would be months before we could witness through the camera's eye the devastation of those two cities. We were still almost medieval in our approach to armed combat, still using machine guns from the First World War, still using bayonets in close combat, still believing that warriors contended with warriors on the battlefield, that differences in politics and policies were settled there and not in the heart of a city filled with women, children, and old men.

On the following day, 10 August, one day short of the fourth anniversary of my enlistment in the Marine Corps, in spite of my unshakeable belief that they never would capitulate, the Japanese sued for peace. The people of two of their cities had been exposed to the most hideous and terrifying experience that mortal man could imagine. It was senseless to continue to resist. I prayed then, and I pray now, that the same experience never will befall my people.

14

The Conquerors

On a chill, dull, rainy morning in late September we sailed into the harbor of Sasebo on the island of Kyushu. The city had been heavily firebombed, evidence of it everywhere, but the dock area, by design or accident, had survived, was fully operable. General MacArthur had stated that when we went ashore there would be a solid shield of aircraft overhead to protect us. As we came off the ships the rain clouds were our only cover. Not an aircraft to be seen or heard.

MacArthur had determined that we would go ashore as peacemakers, an unlikely role for Marines who last had made contact with Japanese on Iwo Jima. No weapon larger than a Browning automatic rifle could be displayed. No crew-served weapons in sight. They would be kept under cover in jeep trailers and in trucks, not immediately available to us should the Japanese elect to take a few of us away to never-never land before we occupied their island. Fear of the unknown, knowledge of Japanese trickery in the past, and uncertainty about our mission bore down heavily upon our minds as we slopped warily through the mud and rain towards an abandoned ammunition factory that was to be our temporary abode. We did not smile, nor did we look like the

German troops entering Paris in triumph, did not exude their attitude of sublime contempt. The cold autumn rain drenched us, the water taken in like a sponge by our threadbare herringbone twill utility uniforms; our footgear was full of water, their exterior coated with mud and slime. I didn't know what a conqueror was supposed to feel like. I never found out. On that march to the outskirts of Sasebo I was just like all the rest—a miserable gravel-cruncher waiting for it all to end, hoping for a dry spot to crawl into. The streets were empty. Discipline, they told us later, had kept the conquered from coming out to view the conquerors. I didn't believe that. The Japanese, like intelligent people everywhere, knew enough to stay out of the rain.

Dry spots were hard to find at the end of the march. The roofs of the single-deck factory buildings had been well worked over by American aircraft that perforated them in grand style. For days, while we waited for the remainder of the division to come ashore, we huddled wherever it was partially dry. We were forced outside to dig heads, install urinals, cover garbage and trash, returning to the dry spots as quickly as the tasks were finished.

Across the river, where they could plainly observe this mass of misery, the Japanese prostitutes watched, giggled, and waggled their heads in derision. They had been instructed to be very careful. These were the American Marines, the most savage and diabolical of the enemy fighters. How could this be? Had anybody ever seen a member of the Japanese Special Landing Force, the Japanese equivalent of the U.S. Marines, dig holes in the ground; had anyone ever seen them construct a *benjo? Never!* That was for the labor battalions, not for the fighting men. No, someone must have been kidding them. These pitiful things were not American Marines, just some labor troops getting ready for the arrival of the fighters.

East of the city lay a naval ammunition depot, its place-name Ushinora. Within its limits were magazines and storerooms filled with a magnitude of naval ordnance items—bombs, torpedoes, explosives, ammunition of various calibers from small arms to aircraft cannon—and such sophisticated items as aircraft cameras and instrumentation. All of this material was still in Japanese hands. Ushinora would be my home for the duration of our short tour in Japan—separate duty, close to Sasebo as the crow flies, but fifteen miles by the twisting, curving road along the seacoast. At the time of my posting to Ushinora I was in the first stages of committing political suicide, a lieutenant battling a major, openly defying the battalion executive officer's orders to provide enlisted working parties from my company to construct an officers' mess before the troops had been provided with adequate living places. Demanding office hours with the battalion commander I had described my feelings for the major and his construction project in terse and colorful terms. The colonel offered me Ushinora, which seemed a most satisfactory solution to my immediate problem, although the assignment there, and the loss of potential working parties for the officers' mess, gained me the devout enmity of the major for years to come.

Living spaces at Ushinora were only marginally superior to those on the fringe of Sasebo, but the tranquility of a separate command, the distance away from the major, made them appear much better. We settled in, the gates of the compound still guarded by unarmed Japanese troops, to inventory, to accept responsibility for, and to provide American security for the depot and its contents.

We commenced our takeover by first moving to the hilltops surrounding the depot. On them, set into solid concrete, were gun batteries taken from damaged Japanese warships in the harbor and painfully, slowly, and deliberately dragged up the sides of the hills, the scars on the earth mute evidence of their mode of movement. Four such batteries were emplaced on the heights above Ushinora, muzzles pointing over the ramparts, toward the west, toward the narrow opening between the rocky bluffs at the entrance to Sasebo Harbor. Invasion forces such as ours could have been blown clear out of the water by those same guns. Standing there with the officer in charge, bore-sighting those guns, I felt a cold dampness break out on me, felt my skin tighten and tingle. What a reception *that* would have been!

An orderly transition, as the brass likes to say, took place. I signed for everything that I could see, and the Japanese gave up control of the depot, leaving behind a naval warrant officer to assist me.

In addition to the interior security of the Ushinora Naval Ammunition Depot, I was charged with patrol duties beyond its limits, sixteen square miles of the prefecture of Ushinora.

A rural area. Farmland and paddies. Small hamlets clustered across the landscape. Beautiful countryside. Motor patrols gave us a chance to observe at first hand the activities of the Japanese farmers. No sophistication here. Shirts of cotton. Trousers of cotton or silk. Utilitarian. As utilitarian as putting a wife or daughter into the traces to pull a plow while the father or brother guided it. Maximum effort by all family members—something of value that once had been known and practiced in America.

Of all the things that we saw in the countryside, the children impressed me most. Their good manners never failed to touch me. At the sound of our vehicle approaching, without a glance to the front or rear, they would face inboard on either side of the road and bow low from the waist, black-haired heads bobbing in unison, looking like handsome dolls.

At the schools I saw the discipline imposed by the teachers on the students, not as masters to charges but as loving parents to children. Watching the way these children were molded in their tender years, one could understand clearly that discipline was an integral part of life. This mirrored with exceptional clarity the reasons why their fathers, brothers, and friends had died so well in the Pacific, choosing an honorable death rather than the shame of surrender.

Our personal feelings toward the Japanese? Throughout the war I never had been able to hate the Japanese soldiers who opposed us. They fought for their country as we fought for ours—fought well, were worthy adversaries. In their country, patrolling their homeland as a matter of routine security, I doubt that any of us were plagued with political or racist thoughts. We had a job to do. We tried to do it well.

Thirty days is not enough to know a people or a country. From what I could see of the Japanese civilians in our area during September and October 1945, they were a hardy, tough, resilient people who believed in their country and their way of life. I had respected their soldiers for exhibiting those same qualities, so it was not difficult to respect them.

15

Malakal

Orders came for the regiment, minus certain elements, to move from the sleeping bag coolness of Kyushu in October to the heat of the tropics, to the Palau Islands, seven degrees north of the equator. There, it was said, 24,000 Japanese impatiently were awaiting our arrival. Impatiently? We were going south to process them for repatriation. *They* were going home!

We knew a little about the Palaus from reading about the landing made on Peleliu by the 1st Marine Division. Peleliu and Angaur, where the Army landed, were coral islands. The Palau group ran roughly south to north a distance of about forty miles. The northern islands, created by volcanic upheavals, were much more lush, more heavily endowed with the finer things of life—tropical fruit, coconuts, bananas, and the like. The largest of these islands, Babelthuap, reminded one of the islands of the Solomons.

We off-loaded from the ships at Peleliu and came ashore by boat. No docks available, a slow process. One battalion plus regimental headquarters would remain on Peleliu. Our battalion reloaded into cargo and personnel-carrying landing

craft and chugged the thirty-five miles north to occupy the
northern islands of Malakal, Koror, and Arakabesan.
Babelthuap contained the Japanese garrison. Marines would
not go there during my time.

Battalion headquarters and two rifle companies would
hold down Koror and Arakabesan. My company would be
based on Malakal, once joined to Koror by a causeway made
useless long ago by the constant bombing of American aircraft.

Our landing craft reached Malakal late in the afternoon,
during one of the many rain squalls that swept across the
islands on a regular basis, and tied up to a concrete dock.
The island was then under the control of a National Guard
company from Hawaii. When we came ashore they would go
home. They might have had little use for Marines under
normal circumstances, but under those they looked after us
like blood brothers. The lieutenant commanding the company offered me the use of his pyramidal tent for the night.
My troops would sleep on the ground in shelter tents, at
some distance from the National Guard detachment, and I
would sleep in my own shelter tent with them. The lieutenant
seemed a little shocked by this approach, but he lived in a
different world. When he had invited me to stay with him, he
had told them to have my *orderly* bring my gear to the tent.
Orderly? Batman? In the Corps a company grade officer
never had heard of such a thing.

The following morning the National Guard company
cleared the area, went south on the boats that had brought us
in. We cleaned up their debris, policed our billeting area, and
settled in. It was not long before our tentage arrived, not long
before we were as comfortable as anyone can be sitting
almost astride the equator.

The island was small, but to me very interesting. On the
western side, the Japanese almost had completed carving out
a dry dock large enough to accommodate a cruiser before
American naval aircraft had denied its completion forever.
On the other side, where we now were billeted, was a three-
sided concrete dock, the water so deep that it could handle
easily destroyers and cruisers. From the top of a small hill
that dominated the island, one could see a number of Japanese warships driven up against the shorelines of the

smaller islands that lined the passage into Malakal, run close
aboard under the overhanging jungle trees in an effort to
elude the eyes of the American flyers, but failing—hit by
bombs and torpedoes, raked by cannon and machine gun
fire. Those islands in the north had been very well organized
and fortified against attack by surface sea forces, but there
was no way to cope with the endless attacks by naval air
power.

The Japanese to be repatriated were transported in small
craft from Babelthuap to Malakal, processed on the dock,
and jammed aboard LSTs for the trip to Japan. Only personal
belongings and a nominal amount of yen, perhaps 500, were
allowed each man. Marine teams, using English-speaking
Japanese soldiers as aides, inspected each man's gear, con-
fiscating all contraband for the island command. Japanese
officers, wearing empty sword scabbards as symbols of authority, moved among their men, maintaining order, keeping
the repatriation process moving.

Some of the repatriates were pitiful sights. They had
been caged in the jungle of Babelthuap for years. Under-
nourished, without enough medical supplies available to be
treated properly, they had succumbed to tuberculosis, dysentery, fungus, and yaws. I had seen photos in *LIFE* magazine
of the survivors of the camp at Dachau. Many of these
Japanese were in the same condition, reduced to skin and
bones, joints hugely swollen, skin pulled tightly over skull-
like faces, not able to move, often not able to speak, the eyes
moving slowly, trying to understand where they were, what
was happening. We saw it all during those days of processing—all the misery of mankind trotted out on those steaming
docks at Malakal in November and December of 1945.

And there were hundreds, maybe thousands who never
would hear, see, or smell their homeland again. Cubes of
cardboard and wood, containing the ashes of the dead,
wrapped neatly in paper, tied off in colored cord, names and
serial numbers carefully painted on their sides, reverently
handled—going home—home to rest with the ashes of their
ancestors.

Processing did not take place every day. The days in
between were drab tedium. Inspections of clothing and

equipment, close-order drill under arms, school of the soldier, garrison duties in the field conducted in 100-degree heat, 90 percent humidity. The crews of the LCI gunboats, the minesweepers, and the PCs came ashore each night after a full day of sweeping and blowing enemy mines in the Malakal channel, ran electric current ashore, and provided movies for us and them. In the morning they would take aboard cases of warm beer, let them set in the coolers aboard the vessels all day, and at the close of operations would make a few cold ones available to all of us on the beach. The skippers of those craft made life a lot better for us. Any variance from the dull routine was all to the good.

November plodded by and December was upon us. In Japan, other units of the 5th Division had been alerted for movement to the States for disbandment, were preparing to make that move.

There were renegades in the ranks of the Japanese Army, soldiers who had taken Micronesian wives, gone native, established another life in the northern Palau Islands. They had moved away from Babelthuap, had found places on the outcropping islands around Koror and Arakabesan. They refused to come in for processing, refused to report to the Japanese officers, from time to time got off a few rounds toward any force who tried to induce them to give up.

To add a little spice to life, to break up the monotony, the staleness of our lives, certain of us went out into the night to attempt to intercept these people, to talk them into surrender or to blow them away. Craig Leman, now the battalion operations officer, was one of the regular participants.

Using rubber boats, we would paddle noiselessly along the waterways that edged the islands, searching the locations where intelligence indicated deserters might be. We would go ashore, prowling through the night more by touch than by sight, entering huge caves that opened just above the high-water mark. There were patrols during which a smidgen of excitement was added—stepping over the side of the boat, feeling something hard and cold against one's thigh, gingerly feeling for the unknown object, discovering the horns of a Japanese hemispherical sea mine that had floated in from the open channel to lodge itself in the shallows—guaranteed to send the blood slamming fiercely through the veins, to dry up the saliva like a desert wind, to make one's eardrums pop.

Such operations were much better for us than any medicine that the doctors could order up. They put us back onto a psychological high, gave our lives some purpose, put some zing back into our flagging spirits. At a cave opening, thick gloom. At the far side, a pinpoint of light from candles or a small fire, smoke wreathing the cave's roof, its acridity assaulting the nostrils. Human forms, indistinct at first, becoming clearer as the eyes adjusted to the dimness. Three or four of them, sometimes more, men and women, often exceeding in numbers the size of the raiding party; but surprise was always on our side, always gave us the advantage. Sometimes shots were fired, mercifully with no lethal results. No great accomplishment, but these exercises kept us on our toes, kept us soldiering even though the war was over.

In mid-December, Bob Follendorf, who had been my first sergeant in "I" Company prior to receiving a field commission, called me on the land line to inform me that Fleet Marine Force, Pacific had sent out a directive which made me eligible to return to the States, Did I want to take advantage of its provisions? Hell, *yes!* I was bored, fed up with the nitpicking peacetime attitude that was pervading the battalion. Put me on the list. Type up the request. Get the colonel's approval. *Salt Lake City* was due at Peleliu in four days to take us to the States. I wanted to be aboard that cruiser when she headed east.

About an hour later the battalion commander called. Why was I putting in for stateside? Hadn't I promised him prior to Ushinora that I would give him a hand, stay with him? The move from Japan was history, and there were damned few Japanese left on Babelthuap to be moved to Japan. I had pulled seventeen consecutive months overseas with the battalion. The war was over. I could be bored just as easily in the States, and much more comfortably. I had a son I never had seen, a wife I had not known in nearly a year and a half. I knew that my decision did not please the colonel, for he squawked as though I had castrated him. I was prepared for some retaliation, but not for his devious countermove.

Unknown to me, a court martial had been convened by

the battalion commander, with two lieutenants and the bat- talion executive officer as members. I found myself to be a member of this court before the day was over, and was drafted to appear as a member the following day. With me on the court was Edgar Crum from old "I" Company, the major, and Craig Leman as recorder. Craig, like me, had been scheduled to go aboard *Salt Lake City* for transportation home. The colonel refused to change the composition of the court in spite of our requests to be eliminated. We could perceive now that he was attempting to hold us past our sailing date, to get yet another month of service out of both Leman and me.

Charges had been preferred against a Marine private by the island commander, Northern Palaus—a navy captain sen- ior to our regimental commander. The private was charged with speeding in excess of the twenty-five-mile-per-hour speed limit, of resisting apprehension, of being insolent and insubordinate.

We sat in court for two and a half days, working at night to beat the deadline set by the arrival of *Salt Lake City* off Peleliu, and acquitted the private of all charges, set him free with nothing on his record, not a charge proven. A number of enlisted men had testified for the defendant and we had believed their testimony. The island commander had taken the stand and we had disbelieved him for a variety of reasons. Some material, highly detrimental to the moral character of the island commander, surfaced; unfortunately it was entered in the record at this time and never deleted from the final typing of the court record.

Leman, Crum, and I signed the record of proceedings, all copies in the appropriate places; turned the record over to the major; and called it a day. Leman and I finished packing our gear and caught the boat for Peleliu, arriving there late in the afternoon, prepared to board *Salt Lake City* the following morning. I settled in with old friends from the 1st Battalion and regiment, ready for a celebration, ready to forget it all, free at last!

About 2030 that night the battalion executive officer appeared with the transcript from which he had deleted those compromising passages concerning the island com- mander. Quite illegal, but anything can and will be attempted when rank is breathing down the neck of some individuals. In addition to the deletions, just to cover his seagoing rump a little more securely, he had submitted a minority report stating that he had not agreed with the court's finding of acquittal—also quite illegal. The island commander had the major in a spin. Leman and I were supposed to sign the new transcript, get the island commander's record cleaned up. Both of us refused. The major left, sweating, mumbling in rage, fearful of his future.

Thirty minutes later a runner came to the tent I occupied. I was to follow him to the regimental commander's billet, *immediately!* Things were warming up!

The regimental commander was elsewhere when I arrived. I had a cup of coffee with the executive officer, who by inference implied that I might be in for a little trouble.

Trouble? I never saw so much, so fast, so furious, as when the regimental commander hove to in the center of his tent. "What in the hell are you doing, acquitting that private? Do you believe the testimony of a bunch of Pfc's over that of a Navy captain? How did all that crap get into the record, and why wasn't it thrown out? *You* have been derelict in your duty. I am going to recommend you for a General Court!"

While he caught his breath I tried to figure it all out. There were two other voting members on that court. Why wasn't he after them, too? It didn't make any sense. The island commander must have had him in a tight wristlock. Whatever the reason, I wasn't backing off. Confrontation with rank never had bothered me before. Why let it now?

"We tried the private, Sir! Yes, I do believe the testimony of a Pfc over a Navy captain when the captain's is illogical and unprovable. The material remained in the transcript because that is the way it was presented by the witnesses—Sir!"

At this retort his face turned purple, his breathing became labored, and, gasping, he dismissed me peremptorily, warning that written charges would be forthcoming shortly.

Lt. Col. Dan Pollock, the former operations officer at Lakehurst, still was commanding the 1st Battalion. It was to him that I turned for help. He was very reassuring and had my fears wiped out before I could get a full charge out of them.

"Shorty," he grinned as he spoke. "In the Old Corps you weren't worth your salt until you had some hack time and a recommendation for a General. It didn't always mean you were right, or that you were wrong, but it did prove that you were doing *something,* not just going along for the ride! In this case, *if* they recommend it, I doubt that they can make it stick. I doubt that you will ever go to trial, but if you do I will defend you. Don't worry about it! You will be OK!"

The old-line-corporal-turned-light-colonel had just the right touch. He got me up and back on my hind legs steering a straight course again, made me feel good.

The information that Colonel Pollock would defend me must have found its way quickly to the regimental commander, for the next morning he sent for me again, told me that he was not recommending a General, that I was to return to Koror to serve out ten days hack time—house arrest, no duties—and that my former battalion commander would give me additional punishment at the conclusion of hack time. After that I was free to return to the States.

I returned to Koror and sat there without duty for ten days, including Christmas. At the close of the tenth day I went to the colonel and requested that he impose his punishment upon me so I could stand clear of the Palaus and head for home.

An unsatisfactory fitness report was his punishment. I never had been marked unsatisfactory in any of the marking categories before. It tore me up a little until I saw how crazy the report was. *Excellent* to *Outstanding* in all the categories that really counted. Unsatisfactory in *Additional Duties, Cooperation,* and *Loyalty.* According to the narrative portion of the report, my additional duties were as a member of the fateful Court Martial Board. Being a member of a court or board is considered under *regular* duties, according to the Manual. I did not know in what manner I had failed to cooperate. Perhaps wanting to go home was uncooperative. And loyalty—mine was to the Corps and to the people that I served, those under me as well as those senior to me. *Never* to rank alone! The narrative portion of the report also stated that I found it difficult to go from a war situation into a garrison situation. The only true statement in the narrative portion—one that I could not contest!

Using a Marine Corp Manual borrowed from Follendorf, I worked past midnight to complete my rebuttal of that fitness report for submission to the commandant, took the rebuttal to the colonel's quarters, turned it over to him, signed the fitness report, and requested permission to leave Koror the following day. I was on the morning boat for Peleliu at dawn, anxious, itching to get away from the Northern Palaus, to start the journey stateside.

I stayed on Peleliu for two days, trying to secure air passage east. In my spare time I walked over portions of the 1st Marine Division's battleground, marveling that those brave Marines ever could wrest that chewed-up mass of coral ridge lines from the Japanese. Looking down from the heights of the old Japanese positions and thinking of the firepower that tore into them as they advanced, it was hard to believe that it was accomplished, that it *could* be accomplished by human beings. But then, as they used to say, Marines don't care. Marines can do anything.

On the third day I wrangled a seat on the mail plane to Guam. My days with the 5th Marine Division finally were over. After twenty-two months in the battalion—stateside, overseas, and in combat—I would miss it, miss the troops, miss the duty we had pulled together. I would see some of the people again, would serve with some of them again. In an outfit as small as the Corps, you always could find a familiar face on any post or station.

As the plane lifted off the runway at Peleliu, I wondered what peacetime duty would be like after so many months at war.

Part Four

THE LEAN, MEAN, IN-BETWEEN YEARS

16

The Peacetime Shuffle

Contrary to the misconceptions of the Flower Children of the sixties, the warriors of World War II really were not popular with their countrymen. With the exception of those servicemen who happened to be stateside on V-E Day or V-J Day, we saw no outpourings of gratitude for our pain and suffering—no bands playing, no ticker-tape parades. The majority of the overseas combat troops slipped quietly back into the stateside camps and forts and were discharged without a smattering of the jubilation, the hugs and the kisses, the dancing in the streets, the popping of corks that heralded the close of the war in Europe and the Pacific. We were just so many more returnees from a war that no longer existed— tools of that war, used, and used again, when the need was great—cast aside now as obsolete, useless. We were faceless outsiders, strangers returning to a homeland that no longer recognized us as citizens. There was no common ground between us, no common experience to share.

So for most of us, when the leave periods ended and it was time to return to duty, it was a relief to be packing up, to be moving back to people that we knew, people that we trusted, people that we understood and who understood us. It was good to be going *home*.

My orders took me to the Marine Corps Base, Quantico, Virginia, for duty at the Marine Corps Equipment Board, commanded by Gen. Clifton B. Cates. It was a testing and evaluation center for weapons, equipment, and vehicles—a valuable and worthwhile organization. My wife and son came south to be with me, the first tour of duty during which we would live together on a daily, routine basis. We lived first in Fredericksburg, sharing a home with its owners, and then in a substandard government housing complex called Midway Island. It was our first real home in the Corps, and we made do with it.

As soon as I could, I got on up to Headquarters, Marine Corps, to see just how badly I had been hurt by my final escapade in the Palaus. Upon requesting my official jacket for examination, I was told that my records were before a promotion board. No one had told me that a board was meeting, nor that I was in the zone of consideration. I left Headquarters in a fog, my uncertainty about the future more pronounced than ever.

On 13 April 1946, I was promoted to temporary captain in the Marine Corps Reserve. My agitation over survival in the Corps as a corporal, of ever making sergeant, could be dismissed for the time being. I disliked the Reserve connotation, but could live with it. A captain in any category was a lot farther up the ladder than I ever had dreamed of going. Count your blessings, as the old adage has it. I counted mine every day, for it was that time in Marine Corps history when reduction in force, reduction in rank, was the order of the day. I *was* blessed, and I knew it.

In spite of all this obvious good fortune, there was locked up deep inside me an insidious turbulence, an unease and discontent directly attributable to the sudden, suffocating, crashing halt of combat operations, generating intense resentment against all of those who had not shared in that combat.

Those feelings hovered in my subconscious, ready to explode anywhere, anytime. For instance, when I entered the mess at Quantico, looking for a table, I found my eyes involuntarily flicking over the area above the left pockets of the officers sitting at the tables, carefully steering clear of tables at which noncombatants were in the preponderance, sometimes not eating at all rather than having to sit with them.

Unfortunately, I let these prejudices enter into my family life, demanding miracles from my son, expecting him to respond to me as would a well-disciplined young Marine, when in fact he was an infant, barely a year old. I was equally miserable to my wife, upbraiding her for imagined failures in her duties as mother and spouse, treating her as I would a less-than-competent Marine Corps subordinate. I was in a new world, not the least bit sure of my place in it, everything in me crying out for a return to the simple, clear-cut ways of the combat Marine, where one accepted his orders, passed them on down, and saw to it that the assigned objective was taken.

It would take years for this blind intolerance to leave me. Like recurrent malaria, it would return for brief periods, its chills and vapors to settle upon me more than once again as other wars, other battles, caught up with me and were fought. A most dangerous occupational hazard, one of the worst that comes with the profession of arms. Fortunately for me, during those years immediately following the war, I had some outstanding senior officers watching over me. Thanks to their patience, understanding, and insight, the malady never got a firm hold.

Life at the Equipment Board was pleasant but too routine, too boring for my taste. The 2d Division was in Japan. The 1st Division was in China. There was no major Fleet Marine Force element in the continental United States. To compensate for this shortage of State Department muscle, the 1st Special Marine Brigade was formed, its headquarters, with the bulk of its force, at Camp Lejeune, North Carolina, and with a battalion stationed at Quantico. The rolls of that battalion contained a high number of combat veterans from all of the World War II divisions, among them Ernie DeFazio. To me the 1st Battalion of the Special Brigade took on an instant appeal, a positive answer to the overpowering ennui that encompassed me at the Board. I made a visit to the battalion, was introduced to Lt. Col. Richard C. Nutting, the commanding officer, and met other officers of the battalion. I was assured by Colonel Nutting that if the Equipment Board

would release me at my own request there would be a job for
me in the battalion.

General Cates was generous and kind to me, approved
my request with demur, and wished me the best of luck. I was
back with the troops again.

I was assigned to "A" Company for duty as executive
officer, with a promise that I would command the first company available through transfer or default. I was happy to be
there, even in a lieutenant's billet. Some people could not
have stepped down in order to get a troop assignment. At that
time I was quite satisfied to do so.

The Caribbean, always politically turbulent, always a
potential source of trouble, began to rumble just at the time I
joined the battalion. The State Department felt an urgent
need to show the flag, to demonstrate the fact that there was
an American strike force available. The 1st Special Brigade
was ordered south, the 1st Battalion with it.

I had been back from extended overseas duty just four
months when we mounted out.

We showed the flag in selected ports and conducted
amphibious exercises on Puerto Rico, where, in the coconut
groves behind the landing beaches, we were met not by
enemy forces but by native hawkers selling Coca Cola, beer,
coconut milk, and rum of the most lethal kind. Once ashore,
we moved onto the ranges of Roosevelt Roads, conducted
training exercises, fired all of our individual and crew-served
weapons, and reembarked.

Upon our return to Quantico, several things happened
almost simultaneously—good news and bad. My good news
was that I had passed an almost forgotten examination for a
Regular commission. Back on Peleliu, in December 1945,
applicants for Regular commissions had gone through a
three-day period of testing—a Naval Officer's Selection
Test—to determine suitability for retention in the Regular
establishment. On a grading curve that must have resembled
the straightest of straight lines, I had passed. In one day I was
mustered out of the Marine Corps Reserve, reinstated in the
Regular establishment as a permanent second lieutenant, and
promoted to temporary captain in the Regulars. On 15 June
1946, my worries about retention in the Marine Corps were

wiped out. The commandant had given me my chance. My cup was full.

The bad news was that the brigade was to be disbanded, the headquarters and the Camp Lejeune-based troops to become a part of the 2d Marine Division scheduled soon to return from Japan. Our battalion was to be phased out and into the headquarters troops of the Marine Corps Base, Quantico. I was out in the cold again, looking for a new home almost before getting established in the old one.

An Air Observation School was scheduled to commence that summer at the Marine Corps Air Station, Quantico. I had applied for the school while still on duty at the Equipment Board. Orders to that school arrived prior to the disbandment of the battalion, so I was not forced to stand around fidgeting, trying to line up a billet with the Base troopers.

The course ended in mid-October. It was easily the best organized-for-training course that I ever had attended. It was the only school in which the instructor-student ratio was adequate—more than one instructor per student. The instructors were able, had excellent backgrounds in their own blocks of instruction, and had a method of teaching more informal than I ever before had encountered.

The course itself brought a new appreciation of terrain and the military observation of it. For the first time in my career I was exposed to the conduct of live artillery shoots, observing registration and fire missions from both the ground and the air, in daylight and night shoots.

And of course the designation as tactical and gunnery air observer, and the award of the gold and silver observation wings, made the course a tangible, rewarding experience.

With the end of the course came a change of station. For me it was the Marine Training and Replacement Command, Camp Pendleton, California.

On 29 November 1946, after a cross-country automobile trip made with our newborn daughter in a wicker laundry basket and our nearly two-year-old son riding shotgun over her, we arrived at Camp Pendleton. I was assigned to the 3d Marine Brigade for duty. I queried the brigade personnel officer concerning an air observation billet. No. Just have one billet on the T/O, and that one is filled. Brigade doesn't need air observers. Needs rifle company commanders.

I reported to the 2d Battalion, 6th Marines for duty and was introduced to the battalion commander, Lt. Col. Leroy P. Hunt, Jr., a highly decorated veteran of World War II and son of a Marine Corps general officer. He was one of the most gentle, considerate, forthright gentlemen I ever would serve with. After further pleasantries, I was sent on down to take command of "F" Company.

In the 2d Battalion, 6th Marines, I found old faces. Red Harper, now a lieutenant, was executive officer of "G" Company. He had been gut-shot on Iwo, but had lucked out with a nice clean hole, belly to back, with nothing vital being touched on the way through. It was good to see the redhead again. Throughout the battalion there were a goodly number of mustangs, some commissioned, some warrants—all of them very capable people. The company was up to strength in officers and staff NCOs, but with so few privates and Pfc's that a training schedule was quite useless. The Marine Corps was into one of its worst failures in the business of bringing basic Marines into the Corps—the experiment with two-year enlistments. Catch them, put them through boot camp, milk a year or eighteen months out of them in the Fleet Marine Force, send them to the nearest Marine Corps activity to their home of record, let them serve out their time, and discharge them. Some time in the Marine Corps Reserve was a part of the contract—*if* you could catch them once you had turned them loose.

I had the world by the tail—a rifle company of my own and a battalion commander who allowed me to run that company the way I thought it should be. In a short period of time I had built a reputation for diligence and discipline that had reached beyond the battalion limits. One full colonel, a friend of Colonel Hunt, had requested that his son, a lieutenant, be sent to the toughest company commander in the battalion. Colonel Hunt sent the lieutenant on down to me.

In spite of the blessings of the West Coast, there still was the old irritation kicking around inside of me concerning noncombatants, kicking around hard enough to come out into the open on occasion, hard enough to provoke a show-down that would prove most valuable to me.

The battalion executive officer was not a bad sort. He just happened to fall into the two categories that I never handled very well—seagoing during the war and no infantry combat on his record. One afternoon he called me on the phone to inform me that my company was going to have to take on another week of guard duty. It hit me just wrong. After a week on interior guard duty, I wanted to get the company back into shape, get it back out into the boondocks. I let the major know what I thought about that. Things got tense. He gave me a direct order and hung up the phone.

Almost foaming at the mouth, I charged up the hill leading towards battalion headquarters, stomped into the adjutant's office, and demanded office hours with Colonel Hunt.

The colonel overheard the commotion outside his office and stood in the doorway. He saw the flush of anger, heard the rapid breathing, the muffled words cascading up out of my throat in half-strangled gibberish, nearly every word punctuated by a standard qualifier, *goddam noncombatant!*

He motioned me inside, heard me out quietly. Just as quietly he motioned me into a chair. My anger was spent, shame at my outburst now the overriding emotion.

"Ave," he said, voice barely audible. "Settle down! Settle down! You had something to gripe about—but it so happens that *I* decided that "F" Company would pull another week of guard—the major just passed it on to you. Your reasons are good, but mine are better. Now—on to something else."

He paused, then moved to stand directly to my front, and continued.

"You have got to get that noncombat chip off your shoulder! Ave, *we* are the lucky ones. We got to practice our trade in combat—got a chance to really earn our pay. We know what combat is about—know how we reacted to it, know pretty well how we will react to the next firefight that we are in. Many of the others—like the major—never had that chance, may never have it. Don't get furious with them. Feel sorry for them, if you must feel something. Recognize your own good fortune. Realize that you are one of the chosen!"

Wisdom, in a small dose, from a very wise combat leader. Leroy P. Hunt, Jr., in his unobtrusive, pleasant way, had given me the best reason in the world to be reasonable.

In the days following the war, there just were not enough Marines to go around. The Corps, as always, was understrength and overcommitted, the postwar apathy toward all things military only adding to the difficulty.

In the winter of 1947, the work force at the Marine Corps Supply Depot, Barstow, California, evaporated for reasons never quite made clear to us. Huge amounts of war materiel—weapons, vehicles, artillery pieces—were in the process of being mothballed for storage when the worker exodus took place. The processing could not be allowed to stop. Why not send a Marine infantry battalion to Barstow to get the work done? Fine idea. Put them on temporary duty for ninety days and let them clean up as much of the existing mess as possible. If they don't get it all taken care of, rotate in another battalion for another ninety days.

Our battalion was selected to be the first into the bullring. Department of the Pacific, the headquarters command for the Barstow installation, expected us to work our men a full eight hours a day in the civilian processing pursuits. The commanding general, 3d Marine Brigade, expected us to maintain a Fleet Marine Force training schedule to maintain combat readiness. A day can be stretched just so far and then there is no time. We met ourselves coming and going. The Good Book says that one cannot serve two masters, but somehow we did just that. Closeorder drill at first light, followed by physical drill under arms, followed by a run—all accomplished prior to 0700, for the troops had to eat and be at their civilian work stations by 0800. We conducted classes after evening chow, sometimes right up to taps. A tough schedule for any unit to follow, a rough way to treat the troops, but we got it done, even with the less-than-motivated, two-year enlistees. The NCOs took up the slack, keeping a taut line, never letting the ship break loose from its moorings.

*   *   *

Those ninety days in the high desert pulled the company close together. By the time we returned to the old barracks at Camp Pendleton, we had come to know each other very well. We had messed together in a company mess for three months—something pleasingly different in the days of cafeteria-style battalion messes—had seen each other more than fourteen hours a day at the work sites and the Fleet Marine Force training activities. I knew my company officers and NCOs. They knew me, knew what I wanted from them, and gave it to me with verve and unquestioned loyalty under conditions often approaching the unreal. We lost nothing on the high desert but a little sleep. What we gained there was of inestimable value to all of us.

The spring and summer of 1947, after our return from Barstow, whipped by in a flurry of activity. The 6th Marines remained the largest Marine infantry unit on the West Coast and was held responsible for the summer training of Marine Corps Reserve officers and NCOs, and Marine Corps Reserve units. The individual NCOs and officers usually were attached to a company or battalion of the regiment—integrated training, it was called. The 2d Battalion, 6th Marines was saddled with the majority of the Reserve training exercises and furnished individual instructors and demonstration troops for live-fire, artillery, and air-supported field problems. We stayed busy, straight-out, with no letup, spending more time in the field than in the barracks, "F" Company catching more than its share of such duty.

Money was scarce that summer, the armed forces budget trimmed so close that there was no trace of fat and imminent danger of permanent muscle damage. The Marine Corps, operating on as ragged a shoestring as one could imagine, still insisted on training as though we had unlimited logistical support. Things were so tight that gasoline for wheeled and tracked vehicles was rationed. The infantry moved from training area to training area on foot, sometimes twenty miles between points A and B. If tank operations were conducted, the tank crews were allowed enough fuel to reach the training areas and remain there during the exercise. There was no fuel to return to the tank farm each night following the day's training. Infantry and tankers bivouacked together, became close friends, came to understand each other's problems intimately. The operations of that summer turned the company into a slick, hard-charging, smoothly running military organization.

Many changes that summer. The 3d Brigade became the 1st Marine Division, the 2d Marine Division taking over from the old 1st Marine Division, its East Coast base. There would be no swaps in the future. The 2d would be at Lejeune, the 1st at Camp Pendleton from that point forward.

Then in September, with just a little more than ten months on station, orders arrived. Coming down off the Pendleton hills one evening, after three days and three nights of continuous maneuver, demonstrating for the last of the Reservists, Red Harper and I were summoned to the adjutant's office and told that we would be moving back east— Red to duty in Harrisburg, Pennsylvania, I to Charlottesville, Virginia. Duty with the Reserve. New Reserve infantry companies were being formed all over the country. Some people thought us very fortunate. As for me, I would have preferred the Pendleton boondocks. In spite of my protest, I had to pack up and move on.

We crossed the continent for the second time in less than a year, two children stashed in the rear compartment of a Ford business coupe, a third starting to grow in my wife's belly. Since temporary duty in Washington, D.C., was set forth in my orders, I headed northeast, dropped the family off in Maine, and went south to be briefed at 5th District Headquarters.

From the moment I arrived in Charlottesville, it was a disaster. I was a Yankee in a strong redoubt of the Confederacy. I was a Marine Corps representative in a city that leaned heavily towards sponsoring its own National Guard unit, replete with a new armory, and not prone to accepting outsiders from any other branch of the service. I was a Regular officer, charged with bringing the most casual, non-regulation, disinterested group of Reserve officers and men I ever had encountered up to a minimum standard of military proficiency. It was my great misfortune to attempt to achieve the desired results the way I had in the Regular establishment.

The company commander and his junior officers did not buy that approach. Brown loafers were worn with the uniform. Socks of various hues, usually red, went with the loafers. Sometimes rank insignia and Marine Corps emblems were worn as a part of the drill night uniform, sometimes not. Drill night normally consisted of checking in, getting one's name placed on the attendance roster for pay purposes, and then off to the cinema or to one of the pubs for a few beers. Conferences with the company commander, who was, it later turned out, the nephew of one of the General Staff at Headquarters, U.S. Marine Corps, brought no change in this sorry state of affairs. Calls and letters to 5th Reserve District in Washington, D.C., brought me only the admonition to walk softly, settle down, be exceedingly circumspect and patient. I felt boxed in, shut out, no place to turn. Things could not go on like that. They did not.

I endeared myself to the local moguls of industry and business almost immediately by insisting that some knitting machines, stored in the basement of the building leased by the Marine Corps as a Reserve Armory, be moved out to make room for weapons and supplies. The owner of the machines, coincidentally the employer of the Reserve company commander, was an influential man and he was not pleased. I gave him seventy-two hours to get the machines off government property and warned him that I would move the machines once the time limit had expired. He did not believe me.

At the end of three days I kept my promise. I moved the machines outside the building on a Friday afternoon; that night I moved the Reserve weapons and equipment into the basement storage space.

On Monday morning the owner of the machines called me on the phone and cut me to ribbons, accused me of being both a Fascist and a Communist—an accomplishment requiring great ingenuity even for such a renegade as I. My reputation as a troublemaker, an enemy of free enterprise, was not long in making the rounds of the city.

And then the coup de grace! One evening after drill, the sergeant major, an amtracker from World War II who rolled through life just about like an amphibian tractor, letting the debris and wreckage fall where it might, decided that he would get into the act. In an extremely abrasive and bellicose manner, he came down hard on one of the company officers

in reference to slovenly appearance. One of the Brown
Loafer Brigade was wearing yellow socks instead of red, with
no headgear and no Marine Corps emblems on his jacket.

Angered, the lieutenant retorted that he suspected he
looked as good in his uniform as any Regular officer did in
his. Being the only Regular officer present, and knowing full
well that I looked far better in my uniform, I took umbrage
immediately. My hands leaped up involuntarily, grasped the
very tall lieutenant by the field scarf, pulled him down to my
size, flipped him back over onto the sergeant major's desk,
and asked him gently if he wanted to buy a new set of teeth
for his bad mouth. In the background, the sergeant major
chortled and capered—his mirth boundless.

A few days later I was invited to 5th Marine Corps
Reserve District headquarters. There I was informed that the
lieutenant—a member of the Shenandoah Blue-Bloods, First
Families of Virginia, and other baronial organizations—had
written directly to the commandant of the Marine Corps,
protesting his public humiliation at the hands of a Regular
officer. The commandant was displeased with me. I was given
my choice of an East Coast duty station. I chose the 2d
Marine Division at Camp Lejeune, North Carolina.

That week my entire staff, including the sergeant major,
were detached and sent to duty stations of their choice. A
clean sweep down, fore and aft. My first, last, and only
association with the civilian component.

Our first two children had been born in Maine. My wife
now was ready to deliver our third. My orders authorized
thirty days in reporting. Why break an established pattern?
Why not three deliveries in the old Pine Tree State? We went
to Maine. There our second son was born. We named him
Craig, after Craig Leman. It was the last week in April 1948.
When I left Maine, I would not see my family again until
autumn of that year.

17

The Mediterranean Shores

There years after the bombing of Hiroshima and Nagasaki, the armed forces of the United States were playing war games as if it was a foregone conclusion that low-yield, tactical nuclear weapons could be utilized with impunity on the battlefield. If one spread one's forces into tactical localities, sometimes miles apart, those forces could survive the impact of enemy nuclear weapons and go on to win. Dispersal was the name of the game—the key to certain victory—although no one had quite solved the problems of adequate communications between dispersed units, nor the problems inherent in the secure movement of units from assembly areas into attack, defensive, or counterattack positions. Mundane things such as mass evacuation of nuclear casualties were "under study." The devastation of two of Japan's largest cities, and the implications of that act, had not made the same impression upon the Americans as it had upon the Japanese.

The Marine Corps was in that game, along with its sister services, by choice or by pressure from the Joint Chiefs of Staff, but in it all the way. Self-contained, self-sufficient tac-

tical units, tailored to operate independently as well as in
concert with other units, were under test by the Army and
the Marine Corps. The unit devised by the Marine Corps to
do its shooting and scooting around the nuclear battlefield
was quite similar to the Army's Regimental Combat Team.
The nucleus of the Marine Corps unit was an infantry battalion of three rifle companies, and a headquarters element,
reinforced by additional administrative, communication, and
support personnel. The battalion was supported further by
the inclusion of a tank platoon, an engineer detachment, a
detachment from Combat Service Group, an air delivery
platoon, and a truck company. Further augmentation of personnel, weaponry, and equipment could be made for special
operations. This team was commanded by a full colonel,
whose next senior headquarters was the Marine division. If
one or more of the teams were deployed, overall command
would be vested in the assistant division commander, a brigadier general. Should all of the teams be utilized opera-
tionally, command would be by the division commander.

In the spring of 1948 there were four such teams in the
2d Marine Division—the 2d Marines, the 4th Marines, the
21st Marines, and the 8th Marines.

On the morning of 9 May 1948, I reported to headquarters of the 21st Marines and from the adjutant learned that
the unit was scheduled for deployment to the Mediterranean
prior to the month's end. I also learned that two captain's
billets were open—the logistics officer and the command of
"B" Company. The colonel commanding, Paul D. Sherman,
was attending a briefing at division, was expected to return to
his office prior to noon chow. He would make the decision on
my assignment.

Enter trouble. The landing team executive officer had
heaved to, out of nowhere, and had come alongside bristling,
ready to sink me with a single salvo. Tall, slim, handsome,
black-haired—everything that I was not. A typical seagoing
type, and that is exactly what he had been. He had gone
aboard a cruiser as a lieutenant, the cruiser had been sunk
from under him, and he had been the guest of the Japanese
for the duration of the war. Upon his release from prison
camp, he had been promoted rapidly up into the grade

reached by his ground combat contemporaries during the conflict, in his case to the rank of lieutenant colonel. He had been sent to the appropriate schools to bring him up to date, but he still had a lot to learn if he was to be of any value in a real, honest-to-God infantry battalion.

On that day he dramatically and emphatically had assured me that there was no need to wait for the colonel. I was to be the logistics officer. The rifle company already had been promised to another. Without drama, but just as emphatically, I assured the executive officer that it was my intention to let the colonel make the decision. His nostrils flared, the patrician countenance flushed a deeper hue.

The colonel returned before the noon meal as promised. From my seat in the adjutant's office, I was able to observe the powwow taking place in the colonel's office, his scrutiny of my qualification jacket, the rapid-fire conversation of the executive officer. The adjutant was standing between the two senior officers as though umpiring. Glancing up, the colonel caught me watching and motioned me into his office.

Introductions were made to a massive individual, who looked more like a heavyweight boxer than a professional law officer. Another flip of the pages of my qualification jacket, then, "Captain, I am going to send you down to command "B" Company." A pause, a smile. "That is— unless you would really prefer to be the logistics officer!"

The adjutant smiled and winked at me. The executive officer did neither. I had made a lifelong enemy, but in the delight of escaping staff duty, I had given no thought to future encounters.

On 18 May 1948, Lt. Ermel D. Bowen and I flew to Newport, Rhode Island, to effect liaison with Commander, Cruiser Division Twelve. Bowen's unit, "A" Company, was to be embarked in the light cruiser *Fargo*, CL-106. My company was to go aboard *Huntington*, CL-107, the sister ship to *Fargo*—the only two light cruisers of that class ever built.

Fargo and *Huntington* were ships of sublime beauty. Racy, lean, mean, in appearance almost like oversized destroyers, and with almost the same agility but infinitely more powerful. Main battery, six-inch guns. Secondary battery 5-in. 38s and 40mm. Floatplanes, for recon and gunnery air spot, hangared beneath the fantail.

Each of the light cruisers had its own Marine detachment aboard. Each ship had its own detachment compartment, its own tailor shop for its embarked Marines. Neither of the ships had room to accommodate an additional 200 Marines, yet before Bowen and I left Newport for Camp Lejeune, we had fitted both rifle companies into sleeping spaces aboard our respective cruisers. It meant accepting the fact that some Marines would sleep in passageway bunks chained up during daylight hours, some would sleep in the seaplane hangar, some would sleep on the mess decks between evening chow and breakfast.

Overhead, a clear, azure sky. A strong wind from the east raised whitecaps across the dark blue-green sea, turning the wakes of the ships into glistening spume. In the formation, heavy and light cruisers, an Essex- and a Midway-class carrier, both launching aircraft. Out on the flanks, the whitecaps on the horizon sometimes obscuring them, destroyers and destroyer escorts. Trailing in the rear, the tenders and the cargo vessels. Everywhere, as far as the eye could see, the American colors snapping and popping from every peak in the stiff breeze. A sight to bring a sudden, smarting moisture to the eyes, a constricting lump to the throat. American naval power—the striking force of the United States in World War II—reaching across the expanse of the Pacific to devastate the Japanese bastions, projected eastward now to counter the Communist threat, to carry the flag along the seething Mediterranean shores, to show the nations there that the Mediterranean was an American sea, that the United States intended to maintain control of it.

In the guts of the warships and the cargo vessels, to help maintain that control, to extend sea power ashore, a Marine Corps landing team was embarked. Such a team had been assigned to Sixth Fleet since 1947.

At day's end half of the naval force, now steaming eastward, would turn and head west, pass through the Gates of Hercules and sail for the United States, its time with Sixth Fleet completed. Homeward bound, with the naval force, was the 8th Marines.

Standing to, off Phaleron Bay, Greece, in the ships of the

arriving naval force, was the relief of the 8th Marines—the 21st Marines, new players for a new game.

It had been a rough, miserable crossing, the Atlantic living up to its reputation as a tough customer, showing no mercy, determined to make certain that we were all fully aware of our fragility. I had seen some tempestuous seas in the Pacific, but nothing that could compare with the battering, frenzied turbulence of the Atlantic.

Now, in the gathering dusk, the ships rocking gently in the waters of Phaleron Bay, that stormy passage seemed remote, the setting almost too peaceful. Our thoughts were not on what had gone before, but rather in what lay in store for us between June and October. There was good reason to be thoughtful.

The exultation of V-E Day had not subsided before the Cold War had begun. The Soviets had infiltrated the power structures of Italy and Greece and, by military power and subversion, had seized the Balkan States.

The Truman Doctrine had come into being during 1947. It was a doctrine committed to the aid of governments threatened by the Soviets. Weapons, supplies, and military advisors had been sent to Greece to assist the Royal Greek Army in its battle to drive Yugoslav-trained Greek partisans from the homeland. During November 1947 the United Nations General Assembly approved the establishment of a Jewish state in Palestine. About the time we arrived in the Mediterranean, in mid-May 1948, Lebanon, Iraq, Syria, Egypt, and Trans-Jordan had gone to war against the newly proclaimed state of Israel.

Before the cruise was over, we would anchor off the southeastern end of the Greek battle line, socialize with the American advisors to the Greek Army, roam both coasts of Italy, get acquainted with the American and British contingents holding a portion of the international city of Trieste and, with them, butt heads with the Yugoslavs along the border—the firepower of our six-inch guns most welcome, should it be needed. We would cruise the coast of Libya, take a long look at "the shores of Tripoli," run picket between Greece and Palestine, provide Marine operators and radio equipment to the Israeli armed forces.

We would stay busy on that uneasy sea. It was not to be a midshipmen's cruise.

We traveled the length and breadth of the Mediterranean that summer and autumn of 1948—at sea for two to three weeks, in port for four to five days. We learned all of the seas by heart—the Tyrrhenian, the Ionian, the Adriatic, the Aegean, the Sea of Mamara, and the southeastern edge of the Black Sea. We knew the straits, some of them extremely well—the Dardanelles, the Bosporus, Messina traversed so many times that its charm was lost completely.

Imperceptibly we became as much a part of the ship as her regular crew and found ourselves remarkably integrated. *Huntington* was our home (despite her many discomforts), our base of operations, our backup, our fire support when we went ashore under hostile conditions. Best of all we became comrades with our Navy and ship's detachment counterparts, able to depend upon them, and they upon us.

18

The Forties Fade

In September the cruise was over, time to leave *Huntington.* I found myself hating to cut loose from a way of life that I had grown genuinely to enjoy.

The 21st Marines disembarked from its Mediterranean shipping at Quonset Point, Rhode Island, and then moved down the East Coast by rail. As soon as we took up habitation in our old barracks, my troubles began. In spite of outstanding fitness reports submitted on me by the commanding officers of *Huntington,* I found myself an outsider in the eyes of the commanding officer and his staff—a loner, not a team player, someone to watch carefully at a safe distance. My insistence on daily physical drill followed by long-distance runs—all accomplished prior to regular working hours—made me suspect in the eyes of the other company commanders, who wanted nothing to do with that early-bird routine. My habit of nonfraternization with the battalion staff made me equally suspect with them. I became one to be suffered for the time being, to be rid of at the earliest opportunity.

The 2d Marines and the 21st Marines became battalions

in the 1st Provisional Marine Regiment. Provisional was a good word to use. One definition from *Webster's* sets it forth as, "Provided for a temporary need, subject to change." Another, in the case of a postage stamp, "For use until a regular issue appears." The latter very well describes a provisional regiment in the closing year of the frantic 1940s—a regiment in name only, with barely enough troop strength to field two battalions instead of the customary three. Everything on paper, nothing of substance. Each rifle company minus a platoon, each platoon short a squad. During field exercises it became deceptively simple to deploy a maneuver element, for in most instances the maneuver element was a phantom without flesh. Phantoms move easily, never take casualties, and always are successful, regardless of mission. Just change their positions with your grease pencil on the map overlay and you have outflanked or enveloped the enemy. A neat trick in training, never to happen for real. The division, the whole Marine Corps, was grossly understrength and overcommitted, so short of troops within the division that personnel transfers from one battalion to another went on constantly in order to keep a full-strength battalion in the Mediterranean. Many individual Marines were on their way back to the Sixth Fleet in as little as nine months' turnaround time, many battalions redeploying within a year.

The Corps is always faithful. In terms of training it always is prepared. In terms of manpower, it often is far from ready. Not necessarily our fault. Just a statement of fact. We do the best we can with what the country allows us.

Manpower was not the only thing that was lost to the officers of the division and of post troops during the fading of the 1940s. During the deployment of the 21st Marines to the Mediterranean, those magnificent combat murals that had graced the overhead and the bulkheads of the bar at the Main Officers' Club at Hadnot Point during the war years had been painted over, completely eradicated. In their place, two shades of "Officer Country" green—one a sickening bilelike pastel, the other a humiliatingly deep, bold green—an obscene assumption of class distinction. In lieu of the murals of the two staff NCOs in dress blues at present arms on either side of the bar entrance were goldfish bowls and tanks filled with tropical fish. Row upon row of potted plants were in the lobby. Not one thing masculine, not one thing left of the legacy of the war years. Some said it was the work of a high ranker's lady. No matter where the blame might be put, the Corps had lost something of inestimable value. The unique had fallen prey once again to the commonplace.

In February 1949, we embarked on assault transports at Morehead City, North Carolina, and sailed for Vieques Island, just off the eastern tip of Puerto Rico, where we played war games for most of the month of March. A division landing exercise, with far less than a division participating. The Aggressor forces ashore could have stood us off forever, having learned the terrain behind the beaches; mined the beaches; and thrown up effective, real, honest-to-God beach obstacles that stopped movement right at the water line. The Navy stepped right into it also. Aggressor submarines, played by fleet submarines of the U.S. Navy, lay on the bottom and torpedoed every transport in the landing area. Once the exercise was over, we surely could not say that we had won, but we truly could say that we had learned from the many mistakes we had made. The critique that followed left no doubt in our minds that there was much work to do.

Returning to Camp Lejeune we slipped, slogged, and slopped our way through the swamps, still training long hours, still giving it a hard go, still minus one-third of our wartime strength. Considering what we had to work with, we turned out a much better product than we might have realized. A good thing that we did, for in a little more than a year many of these same people would be putting this training to the test, would be going up against real aggressors, the kind who shoot live rounds, whose maneuver elements are not fashioned of ghosts.

On 23 May 1949, a change of duty, a change of organization. My orders directed me to the G-3 section (Operations and Training) of the 2d Marine Division for duty as chief air observer/assistant G-3, Training. On 1 June 1949, I received my orders to duty involving flying. I had been waiting for a tactical air observation assignment since completion of training in October 1946.

Country boy in the big city? You had better believe it! I had avoided visits to battalion and regimental headquarters in the past, had become very uneasy if the visits had taken more than thirty minutes. Now I was locked into position, in the same building, on the same deck with all the division wheels, including the assistant division commander and the commanding general. It gave me a bad case of the shakes.

The duty at the G-3 section settled into routine. There were two naval aviation observers (Tactical) attached to the section, I and Robert V. Anderson, a tall, lean and lanky, likeable, capable, and extremely brainy young lieutenant who knew his business and performed his duties in a highly creditable manner. There were naval aviation observers (Gunnery) serving with the artillery regiment, who came under my cognizance only during exercises in which the whole division took part, and they were utilized in tactical as well as gunnery missions. Anderson and I flew the majority of the tactical air observation missions requested by the infantry regiments.

In addition to the flight requirements imposed upon us, we were tasked with the preparation of training orders and memoranda, mainly dealing with the division marksmanship program, one that provided the 2d Marine Division with consistently high marksmanship percentages. I began to learn paperwork, to understand its importance, if not to enjoy it. Good training for old infantry captains who have been out in the weeds for extended periods of time.

Social life, long considered effete by me, now entered the scene. Prior to deployment to the Mediterranean, I had applied for quarters. While afloat, my name came up and I accepted. Upon my return to Camp Lejeune I had moved my family down from Maine and into quarters—the first time we had known such luxury. Three bedrooms, two-and-a-half baths, kitchen, dining room, living room, and screened porch. Compared to some of the civilian hovels that we had occupied, that set of quarters was palatial. In them we entertained the officers and wives of "B" Company and certain other friends from the 21st Marines. For the first time since I had enlisted, we were in a position to enjoy the routine, peacetime evolutions of the Corps, interrupted almost constantly, to be sure, by field exercises, deployments to the Caribbean, and the other things accepted by an overcommitted division—things of no consequence, since everyone was in the same situation.

A year later, I received orders to attend the Amphibious Warfare School, Junior Course, Marine Corps Schools at Quantico, Virginia, with a detachment date of 31 July 1950. I had not attended formal classes, except for the Air Observation School, since early 1943. I was overdue. At least the family would be with me for another nine months—the length of the scheduled course of instruction, which was to be convened in early September.

A month later the North Koreans smashed across the 38th Parallel on their way south. On Sunday, 25 June 1950, a whole new ball game commenced, one that quickly would highlight the shortage of available manpower within the Corps.

When the news of the North Korean attack hit us at Camp Lejeune, I went immediately to the chief of staff and requested that my school orders be rescinded. Colonel Goode assured me that the 2d Marine Division would play no part in Marine Corps evolutions in Korea, stated that the commandant had ordered me to school. To school I would go. He was wrong about Korea. The 2d Marine Division would furnish the better part of two regiments of the 1st Marine Division when it filled up for deployment to Korea.

While flying a routine observation mission on 18 July, I received a transmission from the control tower at Peterfield Point instructing me to report immediately to division headquarters. New orders. Proceed without delay, by 18 July 1950, to report to the commandant, Marine Corps Schools, Quantico, Virginia, by 2400, 20 July. Quarters to be cleaned and inspected for clearance. Household effects to be packed, loaded into a moving van, and sent to Quantico. Three children and a wife to transport via privately owned conveyance, all within forty-eight hours. Don't ask me how, but it got done.

What was the rush? I reported to the Basic School, then under the command of Col. Lew Walt, my friend from Pendleton days, who assigned me to help train members of the naval ROTC program then on board for annual summer training. Important duty? Sure. But important enough to bust your butt to comply with "proceed without delay" orders? I thought not.

By the time I had reported to my course of instruction on 2 September, the 1st Provisional Marine Brigade (remember that word provisional?) had been landed in Korea and by the eighth anniversary of the Guadalcanal landing, on 11 August, had seen its first combat action. Each of the three infantry battalions of the 5th Marines had gone up against the enemy with only two of the three authorized rifle companies present for duty. Each of the rifle companies was short more than a platoon in strength, ghosts still being used as maneuver elements. The battles that raged around the Naktong River on 15 August and 3 September bore bloody testimony to the fact that once the enemy has been weakened, there must be sufficient force present on call to eject him from the main battle position. In far too many cases during the Naktong battles, enemy weaknesses could not be exploited, for there was no reserve element to bolster the attack, no unit to be used as a maneuver element to keep the attack going until the enemy had been killed on position or forced out.

Our country had not been prepared for World War II when it arrived. The opening rounds of the police action in Korea indicated that in terms of troop strength we were starting out with one hand tied behind us in yet another war.

Sitting in an air-conditioned classroom while Marines were sweating blood in Korea was not my cup of tea. Notes from Ernie DeFazio kept a hot flame burning under my tail. Straight scoop from Ernie, no journalism. Early actions within the Pusan perimeter had brought well-deserved fame (if not fortune) to DeFazio. Just as gung ho as he had been in the Pacific war, he now was serving as the gunnery sergeant of the brigade's reconnaissance element. David Duncan of *LIFE* magazine had caught him on camera as he pointed out objectives to his commanding officer. That photo had made the cover of *LIFE*. Good photo. Bad caption. Ernie had been listed as an "unidentified staff officer." A short, terse note from me to the magazine cleared the air, gave DeFazio a name and rank.

Other notes from Korea, after Inchon, indicated a recommendation for a Navy Cross for actions taken during a night reconnaissance across the Han River. We would talk about his actions in Korea face to face in a couple of months.

To ensure direct assignment to the 1st Marine Division upon graduation from school, I made a trip to Headquarters in October and again in November and December. The heat was on in the classrooms—comfortable. The Marines in Korea were on their way back to Hungnam, freezing and fighting down that long road from Hagaru-ri. At Headquarters I talked with several people in whom I previously had placed much trust. OK. OK. Ave, we will get you out there! Simmer down! Go on back to Quantico and relax!

A week prior to graduation a team from Officer Detail came down from Headquarters to issue orders. Some in my class had orders direct to the 1st Marine Division. My name was not called off in that group. I asked for a recheck. Not there. As soon as the session was over I contacted my friends. What happened? Ave, we never told you that we could get you straight to the division. (They had.) We got you to Pendleton. You will have to take it from there.

On 22 December 1950, we jammed all of our travel gear, three children, and Christmas presents into a 1949 Packard sedan and headed west by south. Christmas Eve found us in Ruston, Louisiana. That night, while the children were being bathed and readied for bed by Helen, I slipped out to the car, brought in the Christmas presents, and stashed them in appropriate places around the motel room. For a long time the children were convinced that Santa had spotted us on the road and had followed us to Ruston. When you are six years old or less, life has a special magic.

I reported to the commanding general, Marine Barracks, Camp Pendleton, on 6 January 1951, and was sent immediately to the headquarters of the Training and Replacement Command for duty. Here the mystery of my orders was solved quickly. Maj. Ralph C. Rosacker, the executive officer of the command, had been my company commander in Reserve Officers Class at Quantico in 1943. He had spotted my name on the graduating list and had requested my assignment to his unit. Headquarters, without telling me, had granted his request.

Upon reporting, I was taken before the commanding officer, a full colonel, who stood me at attention for thirty minutes while he harangued me concerning the importance of his command, how hard he worked, how hard he expected me to work, what a wonderful opportunity it was for me to be in his command, how much I would learn, how much better it would be for my career to remain with him than to go to Korea. I had known the colonel in the 2d Marine Division, knew that we never would make it together. When he finally had exhausted all of the superlatives that he could muster concerning his command, he caught his breath and conditionally welcomed me aboard.

Still in a brace, I pulled in a long, deep lungful of air, looked him in the eyes, and informed him that I had no desire to serve in his command, that my only objective was to serve in the 1st Marine Division in Korea, preferably as a rifle company commander.

Not believing what he was hearing, he turned red, his eyes snapped in anger, and he turned away muttering to Rosacker, "Get him out of here! Get him out of here. Send him to the Draft as soon as possible!"

Late that afternoon I reported to the headquarters of the 5th Replacement Draft and was assigned a draft company for training. I had broken down my last door, jumped over my last obstacle. When you *want* to go to the combat zone, why do so many people disbelieve you?

We found a small cottage high on a bluff overlooking Moonlight Beach and the shimmering Pacific in a town called Encinitas, just a few miles down the coast road from Pendleton. During the remaining days at Pendleton and after our return from cold-weather training, the company shaped up swiftly and in the evenings there were chances to visit with Ernie and Peggy DeFazio, to have dinner with them, to share Ernie's experiences in Korea. Ernie had been sent home from Hungnam after the 1st Marine Division had made its march to the sea, for he had been wounded three times, and luck tends to run out after so many hits.

Ernie was wearing a new device on his uniform—the golden dolphins of a submariner. He had served aboard the submarine *Perch,* SSP-313, a troop carrier, during 1949 and 1950. While aboard he had met all of the requirements set forth in BuPers Manual, Article C7608, and ComSubPac Restricted Pamphlet, *Requirements for Qualification in Sub-*

marines. On 1 March 1950, F. W. Scanland, Commander, Submarine Division 51, had written the following of Ernie's accomplishment. "While it is generally recognized throughout the military services that a Marine's accomplishments are without limit, it is felt that DeFazio has now made this an established fact. His associates may feel justly proud of his credit to the Corps!"

February 1946 until January 1951. My family had crossed the United States three times on permanent-change-of-station orders. Three overseas tours, two in the Caribbean, one in the Mediterranean. A variety of duty. Duty in three rifle companies, in command of two of them. A short, sour tour with the Organized Reserve. A tour as a tactical air observer. Duty at the Equipment Board. Duty under instruction at the Air Observation School and the Amphibious Warfare School, Junior Course. Two children born. A Regular commission earned. All accomplished in less than five years.

During those lean, mean, in-between years, the Marine Corps challenged its people to exert maximum effort, to let nothing stand in the way of military excellence. Having observed many Marines during that period of time, I can say only that the challenge was accepted—they gave the best they had in them to give, to the Corps and to the country.

Part Five

THE LONG WALK

19

Replacement

The temperature inside the command post tent was too high, even for Korea in winter. With all of my outside clothing on, it was smothering. In addition to the heat generated by the stove, I had a pretty fair burn smouldering away inside of me. In fact I just about had reached the end of a fuse that was getting shorter by the moment.

It was the end of a long, frustrating day. The USS *Breckenridge* had heaved-to off Pohang early on the morning of 19 February 1951. Six years prior to the day, almost to the hour, I had clambered over the side and down the cargo net of an assault transport, prepared to make the run for Red Beach One at Iwo. On this sixth anniversary there would be no beach assault, but my adrenalin count was still high. A lot of unknowns, a lot of uncertainties on this beach. This would be my first experience in joining a unit already combat-blooded. *I* would be the stranger this time, to be looked over by jaundiced eyes, to be prejudged, to be cut down by the old-timers—not a comfortable position to be in. I had been on *that* side too many times, had been guilty of instant dislikes, of snap judgements, of refusing friendship. I had dished it out with a passion—would again. For now it was my turn to stand and take it.

It had been a clear, windy day, sunlight dappling the dark waters, foam whipped up by the stiff offshore winds. We had clustered at the rail, feeling the bite of winter in the air, gazing landward at the snow-covered hills, waiting for the arrival of the 1st Marine Division liaison teams—the people who would assign us to our units.

When the teams arrived, I learned from an old friend among them of the recent death of John Hancock, a lieutenant who had served in "C" Company of the 21st Marines at the same time I had commanded "B" Company. A fine Marine, comrade in arms, one of those special people blessed with the instinct for small-unit leadership, a mustang who understood the needs of his men and served them well. He had taken command of "B" Company, 1st Battalion, 5th Marines, and had seen some rough going since that October change of command. He was the first of my old acquaintances to die in Korea. They did not have to tell me of the superior manner in which he performed his duties. To me that was a foregone conclusion. The sun lost some of its brilliance, the beauty of the day lessened when I realized that there would be no reunion with him ashore.

Shortly after I digested that bleak bit of information, the liaison teams summoned the infantry officers and we were split up among the three regiments. I was assigned to the 5th Marines. No complaints from me. A good regiment with an outstanding war record in the Great War and in World War II. Korean service only added luster to its reputation as a fighting unit. We boated our gear, went ashore, and were transported to the command post of the 5th Marines at Yongchon. There we met briefly with Colonel Murray, the regimental commander, and then were sent on down to our respective battalions. I received orders to the 2d Battalion, and just at nightfall arrived at the command post. A young lieutenant, who scrutinized me carefully, took my orders inside the tent. I waited outside in the cold and gathering darkness, wondering if I had not screwed up badly by being so insistent on getting to Korea in the first place. From the way I had been shunted around during the day, I started to believe that I was not needed here. About fifteen minutes later the lieutenant reappeared and motioned me inside. As I went through the blackout curtains, I had no idea what to expect, but my expectations were greater, I am sure, than what actually lay in store for me.

A very tall, excessively thin lieutenant colonel stood in the center of the tent, my qualification jacket held in his right hand, his left hand and arm rotating through the superheated air like a huge fan blade. He glanced at me and then down to the open qualification jacket. He gave no greeting.

"Have you ever been in the Fleet Marine Force, Captain?"

"Yes, Sir! A little over six years, Sir!"

"Ever been in a rifle company?"

"Have been in five, Sir! Commanded three of them."

The arm stopped flailing. He placed both hands on his hips and squinted down at me through the haze of cigarette and stove smoke that hung in a loose halo around his head. I was growing weary of this two-bit interrogation. The answer to every question that he had asked me so far was contained in my qualification jacket.

"Ever been a battalion operations officer?"

"No, Sir! Assistant G-3. Aerial and Gunnery Observer, 2d Marine Division. Nothing else."

"Can you write an operation order?"

I was getting hotter by the second, just about ready to blow. He had read my background, knew damned well that I just had completed an intermediate-level school, knew damned well that I could write an operation order.

"Well?" he demanded. "Well?"

"Colonel, I doubt if I could write any plan or order that would please *you!*" The short fuse was gone, the explosion about to take place. To hell with the consequences! They couldn't punish me by sending me to Korea. I already was there!

"I did not ask you *that*, Captain! *Can* you write an operation order?"

"Yes, *Sir!*"

It got mighty quiet inside that tent. There were more people inside it than I thought—clerks, radiomen, and a couple of extra lieutenants. I did not know how this tilting with the brass was going over, but I did know one thing—I had not fought my way through the Marine Corps Schools, Headquarters, Marine Corps, and the Training and Replacement Command at Pendleton to end up in a screwy outfit like this, being treated like a recruit.

My attitude finally must have gotten through to him. He backed off, simmered down, and told me that I would be assigned temporarily as assistant operations officer. He then turned me over to the operations officer, Maj. Ted Spiker, a short, round, smiling little man. We shook hands, as human beings are supposed to do, and went outside. With his help, my gear was moved into the long squad tent that housed the Headquarters Company officers. The canvas cot standing at the far end of the tent looked mighty inviting. I had been standing around somewhere ever since 0600 that morning.

Even then, the day was not to end. There were introductions to the other occupants of the tent, pleasantries exchanged, and then Jack Jones, the skipper of "C" Company of the 1st Battalion, dropped in to see me. We went outside into the crisp, cold night air and Jack cut me in on a number of things.

I last had seen Jack at Headquarters, Marine Corps, where he was serving in operations. His constant nagging at his seniors finally had gotten him sprung in time to make the Marine Corps birthday celebration in Korea.

Out on a combat patrol that 10 November 1950, attempting to cut off elements of the North Korean People's Army during their withdrawal to the north, his company had been inundated by the mass of fleeing enemy troops—cut off and surrounded. It was after midnight before elements of Jack's patrol had been able to filter back into friendly lines, to discover that they had been given up for dead, their personal gear already sent to holding areas in the rear. Jack must have felt the same way that I had felt coming in from Moli Point— why are they so damned anxious to draw a red line through your name? Jack's smile was on the woeful side when he told me that there was no *dead* feeling around the holes in his body when the corpsman had extracted the shrapnel from his wounds, even more woeful when he commented derisively that there was no birthday *cake* ever cut that night!

Of the battle at Chosin he said little, but admitted to having picked up more shrapnel. Counting Iwo, he had been chopped up by shell fragments three times and was still on his feet. Later I would learn of his actions at Yudam-ni, of the predawn attack on Hill 1282 by his company, of the rescue of the casualties of "E" Company, 7th Marines, by members of his command, with Jack himself repeatedly going forward of his lines to bring back half-frozen, immobilized Marines of "E" Company, with enemy fire coming in from all sides. Undeserved recognition, Jack would call it. Others saw his actions as far from commonplace. He was awarded the Navy Cross.

It was good to see him, to find someone from the old days, someone with whom I had something in common, to hear some common sense being talked after my exposure to the irrational, bean-pole colonel, to know that Jack would be around to keep me straight. In the course of the conversation he told me that a lieutenant colonels' list just had been published. The 1st and 2d Battalions were up for grabs between the battalion executive officer with whom I recently had jousted and the commanding officer of the Weapons Company. Command would be assumed, Jack said, within seventy-two hours. I didn't wish Jack any hard luck, but right then I started praying that command of the 2d Battalion would go to the Weapons Company commander.

Prayer can be a powerful thing. The next day it was announced that the Weapons Company commander would take over the 2d Battalion. A lucky day for me. I had learned very much from my first combat battalion commander, Col. Victor H. Krulak, but at a distance—lieutenants and lieutenant colonels are not meant to be cozy. I would learn equally as much from my second combat battalion commander, and at a much closer range.

Lt. Col. Glen E. Martin, U.S. Marine Corps Reserve. Eighteen months older than I. Out of Council Bluffs, Iowa, farm country. Unobtrusive, calm, unruffled, almost gentle in his manner and speech. Easy to talk to, with the ability to extract answers without bludgeoning them out of you. Of medium height, lean, narrow-framed, a slight stoop, almost emaciated in appearance, the hint of a smile always at the corners of his mouth when things were going right, his laugh surprisingly hearty, bursting from deep inside of him when something hit him just the right way.

Behind Nature's camouflage, a creature of quiet wisdom, of fairness, giving every man at least one good chance before throwing him to the lions. A keen mind and the ability to employ it most effectively, answers to tactical problems arrived at with a studied and deliberate ease. He seemed to take immense pleasure in leading others on, letting them believe that he was in fact just the old farm boy they thought him to be, then hammering them senseless with a curt, cutting sarcasm of his own brand, leaving them with no room for verbal retaliation.

He was no boot, you may be sure of that. He came to battalion command with high credentials, with much combat experience in World War II, more recently had finished the long, frigid, exhausting march from Yudam-ni to Hungnam, bedeviled by the Chinese all the way.

As commanding officer of "A" Company, 1st Battalion, 22d Marines, he had landed at Parry-Eniwetok in February 1944 and then, with the same unit, had gone on to the Guam landings. The following year, after his promotion to major, he had made the Okinawa campaign as S-3 of the 2d Battalion, 22d Marines. His actions during the attack on Parry Island, Eniwetok Atoll, on 22 February, for which he was awarded the Navy Cross, were indicative of how his mind worked, how quickly he assimilated the facts of a given situation and cranked out successful solutions.

Landing with the third wave in the vicinity of Valentine Pier, he quickly had taken in the chaos then existing on the beach—troops disorganized, intermingled with empty LVTs and amphibious tanks at the water line or just inland from it—the preceding second wave stalled at the crest of the sand dunes not twenty yards inland and under fire from enemy small arms, automatic weapons, and grenades. Martin raced along the beach, reorganizing groups of Marines into a fighting force, then led them up and across the crest of the sand dunes and through the enemy positions to secure the open flank of the beach. As he surged forward he came under flanking fire from heavy machine guns, which he located firing from positions at the base of Valentine Pier. He quickly arranged with a half-track commander, whose vehicle was just crossing the beach, to deliver direct fire from its 75mm howitzer on one of the pillboxes while he assaulted the other single-handedly. Arming himself with blocks of explosives and hand grenades, in the face of withering fire from the pillboxes and under the additional danger of being hit by shrapnel from the 75mm rounds zipping close by, he charged the enemy strong point, blowing away the guns and the troops that manned them.

We would be together on the hills of Korea long enough for me to learn that he had lost none of that marvelous magic, none of the stamina, none of the get up and go that had made him such a hot company commander in the Pacific battles.

I met him the following morning. Ted Spiker must have told him about the near eruption of the previous night.

"Sure you want to be in *this* battalion?" was his opening remark, offered with a disarming, angelic smile. "Sure you don't want to go to the 1st Battalion?" His next question— what did I want to do?

I wanted a rifle company so badly that I could taste it. I was a captain. Companies were for captains. It was duty that I loved. I came on strong.

Again that wide smile, but this time not so angelic. "No, old captain. You have had your share of rifle companies. You *know* how to run a company. I have three and a weapons company. I want you to help me run those companies. *If* you do the job right, you will find yourself busier than with a company of your own—and you will enjoy it more. I have been a battalion operations officer. I *know* what I am talking about!"

Listening to that low, firm voice and watching the laughter go out of the eyes, I knew that it was senseless to argue. Beneath that placid facade there was granite and spring steel. I ached to run a rifle company in Korea, but knew that there was no chance right then. I couldn't blame the colonel. He had four *knowns* as his company commanders. To him I was new, untried. Why take a chance with me?

He *did* know what he was talking about. Five months later I would not have swapped jobs with any rifle company commander in Korea. I did not realize it fully then, but on that day I had hit pure gold. No replacement officer going in cold ever could have had better luck. The right time. The right place. The right man to serve under.

20

Operation KILLER

About a week prior to my arrival at Pohang, a Chinese Communist attack had been launched against the Central Front. Two Republic of Korea divisions had been driven from positions north of the town of Hoengsong. The town had been lost, and now the Chinese were sweeping south toward the rail-communications center of Wonju. General Ridgway, commanding Eighth U.S. Army, Korea, had watched the attack carefully, and by mid-February had determined that the power had gone out of it. He decided to initiate a limited objective offensive against the retreating Chinese, to regain the high ground around Hoengsong and reopen the roads leading eastward from it, hoping concurrently to cut off and destroy some of the Chinese troop units. D Day for the operation was set for 21 February. The 1st Marine Division would go from control of X Corps to IX Corps, would attack up the Wonju basin, and secure the controlling high ground at Hoengsong.

We moved by truck from Yongchon to Chungju and remained overnight alongside a frozen riverbed. Although Colonel Martin officially had been assigned as commander of

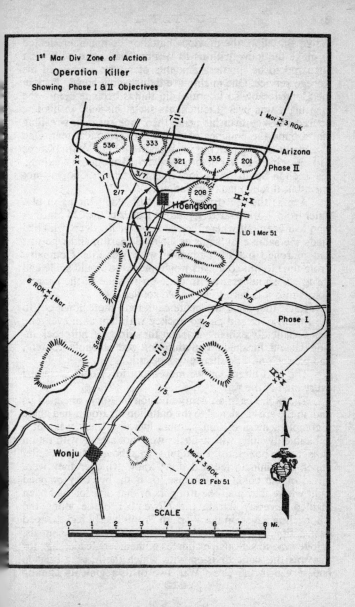

1st Mar Div Zone of Action
Operation Killer
Showing Phase I & II Objectives

1 Mar x 3 ROK

7—1

536   333

321   335   201   Arizona

x x   Phase II

1/7   3/7

2/7

208

Hoengsong   x x x x

1/1   LD 1 Mar 51

3/1

6 ROK x 1 Mar

3/5   Phase I

1/5

3/5

x x x x

1/5

Wonju

1 Mar x 3 ROK

LD 21 Feb 51

N

SCALE

0   1   2   3   4   5   6   7   8 Mi.

the 2d Battalion, the previous battalion commander elected to make the move with us to Wonju. That night, with what appeared to be limitless amounts of booze, he relived his Korean service. One might have thought that he was back in the Confederacy, so informal did things become before the long night was over. Lieutenants sat at his feet, in his lap, poured whiskey over his head, then took turns in wrestling him around the confines of a crowded pyramidal tent. One also might have gotten the impression that the Marine Corps had never been to war before. We learned about the Naktong, the Inchon-Seoul operation, and the frozen Chosin—not once, but through many variations.

Across the tent from me sat "Blackie" Lima, an old-timer from World War II, a platoon leader of the 22d Marines who had been out where the water was *really* deep, who had made the same campaigns as Colonel Martin, and who just had marched out of Yudam-ni with Weapons Company. From time to time our eyes would meet, we would smile and shrug our shoulders, try to doze off in spite of the clamor. Sometimes it is hard to be an old soldier.

Later that night the lieutenants took the colonel out to the frozen river and played hockey with him until everyone was completely exhausted. Then they dragged him back inside the tent, finished off anything left with alcoholic content, and passed out. The silence was beautiful.

The next afternoon we moved out for Wonju. It rained every inch of the way.

There had been an Army division in Wonju ahead of us and, in the area assigned to the battalion, its troops had made a complete mess of things, quite literally. There was not a habitable dwelling whose decks were not strewn with ration cans, ration boxes, used heat tabs, pasteboard cartons, toilet paper, and human feces. I don't know whether they were afraid of the cold, the Chinese, or both, but they crapped right where they ate. The troopers of that division had been mauled severely during the November battle along the Chongchon River on the Western Front, barely had escaped destruction. Perhaps that is what made them act like animals. It jolted me to see such examples of mediocre leadership, for this was the same division with which the Marine brigade had served in the Great War, two of its regiments fighting then with great distinction. Maybe it was the association with the Marine brigade that made them perform so well, but that was another time, another place. In February 1951 my opinion of that division hit an all-time low. Unfortunately, future contacts with it would do nothing to change my mind.

Our battalion came into Wonju with the mission of division reserve. Not a dramatic role, but a necessary one. On the morning of the 21st, just prior to 1000, which was H hour for the operation, the 1st Battalion came rolling into town on trucks. There was no time for a proper briefing and reorganization. They made it to the line of departure as the last minutes ran out and, in concert with the 3d Battalion, started the movement to the north and west. The rain continued, a heavy, freezing drizzle. Mud, slush, and sleet in the daytime. Ice and snow at night. A miserable way to commence an attack.

The time we spent in Wonju was some of the most valuable that we were to know in Korea. Much more valuable than slugging along knee-deep in half-frozen paddies or slithering along slippery ridge lines with nothing but snipers and long-range machine gun fire to relieve the monotony.

Colonel Martin turned out to be the finest terrain analyst that I ever would meet. He could read terrain on the ground and from a map and come up with a plan of attack that invariably would place the enemy at a disadvantage. He also had the uncanny ability of positioning the enemy on the terrain. It might have been pure luck, but I saw it happen too many times for me to believe *that!* In the island battles, we used to assemble in an attack position, hope that fire support would be sufficient, cross the line of departure, and attack— usually a frontal attack, for there was little room to maneuver on some of those islands, and even less cover and concealment to protect a flanking force after air strikes and naval gunfire had ripped away the foliage. Many commanders continued to envisage infantry combat in Korea as a prolonged series of frontal attacks. Colonel Martin did not.

Just before we left Wonju, the colonel took the staff officers, the company commanders, the key staff NCOs onto a piece of high ground bordering the bivouac and there proceeded to educate us. Using his map to point out terrain features in sight of us on the ground, he outlined the tactical techniques that he wanted employed when we were committed to the attack. There were other ways, he said, but this was the *best*, would kill fewer of our people, and would drive away or kill more of the enemy. His method was to attack along the long axis of a ridge line wherever possible, regardless of whether the ridge ran parallel to the direction of attack or perpendicular to it. Gain the high ground from the flanks and rear and then advance along the long axis, rolling up the enemy as you moved. Security elements, squads, or fire teams could work down the finger ridges and clear them from the rear. The attack might be launched using a single company along a single ridge line or, by employing two or more companies, adjacent ridge lines could be cleared simultaneously. If the ridge line formed a cross-compartment, we would forego a frontal attack and, by a series of flanking actions, gain the high ground and attack along the narrow, hard-to-defend, long axis. Of course, he told us, there would be instances when we would be forced into a stand-up-and-walk-in slugging match, but if we were careful and used the ridges properly, we would not get our noses bloodied too often.

Hidebound as we all were, set in our ways from the other war, wanting always to do the John Wayne, it all sounded very complicated and difficult—boxing instead of swinging hard in the time-honored custom. When, in a few weeks, we had to put the colonel's way to the test daily, it worked beautifully, just as the colonel had said it would.

The code name for the operation was KILLER. None of the Marines involved did much killing on the way up to Hoengsong. When the 2d Battalion's duty as reserve was completed, we did not move north by motor transport. No, we walked that road, ten miles of misery from Wonju to Hoengsong, in shoepacs! KILLER damned near killed the mobility of the battalion on that tender little jaunt!

A shoepac is what we used to wear in winter up in Maine. It never was meant to cover long distances on hard, frozen surfaces. We called them gum-rubbers when I was a child growing up. A rubber bottom—sometimes gum-rubber, sometimes plain rubber. Leather uppers, from eight to ten inches high, laced with rawhide. Made to be used under moderate travel conditions in snow and cold weather. If you didn't step into slush or water higher than the rubber portion, you were relatively safe. If you went up into the leather, you could expect cold, wet feet. Since there was no porosity in either the lower or upper parts of the pac, a lot of sweat accumulated, and when movement stopped, your feet got very frigid.

I had an additional problem—small feet. I never could find a pair of pacs small enough to give me a decent fit. Oh! the supply people had said, you will be all right. Just put in a couple of felt innersoles and wear a couple of pairs of extra socks. That will surely do it! On the march to Hoengsong I wore three sets of innersoles and three pairs of socks. I wore holes right through the socks and through the skin on the backs of my heels and soon had both blood *and* water freezing inside the pac every time we took a break. There were a hell of a lot of other Marines in the same condition. I can laugh about it now. I wasn't laughing then!

Coming into Hoengsong from the south and going out to the northwest, I saw two faces of this war that were new to me, faces I disliked very much.

As we entered the edge of town in the bitter cold of February, there they sat. Tiny, brown, dirty. Thick yellow mucus, half-frozen half-coagulated, hung from their nostrils and oozed slowly down toward their weather-cracked lips. Huge black eyes staring vacantly, tear streaks coursing the lengths of their gaunt, filthy faces; naked buttocks exposed to the ravages of the winter wind. The children of Hoengsong, the ones who could not escape the onslaught with their families, the ones whose parents lay stiffly in the streets, killed by the fire of the Chinese or the Marines, never knowing by which, or why.

Coming out of town on the road to Hongchon, a different sight, a different circumstance. Just days ago an American artillery battalion had attempted to move up the road without securing the high ground that flanked it. The Chinese on the high ground had surprised them, caught them in the open, slaughtered them in droves, destroyed their vehicles, turned their own howitzers upon them, killing them with their own weapons. The bodies had been removed after the 1st Marines

had uncovered Hoengsong; but the overturned vehicles just
off the road, the 105mm howitzers pointing toward the town,
gave mute evidence that disaster had walked there. The
Eighth Army, with its propensity for giving even defeat a
fancy name, already had labeled this lonely dirt track Mas-
sacre Valley.

21

RIPPER and RUGGED

KILLER ended on 4 March. It had not accomplished nearly the amount of killing that General Ridgway desired, so we immediately launched out on another operation called RIPPER. I don't know who or what was supposed to be ripped. I never found out. In the bag, already dusted off and ready to be used, was another operation. Its name was RUGGED. It appeared that the more ferocious the code name, the more the troopers were supposed to get fired up. It was amusing, in a way, to see just how many of those fire-eating titles could be devised. There must have been a secret staff section at Eighth Army headquarters tasked for just that special mission.

RIPPER sticks in my mind for a variety of reasons, none of them especially gory. RIPPER, like KILLER, was supposed to trap and wipe out huge segments of the Chinese Communist forces. Like KILLER, it failed for the most part to accomplish that mission. The Chinese would not cooperate, would fight from prepared positions of considerable strength—holding UN forces in place for a few days—and

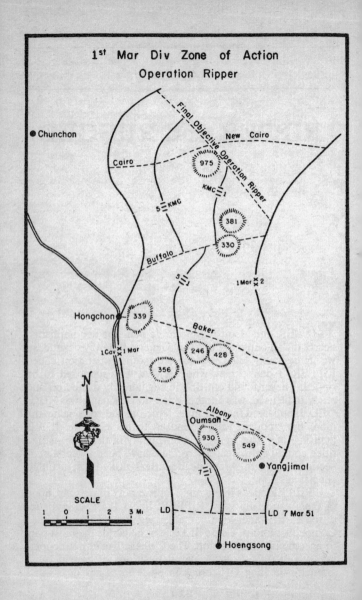

1st Mar Div Zone of Action
Operation Ripper

Chunchon

Final Objective Operation Ripper

New Cairo

Cairo

975

KMC 1

5 KMC

381

330

Buffalo

5 1

1 Mar XX 2

Hongchon

339

Baker

246 428

1 Cav X 1 Mar

356

Albany

Oumsan

930

549

Yangjimal

7 1

SCALE

1 0 1 2 3 Mi

LD

LD 7 Mar 51

Hoengsong

then would move back and try it again from a new defensive line.

We did cover a lot of ground, most of it overland, through terrain unsullied by roads or trails—some thirty-five miles as the crow flies—and ended up with a division front that stretched about twenty miles across. To help us stay busy during the operation, the North Korean People's Army guerrilla units got back into the game, harassing the rear-area units, sometimes hitting the command posts of the infantry battalions. It generally was believed that these troublemakers were remnants of the 10th North Korean Division—the same people who had carried out a similar mission around Pohang in January and February. There was more than enough going on to the front and the rear to keep all of us alert and ready.

During this period of the war, just about everyone that had come to Korea with the brigade—the 5th Marines and supporting units—rotated stateside. After the Pusan perimeter, Seoul-Inchon, the Chosin, and the guerrilla hunt around Pohang, they more than had earned a ticket home. It would be a whole new ball game, a new team, new players. People of the Regular establishment still do not like to admit it, but it was true—during the spring and summer campaign of 1951, the majority of *command* billets were filled by *Reserve* officers, who for the most part had demonstrated superior leadership capabilities in World War II and whose tactical knowledge already had proven itself invaluable to the Marine division. I don't know where the Regular officers were, but that spring there was a definite scarcity of them in the combat leadership of the 1st Marine Division.

Ted Spiker, who had been battalion executive officer since Yongchon, was among those leaving, as was my operations chief. Spiker's relief was unique. He had been assigned as executive officer, 2d Battalion, 5th Marines, *before he left the States!* No palavering around, no bargaining for position for that one. He flew into the regimental command post by helicopter, was briefed by the new regimental commander, Colonel Hayward, and sent on to the 2d Battalion by the same helicopter—the first one to land at our command post in many a day.

There was nothing basically wrong with the incoming major. I had known him in the 2d Marine Division, where he had been in reconnaissance work—duty that he had performed in World War II. He was unfortunate in that his father was a general officer back in Washington. Skids do get greased, whether one wants it to be that way or not, and they had been lubricated properly in this instance. Just the rumor of such things can get you off to a bad start with the locals. And if you happen to act just a little "far out," it sort of puts the sign on you.

The night of the new major's arrival, the North Koreans put on one of their best shows. Explosions from grenades and mortar rounds echoed to our flanks and rear. About a platoon of guerrillas had hit the 1st Battalion area and, after whooping it up there in grand style, had been seen moving in our direction. Periodically I drifted over to the colonel's tent and brought him up to date. The rest of the time we tried to stay abreast of the situation, which was fluid to say the least—plotting contacts, servicing telephones and radios, which were spouting real or imagined enemy information like faucets. I felt no real concern for the moment and was quite sure that the colonel was just as loose.

There was a rustle at the doorway to the tent. The blankets, hung to form a blackout section for the pyramidal tent, were thrust aside with force. A shadow danced on the inside of the tent top, made huge by the feeble light of a dying Coleman lantern. Busy as we were, we paid it scant attention.

I finished my last plot, reminded my new section chief, Cpl. Bob Ramsdell, that lanterns had to have fuel if we were to have light, and glanced toward the tent door just as a voice filled with querulous anxiety sounded off. "What's the counterattack plan? What's the counterattack plan?" The shadowy form detached itself from the darkness of the doorway and leaped into the circle of light.

Steel helmet with no helmet cover. Army? M-1 rifle with bayonet fixed, rifle belt with a full unit of fire, bandoleers crisscrossed over the chest just like Pancho Villa, grenades clipped to upper suspender rings in the fashion of Ridgway. This guy was *ready*, whoever he was! Opening my squinty eyes to the largest aperture, I perceived that it was the new major. Before I could greet him I was swamped by a rapid flow of questions. What force would counterattack? Who was the force commander? When did we attack?

I was shocked nearly out of my senses. I looked at the intelligence officer, at Ramsdell, even at the communicators. I could have saved those looks. They were staring, entranced by the apparition that stood before them. Had I failed somewhere along the way? Had I missed an implied order from the colonel? I couldn't answer, didn't know *what* to say!

Another shadow just off the doorway, this time a silent one until it joined our little group. The colonel. He took in the scene, a smile edging his lips. "Any changes, old captain? Anything going on that I should know about?" Turning to the major, "Everything going OK?"

I breathed a sigh of relief. I hadn't fouled up after all. "Nothing new, colonel. 1st Battalion says that things are slacking off out their way. Might get a little sleep tonight, after all."

The colonel checked the map, had a few words with the intelligence officer, spoke to the communicators, and winked at me. "Major, let's get back to the sack. I want you fresh tomorrow for your first day's work. Ave will let us know before they overrun us!" With that he took the crestfallen warrior by the elbow and propelled him gently through the tent flap.

As I said before, there wasn't anything too wrong with the major. He was just a little tense. In from the States, he thought we were doing things strictly by the book. I think, too, that Colonel Hayward's briefing might have unsettled him a bit. When you learn for the first time that the unit you are reporting to for duty is not tied in physically with another friendly unit, when you hear that a North Korean division is out roaming around in the weeds behind you every night and you suddenly hear them start rattling cages along the line, it *can* make for a case of tight jaws and an even tighter scrotum. It might even shake you a little bit. It shook the hell out of him.

A few days later we received orders to move up. At that time the battalion was issued three experimental armored vests. This particular type was almost like an aviation flak jacket—heavy, bulky, very uncomfortable to wear. The major chose to volunteer his services in the wear-testing of this equipment. He wore it constantly, day and night, for as long as he was with the battalion. The troops gave him his nick-

name—which he wore even longer than the body armor—
Ironsides!

On 29 March, RIPPER came to an end and RUGGED
began. Our first operation during RUGGED was a river
crossing—two battalions of the regiment fording, the other
battalion crossing over downstream in DUKWs.

We crossed at our assigned site without mishap or battle
casualties, mainly because the North Koreans were busily
engaged in mortaring elements of the 7th Infantry Division
that were waiting for us to cross. It remains a mystery to me
why we had to wade that river in order to link up physically
with a unit already across and in position to continue the
attack, in the zone of action which had been ours. A unique,
valueless situation. Ours not to wonder why. Once across the
river we assembled to the west of the road junction and
watched the North Korean shells interdict the road that ran
north from us, and up which an Army battalion was due to
attack.

We were the personification of the term "raggedy-assed
Marines." So many uniforms and combinations of uniforms
that it would have taken a genius to identify us militarily.
Colonel Martin was a case in point. He wore an issue brown
flannel shirt with no collar rank insignia, a pair of green cold-
weather trousers held up by issue suspenders, and on his
head what routinely was referred to as a "Mongolian idiot's
hat"—headgear lined with dark brown pile, with earflaps that
fastened up and over the crown when not in use and a visor
that flipped up and back. On the flipped-back visor was
pinned his only rank insignia—a collar-size silver leaf.

The relieving battalion commander came ripping down
the road in his jeep, his command designator on the front
bumper, those huge Army silver oak leaves glinting from his
collar and helmet, demanding in a deep bellow just *who* was
in command here. Colonel Martin, with a sardonic little smile
playing over his face, walked over to the jeep, pointed to his
tiny rank insignia, and introduced himself.

Formalities completed, we saddled up and headed west
down the road to Chunchon. The weather was taking on a
pattern—warm-to-hot days, cool-to-cold nights. This turned

out to be a hot-to-hotter day. We had been running patrol operations overland. Our feet were tender, not ready for a steady pounding on a hard track. Between the individual loads we were carrying, the heat of the sun, and the beating that our feet were taking, it was not a pleasant march.

All the way to the outskirts of Chunchon we limped and tottered. About three miles east of the city we passed an Army artillery battalion's bivouac. Those boys hadn't seen anyone road-marching for a long time and they lined the roadside just to see *who* these fools might be. They just had been issued a ration of beer and held the cans in their hands as they jeered and hooted at us. We were close to dehydration, water long gone, the sight of that beer really turning some of our people on.

Then a strange and wonderful thing took place. Those artillerymen would not have understood the word empathy if you had thrown it at them, but what they did defines the word in its best usage. One by one they ran back to their tents, picked up as much beer as they could carry, ran back to the roadside, and started lobbing cans of beer into the column. Just about everyone fielded at least two cans, the quick ones even more. We didn't slow down, just shouted our thanks and kept cranking along. The blisters broke, water mingling with blood; the knee joints cracked and ached; the shoulders bent in weariness under the load. But in the ambrosial haze induced by the 3.2% beer, we became immune to all that, coasted right on into the battalion assembly area just at dark.

We never forgot that artillery battalion. The rounds they fired that day were right on for range and deflection, and the fuse settings were incomparable!

The next day we learned that we would have about seventy-two hours and then back to the lines we would go, up to a line called KANSAS, where we would relieve the 1st Cavalry Division and attack north towards the Hwachon Reservoir.

Those days in Chunchon were good for all of us. A shower unit was moved up close to the bivouac area, and for the first time since I had left the *Breckenridge* I bathed in hot, soapy water. As we entered the shower unit and stripped, they took away our old clothing, some of it so stiff with accumulated dirt that it almost could stand alone. And smell! Goats smelled better! After the luxury of the hot water and soap, we drew clean clothing, some new, some reclaimed, all of it infinitely superior to that just discarded.

The next day I bummed a pair of 5EE double-buckle boots from an Army supply unit—the first well-fitting footgear that I had encountered in Korea. Sheer bliss.

22

The Chinese Strike

It was cold for mid-April, and I shivered in the night air. The sky was clear, a jet black, the stars snapping, a bright moon throwing its light against the hillsides. It was a splendid array of nature, calming, deceitful. On this particular night the sound of battle had dimmed for some reason. I stood outside the command post tent alone, gazing up into the heavens, fascinated by the magnitude of the universe, pondering the strange events of the days just past. The background noise from the radio, the cutting in and out when transmissions were made, the voice monotone affected by the operators when sending, the ringing of the EE-8 field phones penetrated my solitude, made me aware that we were still in the business of making war.

The regiment had come up from Chunchon and occupied positions along line KANSAS for more than ten days, patrolling out over long distances, making little contact—an exercise for the leg muscles and respiratory system, good long-range practice for the radio operators. On our right flank the Korean Marine Corps Regiment was involved in a similar mission, had met with more success. One of their patrols had

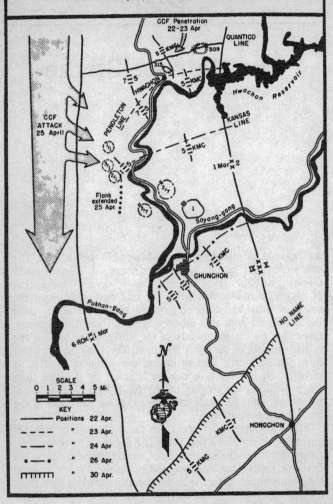

CCF Offensive Starting 22 April
And Subsequent Marine Withdrawals

CCF Penetration
22-23 Apr

QUANTICO
LINE

5 ⫶ KMC   509

313

7 ⫶ 5   HWACHON   5 ⫶ KMC

Hwachon Reservoir

CCF
ATTACK
25 April

PENDLETON
LINE

KANSAS
LINE

5 ⫶ KMC

1 Mar ✕✕ 2

3/1

3/1
2/1   1 ⫶ 5

2/1 ⫶ 7

Flank
extended
25 Apr.

1/7

1

Soyang-gang

7 ⫶ KMC

CHUNCHON   ✕✕✕

5 ⫶ 1

Pukhan-gang

NO NAME
LINE

6 ROK ✕ 1 Mar

N

KMC ⫶ 7   HONGCHON

SCALE
0 1 2 3 4 5 Mi.

KEY

——————— Positions 22 Apr.
– – – – –   "   23 Apr.
— - — - —   "   24 Apr.
• • • • •   "   26 Apr.
⊥⊥⊥⊥⊥⊥   "   30 Apr.

5 ⫶ KMC

made a night river crossing of the Pukhan River by swimming
a guide line across and then, by pulling a rubber assault boat
back and forth ferry-style, had moved the patrol across. The
patrol had penetrated the town of Hwachon and found it
nearly deserted, found and captured eleven Chinese soldiers,
and pulled them back across the river. This all had taken
place on the night of 18 April. The Chinese prisoners had
spilled their guts under the tender Korean Marine Corps
interrogation methods, and had stated that Phase V of the
Chinese Spring Counteroffensive was just about due to kick
off. Trivia, said the higher echelon intelligence people.
Rumors, just rumors. Nothing to get excited about.

On 21 April, the assault elements of the 1st Marine
Division—the 7th Marines on the left, the 5th Marines in the
center, and the Korean Marine Corps Regiment on the
right—were ordered forward from line KANSAS to secure
objectives along line QUANTICO—the high ground west
and north of the Hwachon Reservoir. We moved out against
no resistance and covered 6,000 meters during the day. Even
on the broken terrain over which the Korean Marines operated, there was little activity. The 1st Battalion, 5th Marines
took the town of Hwachon without incident. In our zone, to
the west of the 1st Battalion, we uncovered successive lines
of defense, weapons pits and personnel emplacements newly
dug. Some of the mortar positions had rows of mortar shells
laid out in recesses within the pits—everything in place except for the mortars and gunners. Defensive positions had
been strengthened by the use of abatis—trees felled, pointing
downhill, crossed one over the other, the tips of the branches
sharpened to create a greater obstacle to the attacker. Much
labor had been expended. Everything had the appearance of
a strong, deliberate defense, but where were the enemy
troops? Unsettling. All day long, reports had come in from
observation aircraft that the area to our north was blanketed
by smoke from grass and wood fires, making positive identification on the ground impossible. The Chinese certainly had
something going, but what?

Behind me, the blackout curtains of the tent rustled.
Colonel Martin appeared. He yawned, stretched, and eased
over to where I was standing. "Old captain," he drawled.

"Regiment just called. Said we should be on the alert for an attack tonight. Whatcha think of *that*? Did *you* see any Chinese today?"

I smiled. We both had covered the same ground. Nothing had been out there during daylight, but who could be certain after darkness fell? We stood silently, thinking about the report from regiment, watching the sky, and waiting.

The earth started to pulsate. Flashes of light ran along the northern horizon, outlining the hills. Off to the west, in the area of the 7th Marines, endless explosions of artillery rounds. The rumble grew, intensified, continued without respite. A moment before, all had been tranquil. Now it seemed that the hellish pounding might never cease. I had been exposed to the sixteen-inch salvos of the battleships, had known the air-sucking swoosh of shells from battalions of 105mm howitzers passing overhead, had heard the crash of those shells upon impact, but I never had known such a relentless roar, such countless numbers of shells exploding as now I heard. Drumfire. Over and over again.

"Jesus," the colonel breathed. "Old captain, someone is catching hell out there!"

A shadow fell across the colonel. The radio operator stood behind him, arm extended with the radio handset in his palm. "Regiment, Colonel. Priority message coming in."

Colonel Martin took the handset, identified himself, and listened. He asked no questions, checked out of the net, and wordlessly passed the handset back.

"The 6th ROK Division is taking that beating. The Chinese are between them and the 7th Marines. They say the Chinese are already fifteen miles deep. The left flank of the division is flapping in the wind!"

The adrenalin started to perk. Minutes ago I had been shivering from the chill of the night. Now my shivers were compounded of that same chill, plus excitement, a dash of apprehension, and a lacing of anticipation. One thing now was certain. We did not have to wonder about Chinese intentions anymore.

We didn't get tagged that night, but the 1st Battalion did. They got hit smartly enough to believe that they were in desperate need of reinforcements. "F" Company of our battalion was dispatched to give them a hand. By the time "F"

Company arrived the threat had vanished. The troopers of the Korean Marine Corps Regiment had slipped around the Chinese in the darkness and driven them off. It was a sleepless night—over before we realized it. The field phone never stopped jangling, the radios never stopped chattering. When daylight came we found that we were in good shape. No unit in the regiment had been hurt seriously. There had been a lot of sound and fury in the distance, but up close, little of substance.

During the day the regiment moved back to assume defensive positions along another of the dozens of control lines that Eighth Army had grease-pencilled on the acetate overlays in their operations rooms. This one was called PENDLETON. Along our portion, it turned south and west in order to link up with the 7th Marines, whose positions now faced almost due west in an attempt to prevent the Chinese from turning the 1st Marine Division's left flank. By nightfall we were hooked-in solid, the 1st Battalion on our right, the 7th Marines on our left.

As on the previous night, things started off with an unreal silence, the moon even more luminous, the stars more crisply gleaming. *Too* quiet. A feeling of vague, nagging uneasiness. And then, out of nowhere they stood revealed as plainly as at midday, standing all along the low ground forward of the Marine fighting holes.

No great numbers. Perhaps four squads spread out across the battalion front. Some standing singly. Some in pairs, close together. No shoulder weapons visible. For a few minutes no movement. Then, slowly, carefully they made their way towards the Marine lines, starting a gradual climb. Still no sound except for the footfalls, the crackle of twigs, the snapping of branches. No attempt at cover and concealment. Emotionless automatons advancing.

The Marines on the line had been instructed repeatedly—don't fire the machine guns, don't let fly with the Browning automatic rifles, don't even fire the M-1s or the carbines if grenades will get the job done. The Chinese worked the silent approach as part of their program—frighten, agitate, or anger the Round Eyes into letting go a burst with an automatic weapon. *Pinpoint!* Strong point, there! If they could, they would play the game until several automatic weapons were located. Then they would go about neutralizing those weapons with grenades, mortars, machine guns, and 57mm recoilless weapons of their own. It was a variation of the old Japanese game of World War II. All of the Orientals play the night games extremely well.

The men on the line were nervous, fatigued from lack of sleep on the previous night. To make them even more jumpy, word just had been passed down the line from the 1st Battalion that a Chinese infiltration team had spirited away a Browning A-4 light machine gun and its ammunition. The word said that the Chinese were everywhere. The troopers had good reason to have itchy fingers, but they held their fire. Held it until they could see the unusual amount of potatomasher grenades hanging from the waists of the Chinese. Held until the line of enemy soldiers had crossed through all of the moonlight and had entered the shadows of the trees along the ridge line. Then their own grenades, laid out on the lip of their fighting holes, were thrown. A cloudburst of fragmented metal cascaded over the Chinese, shattering them, driving them twitching and moaning into the ground just short of the Marine foxholes. Carbine fire and a few M-1s. Not a round of automatic-weapons fire had been expended.

The Chinese infantry unit on the reverse slope of the ridge line some 500 meters to our front would note this failure of weapons disclosure, would check off the battalion area as an unlikely place to force a penetration, and would probe along the line to the right or left of us. There would be a weaker spot somewhere, and they would exploit it.

We felt pretty damned good that night. The following morning we patrolled out to and beyond the night positions of the Chinese unit, found plenty of sign that they had been there, but made no contact. We had run the bastards off! No sweat! Spirits rose. The Chinese would not be back, tap-tap-tapping at *this* section of the UN line. It was not just the troopers who felt this way. I did. The colonel did. We all were confident that we could hold forever.

The Eighth Army, who saw the big picture as we did not, had no such confidence.

*   *   *

No professional military man likes to hear the word *retreat!* It goes against the grain. It smacks of inferiority, of defeat, of shame. It matters not what terminology is used to describe it—bug out, as the Army used to say, fire and fall back, pull out, retrograde movement, fighting in another direction. Just plain haul ass. It all comes out the same way. It has a detrimental, demoralizing effect upon the people who must execute that particular maneuver, no matter what great success may herald it upon its completion.

At midmorning on the third day of the Chinese offensive, word came to us that the 1st Marine Division must pull back to the old KANSAS line, perhaps even farther. Why? We were not hurt. Everything was going very well right here on line PENDLETON. I felt like vomiting. I tried to get some encouragement out of the colonel, but he was no help; he felt worse than I did, and for good reason. He had come through one of these same messes a little more than three months ago and was not looking forward to another replay, even though the weather was considerably warmer. Gloom settled on us like a heavy mist with no breeze to move it along. It permeated all the ranks. We despised the thought of being forced back—by the enemy or the Eighth Army! I began to wonder if getting up close to one of the Korean reservoirs had anything to do with this madness. The 1st Marine Division had moved along smartly wherever they fought, until they closed on the Chosin Reservoir in November. We had come up the Central Front in grand style until we had closed on the Hwachon Reservoir. Could it be?

We moved from line PENDLETON in good order, as the military historians like to say; marched down the hard, dusty road that ran along the west bank of the Pukhan; waded the river at a ford that we had come to know only too well; climbed back up the razorback ridge lines; and by late afternoon had reoccupied the same positions that we had held on line KANSAS three days before.

Coming off line PENDLETON, we began to see some of the reasoning behind the move. About four miles down the Hwachon-Chunchon road, a trail had been converted into a wheeled vehicle track in order to help resupply units on the division's left flank. As we came up on the junction of this track and the main road, heavy firing broke out—medium artillery, small arms, and automatic-weapons fire combined. Looking down that track to the west, at a range of about a mile, we could observe a 105mm howitzer battery firing point-blank, flat trajectory, just as fast as the tubes could be loaded. The sound of the howitzers firing, the nearly instantaneous detonation of the shells, told us instantly that the gunners could observe their targets. Out there to the west of the battery, the Chinese had managed to slide around the left-flank units, were trying to encircle the division.

Out on the right flank the Korean Marine Corps Regiment was coming back in, not in a simple column movement on the road as we had done. Some of their units still fought on in the hills around the southern shore of the Hwachon Reservoir, tied up so tightly with the Chinese that contact could not be broken safely. They would be drifting in—individually, in pairs, in fire teams, and squads for the next few days. Those people had chopped up the Chinese badly, all the way from line KANSAS to the town of Hwachon. The enemy troops did their best to return the favor during the dangerous business of breaking contact.

Those Korean Marines—we called them KMCs for short—were some of the most gutty, doughty, dependable fighters ever to grace the planet Earth. They never caved in as other Republic of Korea units did. They never pulled away from your flank during darkness. They fought to win. It would be great to be able to say that all this was the result of United States Marine Corps training. I am sure that a great deal of it did rub off, but inside those Korean hearts and minds there was an eliteness all of their own making. By happenstance or by device, it seemed to me that the KMC Regiment more often than not was given the most inaccessible terrain objectives, defended by the most tenacious of enemy units.

My first operational contact with a KMC unit was a very happy one, and quite by accident. We were in the final days of RIPPER, going into a temporary position known as the CAIRO line. The KMC Regiment was on our right, moving through terrain so rough that their only means of logistic support was by airdrop, and going up against the only real enemy resistance of the entire operation. After securing its objectives, the KMC Regiment came abreast of us and commenced deep aggressive patrolling to the front.

For weeks I had been hounding Colonel Martin to let me accompany one of the battalion patrols that were screening our front. After we had secured our portion of the CAIRO line, he finally cut me loose with the admonition, "*You* don't *do* a damned thing, you don't *say* a damned thing, whether it goes right or wrong! This is not *your* patrol. You just lope along and look things over. Any correcting needs to be done, you tell *me*. *I* will get it taken care of!"

It sounded like a fair trade-off to me, so I made my promise in salt and blood and went off on patrol with a rifle platoon, reinforced with a section of A-4 light machine guns and a section of 60mm mortars. Things *did* get screwed up, there was some bad map reading done, and we ended up everywhere but on the patrol objectives. We patrolled right into a 1st Battalion patrol moving in the opposite direction— Jack Jones out on a company combat patrol. We compared notes. My patrol leader was not where he was supposed to be. Jack's patrol was.

We had patrolled all day and had seen no enemy. We were following a dirt cart trail and a streambed that ran generally west to east. The people out on the flanks were tired and the patrol leader had not noticed them as they moved down towards the track where the going was easier. All it takes is a certain amount of fatigue, of mental numbness, and you can step into it right up to your butt.

Just ahead lay three Korean huts nestled along the edge of the streambed. North of this cluster of huts a hill rose sharply to crest at about 300 meters. It was late afternoon, shadows starting to creep into the valley. Just as the point of the patrol moved past the huts, an automatic weapon on the hillside opened up on the patrol. One, two, three bursts. I was in the center of the column, then suddenly I was alone in the middle of the trail. The platoon had scampered off the road as they should have, had taken cover under the berm that lay alongside the north side of the streambed. The fourth burst punched neat holes in the dirt just inches from my feet and spattered dust and gravel into my face. After six years away from enemy automatic-weapons fire, I found my reaction time ridiculously slow! I made up for that first mistake by plunging toward the safety of the streambed just as burst number five came ripping in on me.

By the time I had reached cover, the A-4s were talking, firing up a storm; the mortars were set up; and a squad was flanking the enemy from the east side of the hill. That young lieutenant might never be the world's best map reader, but he knew how to get his unit into action once he had a target location. The mortar gunners got their rounds in the air, walking them along the top of the hill and down onto the military crest where the fire appeared to be coming from. White phosphorous rounds, very mean to stand against. The North Koreans didn't care for those shells at all, didn't like the steady hammering of the A-4s, whose slugs were whacking into the hillside far too close for comfort. Before the flanking squad could reach their position, the North Koreans had fled.

Once the squad on the hill had rejoined the platoon, dusk was settling in the valley. The platoon leader set off again, due east. If he intended to take the platoon back through friendly lines before nightfall, he would do well to turn south. On we went, the trail and stream now bending sharply north. We made the turn and there they were in front of us, not twenty yards away—an infantry unit of company size! Meeting engagement? A firefight against superior numbers at this time of day? Were we about to be wiped out in the gloom? It *had* to be North Korean reinforcements coming down in response to all that firing!

Thank God! It was a KMC company, patrolling a long way out from their lines. Always looking for a fight, they had come charging toward the sound of battle. A brief conversation. A comparison of maps and map positions in the failing light. A radio message back to battalion, this time with proper coordinates, and soon we were saying a hasty farewell to the KMC company, heading back towards the battalion lines. Colonel Martin had us covered by 81mm mortar fire all the way back in, dropping a few rounds north of us as encouragement as we closed on his position. Just at darkness we passed through the lines. That was my first meeting with the KMCs, and if they had not come along I still might be out there plowing around with that platoon.

I ran into that same KMC company commander several times after that. He told me that in World War II the Japanese had sent him to Japan to be trained in their army. He had been a machine gun platoon leader and had served in combat on Okinawa. I asked him how many Americans he had killed. He grinned, said nothing. I asked, *many, many?* He just grinned again. It really didn't matter. We had won that war. Now he fought beside *us*.

I could tell many more stories about the KMC, but I could not describe the attitudes of the ones I knew nearly as well as one of their own number put it to the American advisors of the Korean Marine Corps liaison group. 1st Lt. Kim Sik Tong's words say all that is necessary: "The Korean Marine Corps' ideal is to complete the mission, regardless of receiving strong enemy resistance—with endurance and strong united power—and always bearing in one's mind the distinction between honor and dishonor!"

The KMC Regiment made it back to line KANSAS just in time to be ordered to fall back again to start the longest leg of our rearward journey.

We moved both day and night, mostly on foot, and with such frequency that it was difficult to remain oriented for long. Four battalions of Marines took up blocking positions on the high ground west of the Mojin Bridge, holding until the remainder of the division crossed over the bridge. We ground on to the south and west, towards the supply-communications center at Chunchon. No hot showers, no change of clothing on this trip to Chunchon. At dusk we entered the city, were herded into assembly areas on its western fringes, knowing only that we were to hold the city until supplies could be loaded and moved south. As the hours passed and the darkness thickened, that order, too, was changed and again we were moving, this time in jeeps and trucks churning through Chunchon and out onto the narrow, curving, climbing road leading south.

Moving slowly up that long, steep grade to the pass, looking back at Chunchon, it seemed like a nightmare, not real. We were beaten down physically, bewildered mentally, heartsick. Back! Back! *Back!* Was there no other direction? The scene below took us even deeper into a numbing sense of disconsolate desperation. Parts of Chunchon were burning. The remaining supplies had been fired. The flames jumped eagerly into the adjacent buildings, devouring thatch, paper, and wood. A pall of smoke enveloped the city, the reflections of the flames dancing against it and through it, spreading the glow of destruction wider and wider as we climbed toward the pass, until it appeared that the whole of the Pukhan valley was ablaze. In the convoy, silence except for the moaning and groaning and grinding of gears, the roaring of the engines laboring under peak load as we neared the pass. We could not even begin to think of what lay ahead. We had not been told our destination. For all we knew, the road might never end until it met the sea.

RIPPER had commenced on 21 February. Two months later we had crossed the 38th Parallel and had gone into Indian country. In less than three days, by one means or another, we had been forced to cross the 38th again, this time going south. A very short stay.

We stopped far short of the sea. The ride over the pass and into Hongchon ended the retrograde. In darkness we turned west and south at Hongchon and kept moving. What was left of the night was spent in an assembly area eight miles southwest of the city. At dawn, back to the hills we went, into defensive positions facing north. That special staff section that had dreamed up all those code names and phase lines for General Ridgway must have been deactivated when the new commander, Eighth U.S. Army, Korea, took over, for this line had no name, was in fact called the NO NAME line! Names didn't matter too much right then. General Van Fleet had determined that we would move south no more. We would fight it out on this ground with the Chinese. On 30 April, the last, worn-out trooper had humped his packboard and weapon up onto NO NAME and we were anchored in, the KMC Regiment on our right, the 7th Infantry Division on our left. The following day the 1st Marine Division went back to the control of X Corps once again.

For two weeks we held that line and patrolled. Some of the longest, deepest, most potentially dangerous patrols of the Korean War were run off the NO NAME line.

The Eighth Army wanted company-size patrol bases established five miles or more forward of the main line of resistance and active patrolling north of the patrol-base line. Communications were tenuous, stretched to the limit of effectiveness, and control of the patrol bases complicated. In order to expedite reporting, a system of lettered and numbered checkpoints was substituted for six-digit coordinates, which of course required additional overlays for patrol leaders, higher echelon planners, and supporting arms personnel. Some patrol bases were pushed so far out that medium artillery could not reach them from the artillery battalion firing positions, necessitating the movement of sections of 105mm howitzers forward of the main battle position. This further complicated communications and security, subjecting the artillery to the same possibility as that of the infantry patrol units—being cut off and destroyed piecemeal.

I never knew a line unit, Army or Marine Corps, that did not despise the patrol base concept. It was strictly bad news. It asked far too much of the troops, the troop commanders at all levels, and the combat support elements. It was a hazardous, mean, nonsensical attempt to correct the Eighth Army's initial mistake of breaking contact with the Chinese too quickly, of losing contact completely for days at a time.

Fortunately for us, enemy contact within the battalion sector was light. We were concerned more with what *might* happen than what did.

Over to the east of us, the enemy was far more active. They probed and probed and finally located the right spot. On 16 May, 125,000 of them on a twenty-mile-wide front smashed a hole through the 5th and 7th ROK Divisions and drove thirty miles deep, threatening the right flank of the 2d Infantry Division, trying to come around its flank as they had tried to come around the 1st Marine Division at Hwachon. The 3d Infantry Division, one of the best in the Eighth Army, moved by motor march from Seoul that night, covering seventy miles in darkness to help stem the onrush of the Chinese.

Sitting over on the left of the division, we still were trying to figure out who was in front of us—North Koreans or Chinese. Two days later we were moved twenty miles to the east and now were on the right flank of the division, attempting to uncover one of the regiments of the 2d Infantry Division—the 38th Infantry. Over on the right flank we did not have to wonder about the foe. We were fighting the Chinese once again.

23

Martin's Way

The midafternoon sun beat down on the bend of the single-lane dirt road running north to Kwandae-ri. There was no breeze on the low ground. In May, Korea was starting to heat up.

The tanks of the regimental antitank company were deployed in platoon firing position, their 90mm guns cooling from the last fire mission. "F" Company of the battalion had just taken the last of our objectives for the day. The colonel, his radioman, Ramsdell, and I sat in the weeds beside the tank platoon—not talking, just sitting—staring at the smoke from the 90mm rounds still rising from the slopes of Hill 402.

It had been a lively one, that 24th of May, with every company committed to the attack and every company making contact slugging it out with the Chinese. Colonel Martin's ridge-running tactics had worked well, keeping our own casualties low, surprising the enemy, forcing him to fight on other than his chosen ground. Aggressive small-unit leadership coupled with this technique had seen every company successful. This day, too, had been a good test of all supporting arms, down to and including the bayonet, for a platoon of

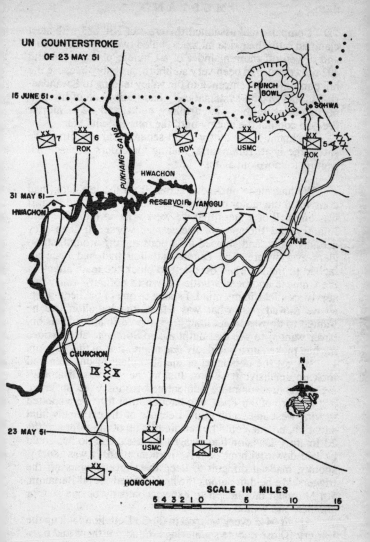

UN COUNTERSTROKE
OF 23 MAY 51

15 JUNE 51

PUNCH BOWL

SOHWA

XX 7   XX 6 ROK   XX 7 ROK   XX USMC   XX 5 ROK   XX 1

PUKHANG-GANG

HWACHON

31 MAY 51

HWACHON   RESERVOIR   YANGGU

INJE

CHUNCHON

IX XXX

23 MAY 51

XX 1 USMC   XX 187

XX 7   HONGCHON

N

SCALE IN MILES

5 4 3 2 1 0   5   10   15

"D" Company had assaulted the crest of Hill 883 with steel clamped onto their rifle muzzles, killed twelve of the enemy, and driven off the remainder of a Chinese platoon. On Hill 402 the enemy had been very stubborn, probably because the hill controlled the entrance to the valley leading to Kwandae-ri. Colonel Martin systematically had utilized all of his supporting arms options—air, artillery, tanks, and 4.2-in. mortar fire—to contain the enemy until the infantry could close.

Regiment knew that we had secured our objective. We sat in the heat, ruminating, waiting for orders to reach us, waiting to move out again.

We had made our move across from the left flank, had completed the motor march during the evening of the 19th. It was one hell of a mess that we were walking into. The 38th Infantry had thought themselves far worse off than they actually were, and showed it—troops milling around, stragglers everywhere. The Dutch Battalion that had been attached to the 38th had been left to block the main attack of the Chinese and been whittled down to nothing—thirty-two survivors sticks in my mind. I spoke to one of the lieutenants as we moved past what was left of the battalion. All he wanted to do was to get away from the 2d Infantry Division, never wanted to see that outfit again! Someone else besides me had picked up a decidedly *bad* impression of that lash-up.

We got the personnel of the 38th clear of our area and took up defensive positions. Just as the sun was disappearing, a hundred or more unidentified troops were observed just forward of our lines, and later another fifty were spotted moving west and south of us. Because of the extremely fluid situation, no one could be certain that all of the troops of the 2d Infantry Division had cleared the area, and no fire could be laid down without positive identification. It was touchy, spooky, made it difficult to keep the trigger fingers off the triggers. We held fire along the line, notified the 3d Battalion, 5th Marines, on our left to expect company of one sort or another, and waited.

About 0445 every weapon in the 3d Battalion took up the war cry. Those people sauntering around out there had been Chinese. They had stumbled into the wrong location at the wrong time. One hundred and fifty Chinese lay dead in front of the lines when morning came; twelve prisoners had been bagged. One can only assume that the Chinese believed themselves to be still opposed by the demoralized 38th. A bad assumption on their part!

We had taken some artillery and mortar rounds in the command post that night—noisy and smoky but no casualties except sleep. Early the next morning the colonel decided to try out another of his supporting weapons—sniper teams.

Back on the KANSAS line—the first time, that is—the colonel had gone over his special equipment and found that the M-1D sniper rifles were not in use, nor were the extra pairs of binoculars charged to the battalion for sniper operations. All that good stuff locked up and doing nothing. Why not use the equipment and weapons? Worth a try.

Gil Holmes, whom I had known in the 2d Marine Division as a platoon sergeant, now a lieutenant, had joined us just a few days before. Among his noteworthy qualifications was duty with the rifle and pistol team. He had a silver and a bronze medal to prove it. When Colonel Martin asked for a likely sniper section candidate, I recommended Holmes. The colonel interviewed him, evidently liked what he heard, and put him to work immediately.

Marines whose service record book indicated qualifications as expert riflemen were the only ones invited to participate. Colonel Martin had settled on six men per rifle company to be trained as three-man teams—two observers (target hunters) and a sniper, but all three trained to shoot or observe or both when more manpower was needed to lay the lead on with more volume.

Practice firing at straw dummies at a range of 200 yards had commenced that day. Before we moved off the KANSAS line the riflemen had been reaching out to 500 yards and getting head shots consistently. Holmes had jawboned enough M-2, boat-tailed ammunition to keep the section operational through three police actions. That had put the cherry on top of the whipped cream—more range and better accuracy from those cartridges, a definite advantage for us. The colonel had checked out the shooters personally before we shoved off for Hwachon, liked what he had seen, and filed the section away for future use.

This would be the first time the teams had been sent out for live game.

Two teams went out. The team operating in "D" Company's sector moved out over a distance of nearly 1,000 yards, closed to within 200 yards of a Chinese company busily bolting down breakfast rice, and killed eight of them. This seemed to infuriate the Chinese, who promptly ran the sniper team off their hill and back to ours. The other team, operating from our right flank, killed one Chinese and captured another. All things considered, we had not done badly from 19 to 24 May.

There had been persistent rumors within the previous seventy-two hours of a grand sweep to the sea, European war style. A tank-infantry end run from Kwandae-ri to Inje and then due east to Kansong on the coast, cutting off thousands of Chinese. Being the realists that we were and knowing how well the Chinese and the North Koreans kept the roads cut, we had not put much credence in those rumors, nor had we worked up much enthusiasm for them. Even then, as we sat quietly in the weeds alongside the tanks, we were to become caught up in the insanity of those rumors.

Overhead, the sound of a helicopter. Looking up we saw a Bell H-13 descending. The pilot, very adroit, brought his aircraft to the ground right in the center of the road, blowing sand and dust over us and the tank platoon. How refreshing! From the right side of the bubble, a tall, heavy-set figure jumped down and walked to the rear, straight into the path of the still-whirling tail rotor. A warning shout from the pilot moved the tall figure away from the rotor just seconds before decapitation would have occurred. As the man approached we could see three silver stars on his cap and jacket. As he closed on us we could read his name tag—ALMOND. The X Corps commander! What was his purpose in visiting our little group?

The general strode up to Colonel Martin, pointed at the tank platoon, and asked, "Whose tanks are those, Colonel?"

"Those are *my* tanks, General. 5th Marines Antitank Company. Been using them to clear that hill over there. General had better have that chopper moved. Still getting a few rounds of incoming now and then!"

"Have you seen any other tanks around—a battalion or more?"

"No, Sir, General. Been here since noon. Haven't seen *anything* come up this road!"

The 187th Airborne Regimental Combat Team had been on our right flank since our move to the east. Its commander, a brigadier, now came sliding up in his jeep in a cloud of dust, jumped out, and in plain sight of the Chinese rendered the hand salute and popped his heels. Military, man. *Military!*

All that pomp didn't make a nickel with the general. "Where in hell is that tank battalion? You were supposed to be mounted up on it an hour ago!"

That brigadier did not know. He was of no help. He knew that he had been ordered to meet the tanks and go charging off up the road with them. His people had been waiting for two hours. He shook his head in the negative. "Don't know, Sir! Haven't seen them, Sir!" All the while at rigid attention.

"God *damn!* You better get your ass into my helicopter—get on down that road and *find* those tanks! You don't come back until you do! You get that tank battalion up here or you will be a bird colonel tonight! I will be at your command post. Get cracking!" The general almost rammed the tail rotor again so great was his agitation, but ricocheted off—just barely!

The brigadier did not want to see crows on his collar at nightfall. He saluted, spun on his heels, dashed for the right side of the Bell, sprang in, buckled up, and the chopper went flashing down the road. The Corps commander nodded in our direction, climbed into the Combat Team commander's jeep, and roared off for the command post of the 187th.

I had heard a lot of chewing out in my time in the Corps, had been chewed out myself by experts, but I never had seen a one-star publicly humiliated. I doubt anyone else in our group had. It was not a nice thing to be a part of, even as a casual spectator. Evidently it was the general's way, and it got positive results.

In less than an hour the tank battalion hove into sight, chewing up the road, throwing sod and dust all over us as they rattled on past. Somewhere down the road they had picked up the troopers of the 187th, for just visible in the dust cloud was the commander's jeep, a solitary silver star still

glinting from the bumper plate. Right behind the 187th, came
a detachment of the 7th Marines. I couldn't see well enough
to identify anyone, my eyes were so full of minute pieces of
the road, but an old friend of mine from the 2d Marine
Division and from Junior School days—Jim Hoey, a captain
commanding "H" Company, 3d Battalion, 7th Marines—
recognized me, let out a whoop, and let me know that *he*
wasn't standing around watching, he was on his way to the
sea! I guess they all had been fed a good helping of that
propaganda, but just up the road another mile, the column
was hit good and hard, and Jim wasn't whooping any more.
He and his company were out of the vehicles and up into the
hills, trying to get the column cut loose and moving before
dark.

In spite of the crucifixion of the one-star, in spite of the
arrival of the tank battalion, General Almond did not achieve
his sweep to the sea or even to Inje. Early the next morning
when we pulled into the crossroads at Kwandae-ri, the tank
battalion and the 187th still were there, still trying to get up
the right fork of the road that led to Inje.

As we moved into our assigned assembly area, the whole
valley erupted with hostile fire, enemy incoming everywhere.
The Chinese, and the North Koreans who now were backing
them up, had it all figured out, just as we had suspected they
would. There was not a piece of high ground on either side of
the river—360 degrees around—that did not have at least a
small group of enemy entrenched upon it. They could see
everyone and everything that moved on the low ground. Fire
from their individual and crew-served weapons, including
57mm recoilless rifles, denied us mobility.

The tank battalion was in column, with the infantry of
the 187th mounted upon them, as the task force slowly crept
forward. On the right of the road the ground dropped sharply
off towards the river—a drop of twenty to sixty feet in places.
On the left the ground rose straight up to form ridge lines 700
meters in height. No security elements were placed on that
high ground or its approaches. The leading elements of the
column, pennants snapping in the morning breeze, clanked
noisily onward. Less than half a mile up the road the column
was taken under heavy fire from 57mm recoilless rifles, mortars, and automatic weapons. Enemy snipers located just

above the roadbed poured fire on the exposed troopers on the tanks and into the trucks that followed. For four hours the column was frozen in place, cut off and surrounded by enemy infantry units. Finally the dismounted troopers of the 187th cleared the high ground and drove off the enemy. With devout caution, not *sweeping* in any way, the column resumed its crawl towards Inje.

I had walked out of the assembly area and on up the Inje road that morning just after the ambush had been sprung. I never will forget the sight of a strapping young lieutenant of the 187th walking slowly down the road towards me, holding his right arm in place with his left hand, the right arm nearly severed at the shoulder by enemy automatic-weapons fire. It hurts me to see any warrior torn up, young or old, but it made me feel especially ill to see such a useless waste of talent. An Airborne Regimental Combat Team, trained for special operations, sacrificed in an operation that had held but doubtful guarantee of success from its inception, and in reality conducted only to try to satisfy an overweening ego.

Dark, heavy clouds skidded across the mountaintops, obscuring the setting sun, shrouding the peaks, the mist cold against the skin. There was rain in those clouds, rain that would beat against our ponchos before morning. Out there to the north, the Chinese would feel it, too, for just before the clouds closed in, we had counted hundreds of them moving along the high ground just to the west and north of us, the officers riding horseback. Artillery and air strikes had broken the enemy column for a brief period of time, but once the bombardment ceased they reappeared. They were beaten, bone-weary, willing to sky-line themselves for ease and speed of movement, wanting only to reach a safe haven, using the North Koreans, as they always did, to block for them, to stay and fight it out while they regrouped.

Our command group was pulled in tight in the center of a perimeter formed by the two assault companies. We were a long way out that night. Artillery from the 105mm howitzers could just cover us. The section of 81mm mortars that habitually moved with the command group—our immediate indirect fire support—already had registered its night protective fires. The battalion was the point of the regiment 2,000 meters ahead, with no friendly units on either flank, the Chinese and North Koreans to our front. We had fought like this—the spearhead of X Corps—since we had left Kwandae-ri the morning that the 187th had stepped so deeply into trouble.

Although we were far ahead of the other troop units of the regiment, we never were worried about being alone. Confidence in one's leader, in the company officers, in the men of the battalion, in the supporting arms people, had a lot to do with the feeling of security that prevailed. Colonel Martin had established a solid reputation among the troopers as a commander who did not throw people's lives away needlessly. They might not have fully understood the tactical aspects of ridge-running, but they thoroughly understood it as a device that kept them alive, in one piece, ready and able to fight again another day.

In addition to tactics, there were many other differences in Colonel Martin's battalion. There were differences in supply, administration, and basic organization for combat.

On the way up from Wonju I learned that the staff section jeeps and trailers did not exist. The colonel wanted each rifle company to have two jeeps and two trailers to expedite resupply. The Tables of Organization and Equipment allowed only one jeep and trailer per rifle company; therefore the extras would come from the staff sections. If I rode anywhere, which was seldom, I rode in the radio jeep with the colonel, roosting on the radio power generator that was positioned between the front seats. It was a hard ride, my rear end always warm, winter or summer.

Unless we were in reserve or patrolling for extended periods of time, we did not operate from tentage. The executive officer, the logistics officer, and the supply section operated in the rear, bringing up supplies and ammunition to the company supply dumps. They were met by company supply personnel and the gear was brought forward to the companies. The majority of the supplies were carried onto position by the strong backs and legs of the Korean Service Corps laborers, who made the final meters on foot, carrying wooden A-frame loads of water, rations, and ammunition through terrain that never had seen a road. Our wounded went out by helicopter, by litter, or by walking. Sometimes we were so deep in the hills that airdrop or helicopter delivery was our only source of ammunition supply. We might go without food for our bellies, but we *never* ran out of ammunition. Colonel Martin's priorities always were lined up properly.

During offensive operations we moved with the companies, in a loose organization tailored for combat and called the command group. It consisted of the colonel, his radioman, his driver-runner; the operations officer, section member, and radio operator; intelligence staff member and radioman; and representatives from the other staff sections. For supporting arms the tactical air control party; the artillery liaison team; liaison member and communications man from the 4.2-in. mortar platoon; and a section of 81mm mortars, with communications means. Very flexible. Members could be added or deleted, the organization structured to fit any given situation.

It was Spartan living on the high ground. Our needs—food, ammunition, water, sleeping gear—were carried on our backs on a packboard, the haversack of the Marine Corps pack strapped to the board to carry rations and toilet articles, the sleeping bag rolled into a poncho or shelter half and secured to the packboard by straps or pieces of communication wire. We slept on the ground, when there was a chance to sleep, with the headsets for the radio and telephone against each ear. When there was an order to be issued, the colonel would call the company commanders in and, under the cover of ponchos, using flashlights for illumination, the next day's operation would be laid out.

Up there on those rocky spines, with peaks rising more than 1,200 meters, it was another world. A gigantic spiderweb of hills and mountains crisscrossed the whole eastern portion of the Korean peninsula, the gorges between the mountains choked with undergrowth. In the mornings and evenings those gorges would be filled with fog and vapor wraiths—mysterious, chilling. On the slopes of the hillsides, coarse, high grass, browned by the sun, dried by lack of moisture. Pines and huge, wind-twisted deciduous trees stood like sentinels along the upward path, sometimes joining to form forests, sometimes quite alone. I loved it on the hills, fascinated by the endless marching of the ridge lines on and on into the beginning of Manchuria, joining other mountain ranges leading into Mongolia. That was the birthplace of the legendary scourge of the world, Genghis Khan, one of the greatest of all warriors. One's imagination soared on the ridge lines and mountaintops. I never liked to be on the low ground for long. Few in the battalion did, although their reasons might have been more prosaic than my own, and more practical. One was far more secure on the high ground.

Moving out of Kwandae-ri, the battalion was on the right flank of the regiment, the 187th on our right flank. A single-lane dirt track ran north in our zone of action for about 3,000 meters before turning sharply to the west. This track would begin as our right boundary and twist through the zone of action until it became our left boundary as the operation progressed. On the right of the dirt track the mountain ranges ran towards the north, with east-west connecting ridges. On the left of the track the mountains ran east to west, with connecting ridges south to north. A mixed-up, rugged, perplexing piece of terrain. A good test for Colonel Martin's ridge-running tactics.

The colonel sent "D" Company across the first high ground to the left of the track, "E" Company across the second. "F" Company moved up along the track, prepared to place a platoon on each of the south-to-north ridge lines that ran off the track after its turn to the west. Both "D" and "E," on the left, ran into enemy resistance—"D" against bunkers facing east, requiring mortar and artillery support in conjunction with an infantry assault to drive the North Koreans out. Yes, the *North Koreans* had slipped between us and the Chinese once again. Two prisoners taken at that time verified this fact and claimed that the high ground assigned to "F" Company was held by a battalion of North Koreans.

"E" Company encountered only riflemen on its ridge line and drove them off easily. The western approaches were secure.

The colonel and the command group moved up the track with "F" Company. Just before we turned to the west along the road, two enemy soldiers popped up out of holes just off the track, hands held high overhead, jabbering and smiling, smiling because in reality they were ROK soldiers captured by their brothers from the North and forced into carrying ammunition supplies. Their information again indicated that there was indeed a strong enemy force just ahead—North Koreans in log bunkers and weapons pits. This would be no picnic.

The North Koreans must have been very confident or very deaf. Both "D" and "E" Companies had fired up a storm with their individual weapons, and a heavy concentration of supporting fires had been called in. Yet as we made the turn to the west, clearly revealed between the two ridge lines forming "F" Company's axis of advance was a squad of enemy soldiers hunkered down around cook fires, apparently unaware that there was a battle in progress. The leading platoon of "F" Company quickly set up a light machine gun and took the enemy squad under fire, killing three and badly wounding two others.

While this lesson in surprise was being taught, the platoon designated to secure the first "F" Company ridge line had reached the high ground. A further advance of 200 meters along the ridge line, then—just as the prisoners had stated—enemy in prepared positions. Fire from the enemy bunkers and weapons pits swept across the ridge. Twelve Marines went down, including the platoon leader, seriously wounded. In spite of these losses, with the help of outstanding artillery support, brought in *very* close by the forward observer, the remainder of the platoon rammed through the enemy defenses and by nightfall had cleared another 600 meters of ridge line.

Meanwhile, the "F" Company platoon that had spoiled the North Koreans' afternoon meal had moved up the nose of the western ridge line. Moving quietly in the twilight, through heavy forest growth, the platoon leader discovered enemy troops digging in and cutting logs for bunkers. He recommended an attack at first light rather than a doubtful wrestling match with darkness rapidly approaching. The colonel agreed. Both platoons of "F" Company held their ground within sight and earshot of the enemy troops, but remained undetected as the North Koreans continued to build emplacements throughout the rest of the night.

The battle plan for the following day was simple. We were eyeball to eyeball with the North Koreans. "E" Company would move north on the right flank, turn west, come up on the junction of the two ridge lines being worked by "F" Company, establish blocking positions, and wait for "F" Company to drive the enemy into them. "D" Company would move north also, but block to the east to secure the battalion right flank.

"F" Company jumped off in the predawn haze. The right platoon found no enemy initially and moved on towards the junction of the ridge lines. With the left platoon, it was a different matter. The North Korean diggers had taken position within the completed bunkers and emplacements, but still were not aware of the Marine platoon within grenade range of them. The "F" Company platoon leader ordered his troops to fix bayonets and move with utmost stealth to the edge of the tree line. Following a sharp, accurate mortar barrage, the platoon charged forward into the enemy strong point. Surprise was complete. The enemy broke and fell back along the ridge line.

At this point the "F" Company platoon on the right was ordered into action, its mission to pass through the left platoon when it reached the ridge junction and to pursue the enemy troops. The North Koreans were not the only ones to be surprised that morning, for at the eastern edge of the junction there were still enemy soldiers firmly emplaced— enemy strong enough in firepower and determination to halt the Marine attack. Supporting fires finally made the enemy position untenable, the enemy pulling back to join their comrades. With both of the "F" Company platoons bringing pressure to bear, some 300 North Korean soldiers streamed from the forest-covered ridge lines—not to the east and into the killing zone of "E" Company, but to the west and into the zone of the 1st Battalion, whose troops would not come abreast of us for another twenty-four hours. The best laid plans, and all that good poetical stuff! Unfortunately, sometimes too true!

Three days later, "E" Company, following the northern extension of the same ridge line, ran into a similar situation. Pressing hard against an enemy strong point for more than two hours, the company assault platoons reached the knob of a hill called 902. As the platoons made the final approach, the enemy broke and raced down the reverse slope at top speed—a North Korean company in full flight. A perfect artillery target. But with the lack of luck that we had been saddled with for the past few days, we lost another chance to destroy massed troops, this time due to radio failure between the forward observer and the firing battery. The enemy loped safely down the hill, crossed over the Yanggu-Inje road, which ran from west to east across our front, and scaled the high ground just north of the road. A steep, narrow spur rising from the roadbed, covered with a crust of flinty rock and partially hidden by sere, high grass, seemed innocuous. Future events would prove it to be otherwise. The map listed it as Hill 800.2.

The next day, we too crossed that road and took Hill 800.2 and the higher elevations north of it, but we paid for it all with more dead and wounded in a single company action than we ever had sacrificed before. It tore the colonel up— *badly!*

A combination of bitchy terrain and execrable leadership caused those casualties. There wasn't anything one could do about the terrain—a thin, knife-edge ridge line zeroed-in on by the North Koreans with automatic weapons and small-arms fire. In terms of numbers there were few enemy left on the hill—grenadiers and riflemen, here and there a Dektyrov light machine gun team to build up a volume of fire. If the "E" Company platoon leader had not frozen on the ridge line, face pushed into mother earth, making violent love with her, his unit could have—*would* have, I am convinced—taken the position quickly and with few casualties. But he chose not to move—a choice echoed by the members of his platoon.

An air strike was requested. Three Navy jets answered the call. The North Koreans stood up in their foxholes and fired burp guns at them, and—can you believe it?—actually put one of the jets out of action with a well-placed burst directly into the air intake of the portside engine. Artillery and mortar fire followed the air strikes. The lieutenant on the ridge line did not budge. Neither did the North Koreans. The remainder of "E" Company attempted desultory charges up the east slope of Hill 800.2. The enemy grenadiers blew them back down again. Finally, as so often happens in battle, sheer guts got the job done.

Gil Holmes, the sniper section leader, was a lot more

than a fine rifle and pistol shot. During the early days of World War II, he had made a name for himself by always being in the point of any attack made by his company, preferring, if possible, to be the point man of the point—the lad all the way out front. In those days he carried a 1928 Model Thompson submachine gun with a fifty-round drum. His company commander told me that when that Thompson started talking, you had better get some people forward in a hurry, for Holmes always let himself get well inside of a group of Japanese before he commenced emptying the first drumload of .45 caliber ammunition into them. He had brought the old Thompson out to Korea with him, forced by the times to use thirty-round flat magazines in lieu of the drums.

On that sorry afternoon at Hill 800.2, the colonel was with "E" Company, as was Holmes. Holmes watched the fiasco, saw all that he wanted to, and walked over to the colonel, paid his respects, and requested permission to try to get things moving. The colonel gave his permission; about that time he would have tried *anything!* Holmes slung the Thompson over his left shoulder in the assault fire position and walked alone up the east slope of Hill 800.2, ignoring the shower of black-smoke-belching, Chinese potato-masher grenades that came down the hill towards him and the small-arms fire directed his way in heavy volume. Reaching the military crest of the hill he let the Thompson have its way and blasted the emplaced North Koreans far out into the land of their ancestors. During the climb he was hit in the arms and legs by grenade fragments. At the crest of the hill he was hit at the front scalp line by a rifle round triggered by the reflex action of a North Korean soldier as he died digesting a full magazine of .45 caliber ammunition from the Thompson.

Holmes himself had broken the stalemate, had opened the way. The ridge line lieutenant and his platoon began to move up when the Thompson stopped firing.

Some of the less dedicated young officers thought Holmes too intense, too gung ho, too single minded in his approach to combat. In their vicious, empty small talk, they put him down as being just on the edge of psycho. Where had *they* been when it was time to stand up and be counted? One of his foremost detractors was the lieutenant on the ridge line of Hill 800.2—the gutless, motionless one. Psycho? I would have liked to have had a Gil Holmes for every company in the battalion!

After it was all over, the ridge line to the north secured, while the heroes gathered together to commiserate, Holmes, covered with blood and bandages, picked up his gear, slung his weapons—the Thompson and the M1-D, and trudged off south of the road to begin the long journey over the hills to the aid station, some 2,000 meters to the rear. We would not see him, or the Thompson, again until late summer.

Anticipating rain, we had rigged our ponchos on branches driven into the ground, providing a lean-to shelter that would shed some of the moisture. I had the EE-8 phone and the radio in my shelter, about five feet away from the colonel. As night settled in on us, my imagination, always fertile, still could picture that long column of enemy troops moving across our front at sundown, still could see that horse and rider sail through the air when the 105mm howitzer shells exploded beneath beast and man. It was not a comforting thought to realize that those same people well might have rested, reorganized, and at this moment might be moving on our positions.

There was no sound except for the wind, the rustle of leaves, the rubbing of tree branches one against the other, the rippling flutter and sharp crack of ponchos as the wind swept up under them, the rattle of the rain on the treated fabric. Although physically exhausted, there was no sleep in us.

"S-ss-ss-t! Sisss-st! Did you hear *that*, Ave?" came from the colonel's hooch.

I listened, throat gone dry, not breathing, eyes and ears straining. Somewhere off to the west, down off the high ground, faintly heard—voices, muted, unintelligible. "Yeah, I hear!"

Just to the west of our perimeter, a deep, steep draw ran up from the valley floor and into our bivouac. It was from this draw that the sounds had emanated. Those bastards had left a detachment on the low ground and now they were slipping in on us! I heard the bolt of the colonel's carbine slide back, pick up a round, slide forward, and chamber it. What a racket it made! I must be quieter with mine, for the voices were growing louder now, the guttural tones informing us that we had North Koreans and not Chinese coming in.

"Better get the company commanders on the phone. One hundred percent along the line! These people are getting too damned close!" This, in a loud whisper from the colonel.

I cranked the handle of the EE-8, cranked and cranked again, hoping to get them all on the line at the same time, hoping, too, that the whirring of the activator would not be heard by our visitors. Then Sam Smith, skipper of "D" Company checked in, quickly followed by the others. I whispered what little I knew into the mouthpiece, told them that the colonel wanted 100 percent alert along the line.

Whoever was coming up that draw was almost upon us. My heart was banging away so hard and loudly that it almost deafened me. I caught movement in the darkness to my right. The colonel was out from under his shelter, carbine raised, ready to let fly once the intruders appeared at the crest. I slipped the telephone handset back into the phone case, swung my carbine in the direction of the voices, and assumed the sitting position. With a little luck we could blow away a few of them before they discovered our location. On they came, thrashing through the high grass, voices in a conversational tone, no attempt being made to cover the sound of movement. What was wrong with that outfit? Not like any North Koreans I ever had come up against before!

Someone slithered into position between the colonel and me, carbine muzzle pointed towards the draw. Captain Kim, our South Korean police advisor/interpreter, had joined us, the smell of garlic a positive identifier.

Over the lip of the ridge line they came, their shapes faintly outlined in the fog and rain. Five clearly seen now. How many more were coming up behind them? My finger tightened on the trigger, eyes straining for a clean target. On they moved, still jabbering, and then Kim was grasping my arm and the colonel's. "No-No! No-shoot!" Shaking our arms, signalling for us not to fire, he pounced forward, swinging his carbine by the barrel, cursing in South Korean, slamming the stock of his carbine across the oncoming faces, kicking low, into the groin, felling them, kicking them again on the ground as they fell. Guttural growls and moans, here and there the embarrassed giggle of the Oriental losing face. Kim stood over them, cursing now in English, no doubt for our benefit, "Goddam fool! Goddam fool! Goddam fool!" Then in staccato Korean he gave them orders. The five stood quickly, bowed in our direction, and scampered off.

"Ahhh-h! Very sorry, Colonel! These people Korean police who join with us at Kwandae-ri. Can speak Chinese. Can interrogate very well, but are very stupid—not like soldier or Marine. Tonight before dark they go into valley for food and drink. Come back now. Very sorry, Colonel. Nevah happen again!" Kim was embarrassed for his people, for himself—knew the trouble that had been caused, the anxiety that had been built up in the last quarter of an hour.

I heard another Goddam! this time from the colonel. I didn't know whether to be angry or just to enjoy the sense of relief that was flooding over me. I decided the best thing to do was to pass that sense of relief along to the company commanders, and got them back on the EE-8. I told them to go back on 50 percent alert for the rest of the night, that it all was a false alarm. There was a long silence along the line. Finally Sam Smith, usually unshakeable—steady as the proverbial rock, an Iwo veteran and winner of the Navy Cross in Korea—spoke up. "OK. OK. But Ave—don't you ever *whisper* at me on the field phone again at night! I was shook when you called. I am *still* shook! That damned whispering has got to go!"

I should not have worried about the Chinese regrouping and counterattacking that night. They were whipped to their knees, no longer an efficient fighting force. They continued to move all night, slept in concealed positions during the day, and moved again the following night. May and June had used up the last bag of rice, the last round of ammunition. May and June had used up their manpower, too, our artillery and air working them over at every opportunity. Time now to let the North Koreans take up the slack; time now for the Chinese to keep moving north, to find a place to reinforce, to refurbish, to relax. From early June the Chinese were out of the fight in our zone of action. For the remainder of my time in Korea, the battalion never again would be opposed by Chinese troops.

*   *   *

June was a hard month for the 1st Marine Division.
Elements of the division were committed to the attack from
Yanggu on the west to the rim of the Punchbowl on the east.
Every regiment, including the KMC Regiment, found itself
going up against a tough, stubborn, well-equipped, well-posi-
tioned force of North Koreans, who repeatedly refused to be
dislodged from the hills and crags to which they clung. The
division lost a lot of men over on the Yanggu side before the
1st Marines and the 7th Marines finally drove the North
Koreans from the high ground forming the southwest rim of
the Punchbowl, and around the hill mass south of the
Punchbowl which dominated the southern approaches. Here
the KMC Regiment fought for nearly a week (after relieving
the 5th Marines, who moved to secure the right flank of the
division) attempting to seize the key terrain feature, called
Taeam-San by the Koreans, Hill 1316 by the Americans. A
night attack on 10 June finally broke the back of the North
Korean defenders, opening the way to the south rim of the
Punchbowl. Bloody, brutal, dangerous operations. Taeam-
San cost the KMC Regiment 500 casualties.

The division lost men, too, to such mundane things as a
lack of replacement footgear. Moving day after day along that
rocky terrain wore out shoes rapidly, pulling heels off, wearing the soles as thin as paper. A man cannot carry his
weapon, a unit of fire, two full canteens, and a packboard
with forty or more pounds strapped to it if he is barefoot.
Some of our people almost reached that state. Casualties
from worn-out footgear were just as detrimental to the combat efficiency of the battalion as bona fide battle casualties.

June took Colonel Martin from us—not as a battle casualty, just a paper one. He long ago had gone past the *qualifying* time of the Regulars in battalion command, but the paper
shufflers had not wanted to pull him out while the going was
so rough. Shortly after we had taken up positions on the east
rim of the Punchbowl, he was gone—first to regiment to be
operations officer and then to division as an assistant in the
operations section. We hated to see him go, but were glad
that we had been blessed with him at just the proper time.
Those months between February and late June were when he
was needed most.

Ironsides took command of the battalion. That had been planned months ago in Washington, just as his assignment as executive officer had been. As a general officer's son it was imperative that he command during combat operations, get *qualified* properly. Since the battalion was now in defensive positions, with a strong likelihood of remaining in them for some time, there couldn't be a better time to break him in. His tour would be brief, marked by neither success nor failure, and then he, too, would move to regiment and division—get his ticket punched all the way.

About the time that Colonel Martin left the battalion, the lining of my lower belly, on the right side, broke loose and a piece of gut started to push through. Too many hills, for too many months, carrying too much pack weight had disclosed a basic weakness in construction. One evening in July, during a visit with Colonel Martin at regimental headquarters, we bathed in the Soyang and I exhibited my breakthrough. Right then he told me not to be foolish—to get down to the hospital ship and get it taken care of. Colonel Hayward, the regimental commander, told me later that night that with the Kaesong peace talks floundering along, the regiment might be in reserve for months. Do as Colonel Martin had suggested—get on down south, get repaired, get ready for the next fight to come along.

I couldn't leave for a little while, for Ironsides' relief—a new lieutenant colonel fresh in from the States—just had taken over the battalion. As soon as he was properly oriented and settled in, I took off for Pusan via medical transportation. I allowed myself three weeks to be cut, sewn, and rehabilitated. With the help of a fine Navy surgeon on the hospital ship, I made it back exactly on schedule.

One other thing. During this same time frame, I turned in my brains and made major. The promotion orders were dated in June, my date of rank retroactive to 1 January. I signed the acceptance papers without any feeling of guilt. I had been performing a major's duties since mid-February. From now on I would be drawing major's pay.

On the way back to the battalion, I stopped off at the headquarters of the 1st Marine Division for a brief visit. A lot of old friends were there, among them Col. Victor H. Krulak—now chief of staff—who offered me a job in the operations section. Looking back, that duty probably would have enhanced my career in the Corps, but at that time I could not become enthusiastic about it. I had started my tour with the 2d Battalion, 5th Marines. If at all possible I wanted to finish it there. Colonel Krulak understood and sent me on my way with his good wishes.

The same day I continued on to Inje, where the 5th Marines now was located. It was to be my day for refusals. The new battalion commander had his mind made up that I was to be his executive officer—his second in command. Another hassle, another go-around. I sure as hell had no intention of staying with the command post, in charge of bullets and beans during operations, which is what I would be doing as executive officer. Running the ridges with Colonel Martin had spoiled me rotten. It was now the *only* thing that I *wanted* to do. Executive officer would have been a step up in the hierarchy, would have put me into position to command should the colonel become a casualty. In the late summer of 1951 such imponderables held little appeal for me, were no bait at all. We rattled our jaws late into the night, with me almost ready to pick up the phone and see if Colonel Krulak still would take me for operations. I finally conceded to do both jobs—executive officer and operations officer—provided the colonel would get a major, senior to me, as executive officer at his first opportunity.

The next few days I just looked around, trying to absorb the changes that had taken place in the regimental units. Most of the company-grade officers had been rotated to battalion staff sections, some back to regiment and division. Colonel Weede, former G-3 at division, had replaced Colonel Hayward as commanding officer, 5th Marines. Colonel Hayward had gone to division. A whole new team was forming up in the 1st Marine Division. The Kaesong peace talks had triggered an exodus of the Regular establishment from the States. With a hint of peace in the air, it was time to pull the nails out of the stateside planks, to come out and play soldier while things wound down, to qualify for the Korean Service Medal and the one for the United Nations. No sense in having empty spaces above the left pocket of the service blouse when there were two free medals to be collected just by making the trip.

A month later the medal hunters would not be so gleeful. The war was not to end in 1951. Peace did not arrive. In their eagerness to get in on the kill, they had trapped themselves into a full tour. Those foot-draggers deserved that—and more!

Those days at Inje, during the final days of summer, were special ones, like none we ever had seen before in Korea. Easy days, gentle days, close to the river. A chance to bathe daily, to shoot the rapids on air mattresses, a time to coast, to reflect on battles over, of people come and gone. A time of strange things, such as the discovery of a Johnson semi-automatic rifle taken from an enemy soldier during a patrol action. It was missing magazine pins—the magazine held in place by filed-down nails—but still functioning. I sent the serial number to the inventor of the Johnson weapons, Capt. Melvin M. Johnson, for a trace. That weapon had its own odyssey. Purchased by the government of the Netherlands East Indies, it had been captured by the Japanese and taken to mainland China. There, at a later date, the Chinese Communists had scoffed it up and put it to use and, for reasons known only to them, had brought it into Korea.

Sometimes, late in the afternoon, the air controller and I would go to the dirt airstrip; hoist ourselves into the confines of canvas, steel tubing, and Plexiglas that made up the fuselage configuration of an OY aircraft; take off; and climb into the coolness of the sky. At 6,000 feet, engine just turning over, we would drift over the Punchbowl, its bottom already dark, the sunlight reflecting from the tops of the ridge lines that formed the bowl, the mists of evening seeping into every hollow, every depression. On the hills north of the Punchbowl the cook fires of the North Koreans would show as tiny flickers of scarlet against the sable hills. Here and there, with no apparent pattern, bursting suddenly, the harassing and interdictory fires of the UN artillery would wink and flash along the roadbeds and the river valleys leading into and through enemy territory. We would hang there in the evening air, enthralled, suspended on that slowly revolving propellor, watching night crawl up and over the mountains until we, too, nearly were overtaken by it. Then, on wings almost as silent

as a bird, we would drop swiftly towards the now faintly
visible airstrip alongside the river, using the engine only for
the final approach and landing.

On 22 August, the Communist delegates to Kaesong
received the information they had been waiting for since mid-
June. Their forces had been reinforced and resupplied suffi-
ciently to continue battle, had established a series of strong
defensive positions in depth all across the peninsula. Secure
in their knowledge of this, the Communist delegates turned
their backs on the UN and walked away from the peace table.

Four days later we received a warning order to be prepared to go back on the offense. Those lazy, hazy days of
summer—as the song says—definitely were over. It was time
to go to war again.

24

That Savage September

The Communists indeed had been busy all across Korea during the two months of UN-granted respite. They had developed a network of defensive installations never before encountered in the war. Fire-communication trenches stretched for miles. Concealed weapons pits, log and earth bunkers blocked every conceivable avenue of approach, with weapons sited along the long axis of the ridge lines, supported by others crossfiring from the "T" or connecting ridges. Every strong point had been plotted and covered by defensive fires of artillery, mortars, and mountain guns, so that once the defenders were forced out of position, the attackers immediately would come under the fire from these weapons. The positions went deep, manned by North Koreans determined to hold at all cost, by volume of fire or by counterattack when necessary. In the combat to come, everyone in the infantry regiments would get a taste of what the battles in the Pacific had been like. Savage. As savage as anything that had taken place on those islands.

The mean aspects of the campaign became evident before we ever reached the attack position.

We moved up in a column of files onto the spur of a steep
ridge line that would take us into the zone of action of the 3d
Battalion, 1st Marines, the unit that we were to relieve. We
squatted down and waited. It was early in the morning, just
after 0600. Autumn was heralded by a chill in the September
air. We shivered and shook waiting there, numb, half-asleep.
Across the valley floor, about twenty feet from me, was a
small ammunition and ration dump belonging to the 1st Marines. A three-man detail guarded it and dispensed supplies
from it. They had been in that dump, on that ground for three
days. As our column inched forward, they drank their coffee
and shot the breeze with us. They were happy. As soon as we
moved through, they would be moving back.

As each man in our column stopped, shifted his gear,
reslung his weapon, and prepared to clutch at the branches of
trees and shrubs to aid in the ascent of the near-vertical spur,
one of the chaplains attached to the battalion approached
them to determine their faith and offer prayer and absolution.
It got me *hot!* To think of him planting the seed of doubt in
their minds, to suggest that they might die angered me beyond reason. It is tough enough to keep the troops fired up
emotionally, to keep them filled with belief in their own
invincibility without having all that effort destroyed by one of
your own sky pilots. I was just about ready to walk over to
that chaplain and give him a confession of my own! Before I
could, the valley exploded.

For more than seventy-two hours those lads in the supply dump had walked back and forth across earth that held a
couple of pressure-activated antipersonnel mines, had un-
knowingly played a game of Russian roulette on a grand
scale. On this particular morning the cylinder had spun, a live
round had chambered. One Marine lay in the center of the
dump, his left foot gone, his right leg shredded. The other two
had been hit by shrapnel, but could navigate.

Those mines, the casualties caused by them, the activities of the chaplain, combined to lay a heavy burden on
the minds of the men of our battalion, moving up into what
was to become one of the bloodiest fights to be fought on a
hill complex that already had torn up most of the infantry
battalions of the 1st Marine Division. As I watched the badly
wounded Marine being placed on a litter, watched his friends

kneel by his side to express sympathy and encouragement, the chaplain scurried toward the small group, determined to pave the way to Heaven. Right then I didn't know which I hated the most—the murmuring of the chaplain or those mutilating mines. As I saddled up to go forward, reason returned. It had to be the mines.

The relief was accomplished prior to noon. "D" Company, now operating without the sure hand of Sam Smith, had taken positions held by "H" Company of the 1st Marines—a ridge line directly across from our battalion objective, Hill 812, separated from it by about 1,200 meters, with a deep, forested valley between. A dangerous position, overlooked to the west by Hills 980 and 1052, from which enemy fire constantly was received. "D" Company tied in with "H" Company, 3d Battalion, 5th Marines, who held an even more exposed piece of ground to the west. Our command group, a section of 75mm recoilless rifles, and the heavy, water-cooled Browning machine guns of Weapons Company were all on the "D" Company ridge line.

Commencing with the mine explosions at the bottom of the hill, the day turned more sour as the hours clicked by. "F" Company, with the mission of making the main effort against Hill 812, had been expected to move out as soon as "D" Company was in position. Instead, it was nearly an hour late in leaving the assembly area, and another hour before the assault platoons started up the winding trail into the valley between "D" Company and Hill 812. All this backing and filling, all this aimless milling around had been duly noted by the North Korean outposts, who quickly passed the information back to the units on the enemy main battle position. The little brown men of the North Korean People's Army took up the slack, waiting—waiting for the lead elements of "F" Company to appear in their fire lanes.

At 1700, "F" Company stepped into it right up to the neck. Two platoon leaders were hit, and the toll of dead and wounded mounted as daylight dwindled. Two hours later one platoon had forced its way forward and upward until it had gained the high ground 400 meters south and east of the enemy strong point on Hill 812. There was no reason to turn back. It was better to stay put, even though it was out of physical contact with the parent unit.

As it had been on countless other nights of combat, the terrain was bathed by the incandescence of a full moon, the hills and ridge lines so well illuminated that every movement could be detected. Before nightfall Ramsdell and I had dug a chevron-type foxhole across the spine of the ridge. In it were the field phone and the radio. The colonel's hole had been dug nearby. We sat by the foxhole, talking in low tones about that *bad* 16th of September, trying to figure it all out. Maybe it was because of so many changes in command. A new battalion commander; new Weapons Company commander; two rifle company commanders with no experience, one with minimal. Maybe it was because "F" Company had held to the low ground, had tried to make it up the draw—operations on a valley floor were always hell—and maybe it was just plain bad luck. A lot of the old crew had joined us just prior to the attack—people who had walked those long miles from east of Chunchon to the Punchbowl, people who had been wounded or become ill along the way and been evacuated. The way things were shaping up, they might well be going south on a litter again. There were just too many intangibles, too many doubts. Not a good feeling to have on the eve of battle.

About 0200, the field phone rattled in its case. It was Colonel Weede with the operations order for the day. I pulled a poncho over my head, flipped on the flashlight, and started copying. Division and X Corps were on the colonel's tail. We *had* to have Hill 812 by nightfall. The time of attack was given as 0400. Thinking back on the snaillike progress of "F" Company the previous day, I almost laughed in the colonel's face. After 0200 now. Get up and *charge* by 0400, all of it to be accomplished in the dark! I thought better of the laughter and quelled it in my throat. The colonel knew full well the impossibility of it all. He just was passing along the orders he had received, and we were to do the best we could to execute them. I said goodnight to Colonel Weede, yawned, put away the phone, and crawled over to the battalion commander's hole to give him the glad tidings. Then I called "F" and "E" Companies and cut the company commanders in on the scoop.

As anticipated, the attack did not materialize at 0400. When dawn broke over Hill 812, there were no Marines moving toward it in assault. Indirectly it turned out favorably, for as first light outlined Hills 1052 and 980—the light fully in the eyes of the defenders—the troops on Hill 812 came out to enjoy the warmth of the sun, to wash their faces, brush their teeth, and cook rice. We watched them through binoculars from the "D" Company ridge, and as soon as everyone on Hill 812 was settling in for a pleasant breakfast we blew them away with a nicely delivered artillery concentration. It started the day off right, but from that moment on, things got rough.

That successful artillery shoot set the mood on our ridge line. Everyone wanted to get into the game. The six Browning heavy machine guns were set up in battery instead of by section. Slightly down from the machine guns was a section of 75mm recoilless rifles from the regimental antitank company, attached to the battalion for operations. Hill 812 was within range of both the machine guns and the recoilless rifles.

Just a short time after the last round of the artillery concentration had been expended, the North Koreans could be seen swarming around the hilltop in great numbers. I guess the colonel must have been reading Rommel's *Infantry Attacks* prior to coming out to Korea. In any event, he favored supporting the attack on Hill 812 with long-range machine gun fire. Rommel had made himself famous by such utilization of machine guns in the Great War. Why not give it a try? What to do? My advice was offered and rejected. The guns went into action. Across the valley the .30 caliber slugs flew, hundreds of them striking the hard ground, kicking up little puffs of dust and dirt around the bunkers. And then the roar of the recoilless rifles, the backflash vivid against the green foliage, high explosive rounds reaching out to tear at the tough skin of Hill 812.

Up on Hills 980 and 1052, the North Korean forward observers were watching. They turned to their communications, gave fire commands, and turned back to watch the machine guns once more. The 120mm tubes were laid, the bubbles levelled, the rounds dropped in. One over, one short. The ridge line that we were on had been shot-in by these same gunners weeks ago. The initial rounds were just a little insurance. No sense in wasting ammunition. *Fire for effect!*

Six of our Brownings neutralized, water jackets pierced. Four of the gun crews wounded. The recoilless rifles forced out of position. That sudden. That smooth. Korea was not Austria or even Italy. Korea was Korea. Eventually that fact would sink in.

Well hidden in the undergrowth on the southeast flank of Hill 812, the 2d Platoon of "F" Company, still operating independently, was watching also. When "F" Company commenced its attack, three hours behind schedule, the platoon established radio contact with the company and began making its own approach towards the enemy bunker complex, halting when the platoon was but 100 meters from the enemy.

Caught in a crossfire as it moved forward, "F" Company stalled. From positions in the rear, "E" Company executed a passage of lines and immediately was subjected to the same withering fire. An air strike was called. No aircraft appeared. After two hours of waiting for the arrival of air, the colonel ordered up artillery—4.2-in. mortar and 81mm mortar support—and told the "E" Company commander to make a move. Word of this action was passed to the platoon leader of 2d Platoon, "F" Company, now under operational control of "E" Company.

With the lifting of supporting fires, the 2d Platoon, "F" Company charged into the North Korean strong point. Thirty-five minutes later, after hand-to-hand combat and grenade duels, the southern portion of Hill 812 was secure, allowing the 1st Platoon of "E" Company to clear the northern tip, to pass through the "F" Company platoon and attack toward the base of Hill 980. By midafternoon, "E" Company was climbing toward the crest of that hill. At that time, permission from higher headquarters was requested to attack and seize this vital terrain feature. For reasons never divulged, the request was refused and "E" Company was ordered back onto Hill 812. It was one of the many serious errors in judgement made by people far to the rear, people tracing front-line positions on acetate overlays with grease pencils, and apparently with no ability to read a map, with no idea what closing contour lines meant on a map. Ignorance of the most shameful kind.

We had taken the objective for Colonel Weede well in advance of the time limit imposed upon him. A Marine rifle platoon had given him his prize after supporting weapons had failed.

Colonel Weede had produced. *He* looked good. The regiment looked good. Division looked good to X Corps, and X Corps looked good to Eighth Army. *Outstanding!* But what did the lads up on the hill *really* have?

In a short period of two weeks, the hill complex of which Hill 812 was a part had ground up the 1st Marines and the 7th Marines on the eastern slopes and now was whittling away on the 5th Marines to the west. Hills 673 and 749, connected by a ridge line running south to north, had decimated the other two regiments. Hill 812, which was in essence a western extension of the north-south ridge line upon which Hills 673 and 749 were located, had cost our battalion dearly. With Hill 812 secured, we still would suffer heavy casualties, for we had no *safe* ground from which to operate. We could defend the north-south ridge line of 812 from the east just as the North Koreans had from the west, but here the similarity ended. To the west, leading from Hill 812, lay those two dominating peaks, 980 and 1052, from which the North Koreans could observe our every movement on the south side of the east-west ridge line *and* the western slopes of the north-south ridge line. Movement in daylight was extremely dangerous anywhere within the position that we held.

Out along the east-west ridge line, at a distance of about 200 meters, lay a gigantic rock formation rising into the air a dozen feet, blocking the ridge line. We called it what it was— The Rock. We outposted the eastern side, the North Koreans the western. Just east of The Rock were useable North Korean positions, including a bunker. A platoon from "E" Company outposted the ridge from these positions and furnished a fire team for The Rock. The remainder of "E" Company existed during daylight hours on the east slope of the north-south ridge line. At night they moved into fighting holes on the western slope. "F" Company linked up with "E" Company at the northern tip of the 812 complex and defended to the north along the ridge line running east toward Hills 673 and 749. Two rifle companies, watched relentlessly by the enemy, not able to move in daylight, hanging on by their fingernails and not much else.

I often have thought of how satisfying it would have been

to have exposed the planners at division, X Corps, and Eighth Army to a couple of days on Hill 812. I have an idea that considerably more attention would have been paid to Hills 980 and 1052 had those gentlemen spent even one *hour* on those ridge lines in daytime.

There was another small item to make things even more enjoyable. The 3d Battalion, 5th Marines had made no progress at all along its ridge line, remained essentially in the same positions that had been held since 16 September. This left us with our left flank dangling just down off the southern slope of Hill 812, with the valley wide open to the North Koreans should they decide to use it for an end run during darkness.

This was what the troopers had to contend with on Hill 812 when 19 September dawned.

On the morning of the 19th, the colonel decided to leave the "D" Company area, go up to Hill 812 for a look-see, and establish a command post closer to the lines. Going up that valley trail was a hard thing for me. Blood from the "F" Company dead and wounded was everywhere. Too much of it, too many people gone south again, too many off on the journey from which there is no return. I had been correct in my premonition, but took no pride in the fact. A lot of the old crew had caught it—among them Gil Holmes, just back from the hospital after recovering from the wounds suffered going up Hill 800.2, back just in time to be assigned a platoon in "F" Company and head out for Hill 812. Holmes collected Purple Hearts the way some kids collect baseball cards, and he would live through this wound to collect another.

The main ridge line was a dreary sight. Colors of dark brown and gray, the foliage down off the crest frayed and torn, the main battle position pulverized, a heavy mist or a light rain covering the entire hilltop. The North Korean snipers opened up on us at once. Might as well get in a little practice, firing at this group of idiots who had not yet learned to stay on the east slope and off the skyline. Just to let us know that they had better things than rifles in their arms inventory, the gunners of the 76mm mountain guns gave us a demonstration. Believe me, until you have heard one of their projectiles sing, you don't fully appreciate music. Extremely high velocity, splitting the air with a wicked snap, as accurate as rifle fire and packing a hell of a lot more wallop. Those gunners could have picked us off, one by one, if they so had desired.

While the colonel was talking with the company commanders, Ramsdell and I were moving along the line talking with the troops. It came through in a rather hesitant manner, but it all came down to one thing—the troopers were having the same feelings of insecurity and doubt that had hounded Ramsdell and me the first night of the operation. By the time the colonel was ready to go back down the hill, I had made up my mind. Unless there was a good reason not to, I was staying. Things didn't look right, didn't feel right. I had been with the battalion longer than any other officer at this point in time. I had humped the hills longer, been shot at more consistently, had shared the long days and the longer nights with these people. This had been their hardest fight. It was my job to stay, to look after them the best way I could. Ramsdell, an old Raider from World War II, was for it— charged up and ready. My radioman wanted to stay. When I spoke to the colonel about it, he gave me no contest. He understood the responsibility that I felt. He gave me a wry smile, a thumbs-up, and headed down to his new command post.

That afternoon we cut trees, revetted, roofed, and sand-bagged a bunker just down from the intersection of the north-south, east-west ridge lines, just a few steps from the ridge line leading to The Rock, and a few more to the junction of the "E" and "F" Companies' lines. It seemed the logical place to be. Patrols from both companies had gone north into the Soyang valley without contact. If trouble came, it would come from the high ground to the west. By nightfall we had a land line back to battalion and the radio was properly netted. We were ready for the North Koreans to make their move.

About 0200 the next morning the sky fell in. Like a cloudburst, 120mm mortar shells came down around us, saturating the whole defensive complex. The hills trembled, shuddered, the roar of the explosions unbroken, deafening, the deadly whir-rr-rrr of the cast iron shell fragments like the whine of giant bees. Loose sandbags fell from the sides and overhead of the bunker, attesting to our less-than-perfect engineering techniques. The land line was hit. We sent a message by radio to inform the battalion of our situation, although there should have been little doubt in their minds.

We suffered through thirty minutes of shelling before the North Korean gunners shut it off and the enemy infantry made its play around the north side of The Rock. An attack in company strength—the main body moving against the "E" Company platoon on the east-west ridge line leading into Hill 812, a separate force advancing its members cautiously, one by one, slipping far below the Marine fighting holes, silently stealing their way into position to attack the northern tip of Hill 812 at the junction of the two rifle companies.

Out around The Rock, the Marines and the North Koreans were in a real cat fight, tearing each other to pieces. The Marines were holding, counterattacking in the darkness, trying to eject the enemy. In the close combat the platoon leader was badly wounded. Attempts to evacuate him destroyed the cohesion of the defense. False priorities. They got him out, but lost the position. The North Koreans quickly manned their old strong points and started raking the north-south ridge line with automatic-weapons fire, pinning the Marines low in their fighting holes.

Throughout all this action the company commanders and platoon leaders within the main battle position had been conspicuous by their absence along the line. Here and there troopers were slipping out of the forward positions, ducking back behind the hill. Ramsdell and I turned three of them back with a bayonet and a .45. Something positive had to happen or the North Koreans just might knock us off that hard-won hill. I got the colonel on the radio and asked for operational command of the two companies, received an affirmative, and asked him to relay his decision to the two company commanders. I didn't want any contest from anyone once the dice were thrown. At the same time I gave him my fire-support requirements—no real sweat, for the whole hill mass and the connecting ridges had been shot-in during the initial attack. It just would amount to calling for previously coded concentrations when the time came, but with precise timing.

The troopers were getting spooky. They had reason to

be. It was a sticky, uncoordinated, confused situation. A couple of A-4 light machine guns started to rattle with no targets in sight—a sure sign of increasing nervousness. Just tickle that trigger to bolster your confidence. I had to give one of the gunners a smart rap on the helmet with my .45 to get him to knock off firing. He looked up and back over his shoulder, saw who it was, and gave me a grin of embarrassment. His gun stopped firing immediately.

The average trooper, enlisted or commissioned, wants to see rank roaming around when things turn hot. *That* is what rank gets paid for—at least that always has been my contention. It is a lot like a hard-fought football or basketball game. Someone has to be there to talk it up, to do the coaching, to be responsible for the team. If you stand with the troopers in a firefight, they will put on one hell of a show. If you crawl into your foxhole and pull it in on top of you, why shouldn't they do the same? There was far too much rank in the foxholes that night. That is the reason I had asked to command. There really was nothing to it. I had Ramsdell to do my running for me, to back me up with his M-1 and bayonet. I had a cool radio operator who knew my communications requirements almost before I voiced them, and who kept my contact with battalion intact. The Marine Corps had sent me to school, had taught me what to do. I just had to be smart enough to remember all those things!

Ramsdell came back from the junction of the east-west ridge line and Hill 812. "Easy platoon is all back in, Skipper. Gooks are about 100 meters out from us!"

It was time. Time to rock The Rock and everything around it. A few words on the radio to let the colonel and the artillery people at battalion know what we wanted, that we wanted it right *now!*

Rapid booms in the distance, the swish and swoosh of incoming 105mm howitzer shells, the sound of the 4.2-in. mortars firing at regiment, the steady thumping of the 81mms kicking out of the tubes in the valley behind us. The east-west ridge line blossomed into a solid sheet of red, crimson, orange, yellow, and blinding white. In the light of the detonations, enemy soldiers could be seen darting to the rear, sprinting forward, leaping from the ridge line. That fire was *close*—the kind you read about in the manuals but seldom see, the kind you dream about when you are about to play out your last card. Other concentrations came down on Hills 980 and 1052, a thousand meters of pulsating flame reaching from Hill 812 to the peak of 1052. Now the eight-inch guns added their power, splitting rocks, tearing out chunks of earth, disintegrating trees, throwing bits of enemy soldiers into the air. The barrage moved west, and then east again—searching, searching.

Ramsdell, standing close beside me in the center of the line, nudged me and pointed toward the north. "Incoming mortars, Skipper—on the right flank!"

Dawn was crawling up the eastern slopes. In the half-light, puffs of black smoke appeared at the junction of the company lines. Something clicked in the back of my mind. Once before those puffs of black smoke had been identified as mortars and had not been. That same black smoke had covered the hillside the day Gil Holmes had gone up against the grenadiers.

"Mortars, my *ass!* Those are grenades! Pass the word along the line!"

The North Korean grenadiers had slipped across from The Rock and now were just below our forward-slope fighting positions. Courageous, tenacious, tough as the rocks they had crawled over, they came up the steep slope, whipping grenades up at the Marines as they moved, trying to break through on that right flank while the main effort was attempting to break through on our left. Marines started pulling pins, letting the spoons fly off, holding the grenades to shorten fuse time, and then rolling them downward toward the North Koreans. Marine small-arms fire joined in the sound of battle. The enemy was at the crest, died bravely just short of the line, in some places just over. Not one broke through alive. That right flank had been a very close thing.

When the firefight had started out at The Rock, I had asked for a standby platoon to back up the left flank and to counterattack when the time was right. The 2d Platoon of "F" Company—the same lads who had taken the south portion of Hill 812 during the initial attack—were to make up this force. They stood at the rear of the main bunker in a line of skirmishers—bayonets fixed, weapons and grenades ready—just down from the bunker, out of sight. It was like watching a World War I movie, the Kaiser's men charging into friendly lines, the Marines ready to go over the top and stop them. Psyched-up, confidence bolstered by the fact that the Marines had given ground, the enemy swooped over the bunkers, to be met at point-blank range by a fusillade of grenades, small arms, and automatic-weapons fire—fire so heavy that it stopped the North Koreans, turned them, and sent them flying back along the ridge line and into the western bunkers.

The sky grew brighter. Visibility increased. Now it was time for all those anxious light machine gun gunners to run a few belts on through, to keep a stream of fire moving into the embrasures of the bunkers. Easing out onto the ridge line, 3.5-in.-rocket launcher teams moved up close under covering fire and blasted the enemy out of the bunkers, driving him beyond The Rock and up the slopes of Hill 980 towards safety. Time now for the counterattack force to move—the point—a squad in column, racing along the top of the ridge line, bayonets prodding bodies of fallen enemy, riflemen stopping, taking up the offhand position, firing with deadly accuracy into the backs of the fleeing North Koreans, and, typical of that platoon, one Marine sauntering along the way, Brownie camera in hand, photographing the carnage around him for posterity. By full light the enemy was nowhere to be seen, driven back into his lair on the high ground. The "F" Company platoon reorganized, pulled back to the bunkers, and outposted the top and the north side of The Rock.

The sun was greeted by us that morning in much the same manner that it must have been by the ancient Incas—with gratitude and great affection. It had been a grueling night, things happening in that shadowy interlude best left in the shadows. The weak are always there, in small numbers but ever present, and others must carry their loads. The strong had survived that night, had stood fast, had changed the enemy assault from almost certain victory into a rout. The lessons learned so well in other battles, in other places, were borne out once again. Look after your men, and they will look after you.

* * *

The battalion was ordered down from the hill that morning. Ramsdell and I just had finished shaving, were wiping away bits of lather when the relief battalion—3d Battalion, 5th Marines—with "D" Company of our battalion attached, staggered in. Dirty, sweating, five days of accumulated beard showing, a Hollywood depiction of combat Marines if I ever saw one, although they had done little more than lean forward in their foxholes while the fight for 812 was going on. Some of them stood around the bunker not believing what they saw. They couldn't get it through their heads that people could, or would, clean up in combat, especially after the rather tight little night session that we just had put in. Being clean, shaving, trying to keep a little polish on my footgear had become routine with me over the years, routine with the officers and NCOs in the units I had commanded. No big thing, and surely not done with any knowing sense of bravado.

Twenty-eight years later, a retired Marine master sergeant, Hubert Ivie, who had been Gil Holmes' runner on the way up to Hill 812, wrote to tell me that as an eighteen-year-old Pfc, he had thought that standing on that bunker, shaving, after that hot little fight *was* sheer bravado, that it had perked him up like a fresh cup of strong coffee. I can take no credit for that. That credit must go to Col. Victor H. Krulak's order for the Choiseul operation. He had set me straight, got me started out right, made it a habit with me. If, on Hill 812, it came off as bravado, I am sure that Colonel Krulak would not dispute the fact that a little showmanship does not hurt from time to time.

None of us knew it as we came down off the hill on the morning of 20 September 1951—there was no way we could have known it—but there never would be another battalion-size attack in Korea, the regiments never again would rise up to storm the heights. The Marines' war—the war of movement—had ended. The war of position had begun.

For me, the war ended on that day. I remained with the battalion for another twenty days and then was transferred to regiment to be operations officer. I had seen three battalion commanders come and go and was about to leave a fourth. There were still some old-timers among the enlisted men, and it hurt me to leave them before my tour was over. We had shared so much together, had learned so much together, had known so many things—happiness and sorrow, victory and defeat, the bitter cold of winter and the staggering heat of summer—the long walk finally completed after all those months of surging back and forth across the 38th Parallel.

Part Six

THE SECOND DECADE

25

The Second Time Around

Headquarters cut me loose from the 5th Marines and the Land of the Morning Calm in mid-December 1951. I arrived in San Francisco by air on the evening of the 20th, the city shining, shimmering in anticipation of the holiday season. My contingent was met at the airport by representatives of the Department of the Pacific and driven to 100 Harrison Street for processing. Everyone in the contingent had orders but me. After a night spent in San Francisco, on the off-chance that orders would arrive the next day, I was sent on leave to Encinitas to spend the Christmas holidays with my family. I was told that when my orders reached San Francisco, they would be mailed to me.

Orders came down sending me to Headquarters Marine Corps in Washington. Then a few days later came a modification sending me to Quantico. Couldn't get shed of that place, had been assigned there four times for a variety of reasons during my first ten years of service, and in the years to come would serve there again. What I had hoped for in Korea—immediate assignment to a Fleet Marine Force unit—was not to be.

The time spent at the Marine Corps Schools, while not my choice of duty, was not without tangible rewards. My assignment was as an instructor at the Amphibious Warfare School, Junior Course, where I taught offensive and defensive tactics at battalion level and patrolling, raids, and special operations at company and battalion level. During the summer months when no instruction was given at the Junior School, I was given additional duties as senior instructor, Air Observation School. At that school there were hours of flying time—both day and night, fresh air and sunshine—and, to make things even more palatable, flight pay for four months out of the year.

Living, too, was on the plus side. We were assigned government quarters on post in an area that had been known by generations of Marines as Whiskey Gulch. On the high ground behind the quarters lay the officers' swimming pool and the golf club annex. All of the basic ingredients for the good life, none of them to be wasted by me or mine while at Quantico.

Old friends—Red Harper, Red Morton, Glen Martin— made the tour more bearable. It was a godsend to have them close at hand in a political arena like Quantico, where it behooved one to check constantly one's flanks and rear.

The Marine Corps Schools in the early spring of 1952 had become the crossroads of the Corps, the personnel there teaching, learning, innovating, trying to keep the pipeline to the 1st Marine Division filled with qualified leaders. Since the late summer of 1950, a steady stream of Korean combat veterans had been picked up in the muster rolls of the schools to serve as instructors. On board when I arrived were returnees from the 1st Provisional Marine Brigade—the people who had held fast and defeated the North Koreans in the Pusan perimeter and then gone on to make the landing at Inchon as part of the newly arrived 1st Marine Division; people from the Inchon-Seoul operations; those from the Chosin Reservoir; and my compatriots from the East-Central Front. Before the year had passed, another group, those from the static defense, the trench warfare of the Western Front, had entered the lists of Korean conflict representatives. It was about as complete a mix as could be imagined—each group intensely parochial in the most parochial military organization in the world, each group quite convinced that it was its operations, its arrival in Korea, that had made the most important contribution to the combat effort on the peninsula.

It was an amazing thing that we could deliver our separate assessments to the student body—made up of representatives from every combat grouping—without becoming involved in petty differences of opinion from the platform, but it happened. Different thoughts, different personalities, different tactical beliefs were sublimated for the good of the common cause. It is called closing ranks. Marines always have performed this evolution well. Normally it is done to protect the Corps from outsiders, both civilian and military. Sometimes we do it to protect us from ourselves.

On 10 June 1954 orders were delivered to me, detaching me from the Junior Course and directing me to report for duty to the commanding general, 2d Marine Division. So once again we packed up and left Quantico. We had not lost anything there, had in many ways made positive gains. On the family side, Quantico definitely had given us something that would endure. After nearly six years of girlish slimness, Helen was pregnant once more.

The personnel commitments of the 2d Marine Division had changed little since I had left it four years earlier. Every officer reporting in was up for grabs. I was assigned to the 6th Marines as assistant operations officer. Ten days later I was placed on temporary duty with the 1st Battalion, 8th Marines, to serve as an umpire during Atlantic Fleet Training Exercise 1–55 to be conducted on Vieques Island. On 3 August I moved to Vieques and on 22 August rejoined the 6th Marines at Camp Lejeune.

In spite of the temporary hassle, the heat, the sweat and dirt of Vieques, and the separation from my family, I felt good, alive once more, back with the troops after the deceptive placidity, the politics, and infighting that characterize a place like Quantico. It was a duty station far too close to Headquarters, where, in my opinion, it was not what you knew but whom you knew that made a perceptible difference

in how Marine Corps business was conducted. There were
just too many contingencies to cover, too much training to be
accomplished to allow *that* attitude much leeway in the Fleet
Marine Force, especially in the 2d Marine Division.

The division, in 1954, was blessed with a heavy sprinkling of some very colorful and talented individuals, people
with much combat to their credit. The ranks were filled out
with veterans of Korea, veterans of the Big War, and in some
cases people who had been through both conflicts. Unhappily there was a dearth of such experience at the command
levels of the regiments and battalions, the proponents of the
qualification system still firmly entrenched at Headquarters,
Marine Corps, still adamantly refusing to concede that the
combat elements of the Corps should at all times be provided
with the ultimate in combat leadership. In peacetime it was
easier to live with such faulty reasoning. In peacetime no one
was getting *killed* in the qualifying process as they had been
in Korea.

The commanding general was Maj. Gen. Lewis B.
"Chesty" Puller, a living legend in the Corps, the only Marine ever to be awarded five Navy Crosses. During Korea,
"Chesty" had commanded the 1st Marines at Inchon-Seoul
and the Chosin Reservoir, been promoted to brigadier general in January 1951, served as assistant division commander,
and, very briefly, during February and March, commanded
the 1st Marine Division. Except for that period, I never had
served with General Puller. Before my tour in the division
was over, he would be gone from the Corps, retired medically
over repeated protests from the general, gone from the sight
and imaginations of thousands of Marines, including myself,
who, moved by his flamboyant abrasiveness, his obvious,
open love of the Corps, his admiration for physical courage—courage displayed by him so many times, in so many
places—had sought to emulate him, people who could feel
the stirring of a fierce pride welling within them should one of
Puller's old NCOs say "Skipper, you remind me of 'Chesty.'
That is just the way that he would have done it!" I never
personally had known General Puller, but I had known of and
cherished his style from the moment I entered the Corps.

General Puller's "welcome aboard" ceremonies were

well worth attending, to hear what the general had to say and observe its effect upon newly arrived personnel. From the moment he entered the room, one could feel challenge in the air, the general's sharp eyes darting up, down, and across until he had established eye contact with every person in the audience, a ghost of a crooked smile hovering over his lips. The left breast of his uniform was a splash of color, personal decorations and campaign ribbons reaching from the upper seam of the left breast pocket to the left shoulder strap.

And when the words came they were not idle, empty chatter. Rather, a statement of purpose, of creed, of faith and belief, of a way of life.

"Welcome aboard. I have been a Marine, boy and man, for nearly forty years. The Marine Corps is my life, my reason for being. I love it above all else—more than country, more than family. There is nothing as fine on the face of the earth as a *good* Marine—nothing more sorry than a bad one. If, as I do, you feel that the Marine Corps must, and does, come first in your life, I will be glad to have you with me in this division. If you do *not* feel that the Corps will always come first in your life, *I* don't need you, the *division* doesn't need you, the *Corps* does not need you! If you have any doubts, report to the adjutant for reassignment outside the division—and don't drag your feet!"

There were many at those gatherings who did not feel as General Puller did about the Marine Corps, many who blanched at the thought of such single-minded dedication, whose breathing pattern changed from slow and steady to fast and ragged as the general's words registered, who wished to be anywhere but the 2d Marine Division if General Puller's rules must be followed. You may be sure, though, that in spite of the trepidation felt by them, the passageway to the adjutant's office never was clogged by Marines attempting to escape duty in the division.

The battalions and regiments contained people, both enlisted and commissioned, who believed as General Puller did and had shown it in both World War II and Korea. Two whom I knew well come immediately to mind. Bill Barber, operations officer of the 2d Battalion, 2d Marines, and Carl Sitter, executive officer, 2d Battalion, 6th Marines. Both were mustangs, commissioned early in World War II. Both had been wounded in action. Both had won the Silver Star—Carl's won at Guam, Bill's at Iwo.

During the breakout from the Chosin Reservoir in Korea, along the lonely, frozen, wind- and fire-swept road from Yudam-ni to Koto-ri, in two different types of action, both men had won the Medal of Honor.

Bill, as commanding officer, "F" Company, 7th Marines, had held, for five days and six nights, Toktong Pass, a tactical area vital to the security of the road, against an estimated Chinese regiment. Painfully wounded during the fighting of the second night, he had refused evacuation and maintained personal control of his company throughout the battle. His tenacity, personal courage, and tactical skill were instrumental in the destruction of 1,000 enemy troops and the neutralization of the enemy regiment as a viable fighting force.

Carl, commanding "G" Company, 1st Marines, was ordered to break through an enemy-infested area between Koto-ri and Hagaru-ri, to reinforce his parent battalion, guarding the division command post at Hagaru-ri. Carl had led his company forward in the face of intense enemy fire and, despite taking 25 percent casualties, had driven through to his objective. The following morning he had assumed responsibility for attempting to seize and occupy critical high ground overlooking Hagaru-ri and the division command post, upon which was entrenched a Chinese regiment. After a daylong fight, the enemy, under cover of darkness, counterattacked. Wounded in the face, chest, and arms, Carl refused to leave his company and continued to fight on until the high ground was secured by "G" Company and reinforcing units. At the close of the action, Carl and his troops had been involved in bitter combat for more than thirty-six hours. His leadership, personal valor, and superb tactics had made the difference.

Serving with Carl in the 6th Marines was Bob Barrow, who, as commanding officer of "A" Company, 1st Marines, in Korea, had won the Navy Cross. Barrow, a cool, unhurried, astute troop leader, would become the 27th commandant of the Marine Corps.

Outstanding people. Spread thin to be sure, but there for all to see, to furnish inspiration, to be emulated by their contemporaries and juniors in the 2d Marine Division, others like them to be found in the units of the combat and supporting arms. The division had much to be thankful for in 1954.

Upon my return from Vieques, I was assigned to 3d Battalion, 6th Marines, for duty as operations officer. The commanding officer was Lt. Col. Richard J. Morrisey. Had I been able to make a choice of commanding officer from all of the 0301 lieutenant colonels who had been assigned battalions to qualify as infantry officers, I could not have picked a better one to work with than Colonel Morrisey. He was a man who knew how to use his staff effectively, one who knew how to extract maximum performance from them. He gave me a free hand, took my recommendations, considered them, and made his own decisions, just like the book says to do.

One of my first recommendations to Colonel Morrisey was to conduct physical drill at battalion level. I submitted it in writing and immediately followed through with strong talk—volunteering to supervise the program, if approved. With unbelievable ease the program was sold, permission was granted, and the proper training directives were issued to battalion units.

Immediately, certain of the company commanders contested the concept, went directly to the colonel to voice their displeasure. Commander-to-commander talks were held. A lot of tight jaws, a lot of high- and low-toned muttering, but with the first formation they were all present.

At 0645 every morning, Monday through Friday, the battalion formed a hollow square outside battalion headquarters. The three rifle companies formed three sides of the square; Weapons Company and Headquarters Company formed the fourth. Company officers formed the first rank, facing inboard; the companies in three ranks, extended for physical drill, provided the mass of the square. My position was the center of the square, from which I performed the exercises and simultaneously counted cadence for the battalion—a technique learned from Gunner Blasingame at Lakehurst. Following calisthenics, which consisted of body bends, pushups, four-count sit-ups, squat thrusts, deep-knee bends, and the one-footed hop, we were off for a run, which began at a distance of one-half mile and graduated to a full five miles.

A full-strength rifle company of about two hundred men, in utility uniforms, running at lockstep, calling cadence or delayed cadence or just slamming the soles of their combat boots down on the pavement in silent cadence, is an imposing sight. To run a company properly demands tight control. To run five elements of company size in formation, the control required seems almost unattainable. Yet if one is determined, it can be done, and with excellent results. In the 3d Battalion, 6th Marines, it was attained by me running from the center of the column to the front, letting the troops come up on me, and dropping back to check the rear. Of course this caused me to run twice as far as the others, over the same distance, but it was well worth the effort. To aid me in control, the companies would call cadence in sequence—front to rear, rear to front, and in between run at silent cadence.

From the fall of 1954 until the summer of 1956, for as long as I was assigned to the battalion, it was seen and heard throughout the division area as its members, in perfect cadence, ran through the other regimental areas and past the front of the division headquarters building. There was no one in the division who did not know of the battalion, for they saw us and heard us every working day. As before, a fantastic esprit de corps developed. This time not in a two-hundred-man unit, this time in one that ran close to a thousand Marines, and all of the program accomplished before the first event of the formal training schedule, all of it done before 0800.

Why the preoccupation with physical drill and running? The stock question thrown at me over the years by my contemporaries and seniors is still being echoed—"*What* are you trying to *prove?*" I wasn't trying to prove anything, just trying to be sure that my units could move from point A to point B in good order, at good speed, and arrive in condition—physically and mentally—to enter combat, to fight, and to win. And there was an additional bonus to be gained by all the humping and sweating—a bonus quite important to me if not to others. It has been proven beyond a reasonable doubt that one's powers of recovery from serious injuries relate directly to one's physical condition, survivability itself linked to it. Would any good commander deny that additional insurance to his troops? I think not.

When you come down hard on the troops during their training, as I then was doing, you can expect to become cognizant of disagreement, irritation, bitching, and the airing of colorful epithets. A few months later, in Barcelona, following an afternoon of bullfighting, I was made aware of one of the terms of endearment bestowed upon me by some members of the battalion. During a discussion of the *corrida* with one of the ship's officers, he chuckled and asked me if I knew what the troops called me. "Negative—tell me." He chuckled again and said, "Iron Balls—Old Iron Balls!" I had been called worse. At least they thought *that* part of me was pretty solid!

At autumn's end the battalion went aboard ship for a division landing exercise off the Onslow, North Carolina, beaches. Then the Christmas holidays were upon us, days and nights made more precious, more poignant by the knowledge that in another month the battalion was to mount out once again—this time for an extended overseas tour. Helen, the children with us, and the life growing inside her created for me a Christmas season of unusual warmth and satisfaction.

My second Mediterranean cruise. Many differences in shipping, in command relationships. The Mediterranean was still "our sea," but with the Soviets making their move to change the status quo. Our basic mission remained the same—sell the American presence, continue to show the flag.

In lieu of ships of the line—warships—the battalion was carried in troop transports and a landing ship. As in 1948, we would prowl the length and breadth of the Mediterranean, would pull liberty in Genoa, Naples, La Spezia in Italy; Marseilles in France; Izmir in Turkey; Salonika in Greece; Barcelona in Spain; and Oran in Algeria. We would practice the amphibious trade, would make two turn-away landings and five across the beach, to include a NATO exercise with the 4th Turkish Division at Saros Gulf and a landing against the students of the Greek Military Academy on the island of Crete.

Porto Scudo, at the southwestern tip of Sardinia, was our

Mediterranean home away from home. We conducted three landings there—each one more valuable than the last—the ashore training adding immeasurably to the combat efficiency of the battalion and its supporting elements.

February 10, the initial landing. The first time since the troops had left Morehead City that the entire battalion was in bivouac together. Three days out of the ship's holds. Three days of physical conditioning, crosscountry marches, and the live-firing of weapons. Being on solid ground, actively employed in the practice of their trade, did wonders for troop morale.

The second visit proved to be the high point of the exercise—the landing of a rifle company from the high-speed transport *Carpellotti*, APD-136, several miles northwest of our regular landing beach, and the subsequent attacks of that landing force against the battalion, in total darkness. Infinitely less exciting, but of great value to the unit, was the night withdrawal of the battalion to the beach and its subsequent night reembarkation of troops and equipment—a technique that until that night had not been mastered by the battalion. The landing force was shaping up in a variety of ways.

The third landing put us on the beach for five days—time for training of all kinds, highlighted by rubber-boat training, the throwing of live grenades, and a demonstration of the defense of a forward slope by an infantry company—to include the digging in of individual positions and weapons pits, the camouflage of them, and the live-firing of a final protective line.

What of port calls on this second cruise? For me they were of little consequence—too much work to do. Following every port call a landing exercise was scheduled, with all of the paperwork that goes with it. To complete plans, to coordinate with the naval units involved, to get the necessary signatures, to publish the appropriate plans/orders in time for execution took more hours than were available during a normal working day, so there was little free time to go ashore.

The battalion returned to Morehead City, N.C., on 25 May. Many things had changed since we left; many more changes were coming up.

Helen had accepted government quarters on St. Mary's Drive and had accomplished the move from Jacksonville with the three children. A fine set of quarters, one I thoroughly would enjoy. Helen was larger than I ever had seen her during a pregnancy, and with good reason. A little less than a month following my return, she presented me with a set of twin boys. Change number one.

Within weeks of our arrival back at Camp Lejeune, I moved up to become executive officer and, concurrently, operations officer. Change number two.

On 25 August, Colonel Morrisey was detached for duty with G-4 section, Headquarters, 2d Marine Division. I moved up again, to become commanding officer and, concurrently, executive officer. Change number three.

About the time I became commanding officer, 3d Battalion, 6th Marines, my friend Carl Sitter became commanding officer, 2d Battalion, 6th Marines. The regiment was in for trouble—two mustang majors in the command slots. We had some times, Carl and I, times to look back on and relish.

Majors do not command battalions for long in peacetime. I knew this, so made no plans for changing the Corps. I was, though, determined to give it a hard go in whatever time frame belonged to me. No great innovations. Things needed to be tightened up and they were, a few heads rolling in the process. The battalion fell back easily into the morning physical drill and the runs with no strain after the long months at sea. Once again the division troops saw and heard us on the move.

Going to and from training areas, we refused motor transport and speed-marched. On field problems we operated on reduced rations, ate only what the individual could carry in his initial load, no resupply for the duration. Aggressors were furnished by the reconnaissance battalion; also operating against us routinely was a tank platoon. It was dirty, tough, miserable training, sleep an unknown commodity. It made the lads confident in themselves, ready to roll, proud of the battalion, proud enough to fight for its reputation, which periodically they did, and always won.

Sure enough, my tour was short. It lasted a month to the day and then a lieutenant colonel, already selected for colonel, was brought in to be "qualified." It had been great to have the wheel for thirty days, maddening to have to turn it over. I returned to my billet as executive officer. Prudently I had not moved into the commanding officer's office, so it was an easy transition.

The fall and winter flew by. Life was good on St. Mary's Drive and in the battalion. In the early spring we mounted out for Vieques again. I had commenced my second tour of duty with the 2d Division at Vieques. It seemed only fitting that I should close it out there.

26

Sister Service

Headquarters, 1st Force Reconnaissance Company, Camp Pendleton, California, 19 January 1958. I had flown there from Fort Benning, Georgia, my duty station, to participate in an evaluation of a sleeve-deployed, blank-gore, steerable parachute and to determine the feasibility of incorporating basic skydiving techniques, mainly the stable-body position, during the parachute insertion of Force Reconnaissance teams. Use of the parachutes and the skydiving procedures had been proposed to the commandant of the Marine Corps by Capt. Jacques Andre Istel, U.S. Marine Corps Reserve, an expert in international parachute competition but with little experience in jumping from military aircraft and little knowledge of the equipment requirements of military parachutists.

It was an unforgettable experience. A total of thirty-nine jumps were made, twenty-five of them with Istel's blank-gore parachute using both the twenty-eight-foot and the thirty-two-foot versions. R4D, TF-1, and F3D aircraft were utilized for the jumping, with exit speeds from 80 to 150 knots. Delayed openings varied from ten seconds to sixty, from altitudes up to 12,500 feet.

The team concluded, as a result of the tests, that the Istel parachute was far superior to the modified T-10. Among its advantages were sleeve deployment of the lines and canopy, providing a slower, easier opening of the parachute with far less opening shock; the dual-purpose pack, which permitted static-line or free-fall usage with only minor adjustments; faster packing time than the T-10; excellent steerability provided by the blank gore and the steering lines; ease of student instruction in the use of the parachute; and the provision of Capewell canopy releases for greater safety in high-wind landings. In two separate recommendations to the commandant of the Marine Corps, from 1st Force Reconnaissance Company and from me, it was recommended that six Istel parachutes be purchased by the Marine Corps for further testing and that the technique of body stabilization be taught to all Marine parachutists as part of routine free-fall training.

As I headed back to Fort Benning by air, my mind was filled with a variety of thoughts. During one ten-day period I had made my first free-fall, closely followed by seven others; had jumped two aircraft strange to me—the TF-1, a high-wing, carrier-capable, liaison aircraft, and the F3D, a two-place, side-by-side jet night fighter with the exit made from its escape hatch; had gone through delayed openings of up to sixty seconds in duration; and, in spite of the scoldings received from Istel concerning my terrible body positions while falling, thoroughly had enjoyed each of those challenges. I felt a sense of satisfaction in those accomplishments, but felt even better to have shared those experiences with the best of the new breed of Marines—members of the 1st Force Reconnaissance Company—and to have been accepted by them as a teammate, with mutual respect and admiration openly displayed. A good feeling to have for a thirty-nine-year-old lieutenant colonel with two wars behind him, good to know that at least in the business of deep reconnaissance the Corps was in good hands.

Fort Benning, Georgia. I went there with mixed emotions, but it was either "sister service" with the Army or back to sea on the staff of an amphibious transport squadron. Not much of a choice. As much as I disliked the thought of duty with the Army—after bad scenes with some of their units in World War II and Korea—the thought of two more years on a rust bucket away from my family was just too much.

The people at Benning could not have treated us more nicely. After a short stay at the Main Officers' Club, we moved into government quarters on post, not far from Continental Army Command, Board #3—my place of duty—and near the chapel, commissary, and post exchange. There were good schools on post, and the best youth program I ever have seen on any post in the military service.

Duty at Continental Army Command, Board #3 (the Infantry Board) was interesting and worthwhile. At this time, new weapons, equipment, and uniforms were under study to support new tactics and techniques being developed at the Infantry School.

A short distance from Fort Benning, at Fort Rucker, the Army was experimenting with armed helicopters in a unit called Sky-Cav—Sky Cavalry. I was introduced to its commanding officer, a full colonel, and was invited to fly with him during a demonstration of his unit's capabilities for members of Congress. Whipping through the tops of the Georgia pine forests, rotor blades just above the trees, both doors of the Bell H-13s removed, branches slapping one half-insensible as the plastic canopy passed through the pine tops induced a certain sense of hazard, but the surprise achieved by this type of covered approach made it all worthwhile. The VIPs, seated in bleachers, were not aware of the H-13s until they leaped from the forest behind them and began to deliver machine gun and rocket fire from weapons attached to their skids and fuselage. The H-13s, one at a time, rose from the defilade of low hills, fired in support of infantry troops, and dropped out of sight again, bobbing and weaving to escape detection. New, unrefined techniques—raw material to be sure—but indicative of the willingness to seek new solutions to fire-support/fire-suppression problems present in the wargaming that was taking place in the late fifties.

The Marine Corps was not messing with armed helicopters at the time, would be the last of the services to adopt such weaponry. The fighter-attack aircraft people were convinced that they could, and should, render all air support for

Marine ground operations. They did not even want to hear or read about such experiments as Sky-Cav. I was castigated thoroughly by one of our senior aviation officers when I submitted a laudatory report on Army armed helicopters and the formation of helicopter transportation companies. He was so incensed that he invited me to change the color of my green service uniform to conform to Army greens since I was such a stout supporter. C'est la guerre!

Not as exotic, but equally important to the scheme of things, was a number of new infantry weapons under development and test at the Board. The Browning machine guns—the water-cooled heavy and the A-4, A-6 light machine guns—were due for replacement. The M-60 still had bugs in it but seemed adequate to cover all of the machine gun requirements. There was also need for a lightweight, fast-firing, high-velocity, small-caliber shoulder weapon, with prototypes submitted by Winchester, Remington, the Belgian FN, and Fairchild (Armalight). The AR-15, submitted by Fairchild, held a comfortable lead. And there were night-vision devices, antitank weapons, mortars, and infantry armored vehicles under test. Body armor, new helmet liners, new helmets, field uniforms, and mess kits were also on the agenda. The project officers at the Board were well grounded, knew their business, and were most cooperative in matters of mutual concern.

As soon as we had settled in at Benning, I wrote to General Snedeker, then serving as G-3 at Headquarters, Marine Corps, and requested jump status for the duration of the tour. Within a reasonable length of time I was ordered to jump status and on 5 September 1956, after a thirteen-year layoff, made my first parachute jump at Fort Benning. Even from a bucking, staggering, roaring, just-able-to-get-off-the-ground C-119, it was a good feeling—one that would become second nature to me before leaving there. From 5 September 1956 until 8 May 1958, with the help of the Basic Airborne Committee and the Airborne-Air Mobility Department, I logged 118 jumps of which 66 were with combat equipment. Jumps were made from the C-119, C-123, C-124, C-130, L-20, U1-A, H-19, and H-21 helicopters.

On 20 March 1957, I was qualified as a senior parachutist and was so designated in Special Orders Number 58,

Headquarters, U.S. Army Infantry Center. Thinking it to be a feather in the cap of the Corps as well as in my own, I sent my designation forward to Headquarters, Marine Corps, with a formal request to wear the device as part of my uniform. After a lengthy delay, a letter arrived from Headquarters congratulating me on my achievement but denying permission to wear the device.

On 20 March 1958, exactly one year later, I was presented with the master parachutist badge by the deputy commander, XVIII Airborne Corps, during ceremonies at Fort Benning. The general was pleased to pin the device on my uniform and I was equally pleased to receive it. This time I did not report my achievement to Headquarters and continued to wear the basic badge, issued long ago at Lakehurst. Two years later, under a different commandant, I requested permission to wear the master parachutist badge as part of the Marine Corps uniform. Permission was granted in writing in less than a week. To wear that badge was an honor worth waiting for.

Duty at Fort Benning and Continental Army Command, Board #3, was singularly good for me and for my family. The officers and men of the Board, the Airborne-Air Mobility Department, the Infantry School, and Sky-Cav made a lasting impression on me, changed a very negative attitude towards the United States Army to a very positive one. Duty with a "sister service"—liaison duty, call it what you will—had opened my mind, had removed the prejudices once held. Nowhere in my military career was my family or I treated better, made to feel more at home.

Benning taught me, too, the respect in which the Corps is held by the other services. It was the time of Ribbon Creek, when a gross mistake in judgement by a solitary drill instructor at Parris Island had threatened to explode the traditions held by generations of Marines. Headquarters, Marine Corps, the commandant himself ran for cover, willing to sacrifice the finest recruit-training methods in the world in an effort to compensate for the deaths of six recruits. I could have taken a lot of static from my Army compatriots during that episode, but I did not. They understood the problem much better than the professional politicians of the Corps, gave me sympathy instead of sarcasm.

A decade later, on the hills of Phu Bon Province, II Corps, Republic of South Vietnam, I would meet some of them again as members of the 1st Brigade, 101st Airborne Division. They would remember me and the old days at Benning, would reach out to me as they had there, would provide aircraft in which I might travel to a forward position of the brigade to visit briefly with my nineteen-year-old son, who was now one of them.

27

The Challenge

A short time after my return to Fort Benning from temporary duty with 1st Force Reconnaissance Company, I received a call from Headquarters, Marine Corps, from Capt. Paul X. Kelley, special assistant to the director of personnel. I had jumped with this forthright, well-mannered, and energetic young captain at Benning and came to know him rather well. He had fielded my name to the director as a candidate for command of the Marine Corps Cold Weather Training Center. A full colonel's billet with some strings attached. Would I be interested in the assignment?

I originally was cool to the idea. I had been promoted to lieutenant colonel in December 1957 and felt that I was due a rifle battalion upon detachment from Fort Benning. I was not anxious to become involved in any assignment with "strings attached." I so informed Captain Kelley, thanked him for his consideration, and asked for time to think about it. Within a week I had called personnel at Headquarters in whom I placed implicit trust—among them Col. Lew Walt, my friend from Pendleton days—and asked for their opinion of the assignment. All of them encouraged me to accept it, stating that they thought the assignment would prove to be an especially rewarding one—on my own, in a separate command 400 miles from the nearest administrative headquarters, and under the direct supervision of G-3, Headquarters, Marine Corps, in matters of training. I had received no assurance that I would be given command of a rifle battalion upon leaving Benning, so the assignment sounded better as time went by. But what of those "strings attached"? Better find out.

Back to Captain Kelley for the details. He gave them to me fast and straight.

The Center had opened in 1952 to train Marines for duty in the winter weather and mountainous terrain of Korea. At the end of the police action the Center had remained open for mountain training of selected Reserve units and for mountain and cold-weather training of Fleet Marine Force units. During the mid-fifties, Headquarters, Marine Corps had authorized a Mountain Leadership Training Course—assault rock climbing and military mountaineering in summer, alpine skiing and cold-weather mountaineering in winter, and an Escape, Evasion, and Survival Training Course conducted on a year-round basis.

Some 400-plus personnel manned the Center, with such manpower luxuries as a full-strength aggressor platoon, to be used against trainees during field exercises, included in the Tables of Organization.

In 1957 an evaluation team had been sent to the Center to take a hard look at its value to the Corps, to determine whether training results were worth the manpower levies and the monetary expenditures. The team returned with a strong recommendation that the Center be reduced to caretaker status and that all organized training there be dropped. The commandant had taken exception to these findings, had decided to keep the Center active (and here come those "strings") with the provision that there must be a 50 percent cut in personnel, with no reduction in annual trainee input. If the half-strength training cadre could meet the commandant's training demands, the Center would continue to be funded. It was Captain Kelley's opinion, based on what he had seen of me at Fort Benning, that under the circumstances imposed I could give the commandant the results he desired at the Center. Did I want to give it a whirl?

No more games. I agreed to the assignment with no stipulations, loving a challenge more than anything else. In later years I would thank P. X. Kelley more than once for his recommendation to the director of personnel and for being patient while I made up my mind. Good training in forbearance for a young captain who one day would become 28th commandant of the Marine Corps.

A simple written agreement between the U.S. Forest Service and the Marine Corps in 1952 had made 64,000 acres of the Toiyabe National Forest available to the Marine Corps for mountain and cold-weather training. The northern rim of Yosemite National Park formed the southern boundary of the training area, Sonora Pass the western, Highway 395 the eastern, and the area around Markleeville the northern.

During the summer months there were tourists everywhere; in autumn, during hunting season, the hills took on the sounds of pitched battles. But when the snow came, there was only the Marine encampment.

There was a decided nip in the mid-September air, the sunlight masked by the western crags behind us. I stood on a two-inch ledge, eighty feet up on a rock slab that I was attempting to climb. My right ankle, injured badly during a parachuting accident prior to leaving Fort Benning and held in place by a three-and-a-half-inch diagonal pin, was swollen and stiff, just painful enough to keep me constantly aware of the fact that I had only one dependable foot to maneuver with.

I could not find a handhold for either hand, no holes in the rock for a jam hold, no outcroppings for a push or pull hold evident to me. My bad foot did not afford me the agility required to bring me around, up, and over a small rock formation to my right, which appeared to contain both hand- and footholds. My right leg trembled and shook spasmodically from the increasing pressure on it. I was in a bad spot and knew it, but possessed neither the technical know-how nor the physical strength to move myself higher on the rock wall.

Above me, laughter. Then a foot of nylon sling rope dangled invitingly just within reach, swaying back and forth—temptation to the highest degree.

Laughter again, then "Want the rope, Colonel? You can have it if you want it, *Sir!* Ready to call it quits and come on up?"

Cpl. Roger Shelton, my instructor, was enjoying himself. A nineteen-year-old young bull, he had rigged the big top in circuses and carnivals in civilian life, had absolutely no fear while climbing, scampering over the faces of sheer rock walls with abandon, as though there was glue on his hands and feet, his eyes taking in every potential hand- or foothold, quickly and efficiently planning every move. Lt. Ralph Walker, officer in charge, had known instinctively whom to work me under as I attempted to complete the Mountain Leadership Training Course.

We had arrived at the Cold Weather Training Center late on the afternoon of 1 August 1958 after a short briefing at the Marine Corps Base, Camp Pendleton, my administrative headquarters. Our quarters, the only set on station, had been prepared for us—two Quonset huts had been butted together to form a "T." The head of the "T" contained the living-dining-kitchen areas, the leg of the "T" the sleeping-bathing areas. Adequate in all respects and furnished surprisingly well by a former occupant who had close ties with the quartermaster general of the Marine Corps. Thick, heavily padded carpets throughout the living areas, a huge fireplace with a massive hand-hewn solid mantelpiece. The main source of heat for cold weather was propane gas, which would keep us snug through two winters of bitter cold and heavy snows.

The three older children had been introduced to something new to them, the country schoolhouse, this one seventeen miles north of the Center in a town called Coleville. But after a few weeks they had acclimated, as Marine Corps children must, in spite of a thirty-four-mile round trip each day and the anxieties that attend all outsiders to the local scene.

In terms of living accommodations, we were the most fortunate of the command. Other Marine families lived up and down the length of Highway 395 from Bridgeport, seventeen miles south, to Coleville, seventeen miles north, and on up the road to Gardnerville and Minden, still farther north. There were families, too, in Carson City and Reno, and some in public housing at the Naval Ammunition Depot at Hawthorne, Nevada, 100 miles to the east. If ever there was a pioneer spirit exhibited in the Corps, it never was displayed in a finer manner than by the families of the Cold Weather Training Center, who took their licks and backed their men without the whimpering and nagging that can destroy a man's proficiency during normal operations, that quite literally could destroy *him,* and other Marines, in the course of performing the hazardous duties common to the Center.

By the time I had arrived on station, the personnel cuts had been initiated, the Center complement standing at eighteen Marine Corps officers and two hundred thirty-five enlisted plus three Navy officers—a doctor, dentist, and chaplain—and eight medical corpsmen. Training was coordinated through the efforts of a Training and Operations section of two officers and three enlisted men and accomplished by a Mountain Leadership Training Course manned by four officers and nine enlisted men, an Escape, Evasion, and Survival Course of one officer and seven enlisted, and a Fleet Marine Force/Marine Corps Reserve Section of one officer and twelve enlisted.

The doctors at Fort Benning had told me that I would be able to go back on jump status by 5 September, that my ankle and leg would be able to withstand the stress and strain of jumping by that date. On 17 September, Mountain Leadership Class 3-59 (Summer) had been scheduled to convene. For several reasons I had wanted to train in that class—first, I had no formal training in mountaineering and wanted it; second, during my time in the Corps I never had asked a Marine to do anything that I could not or would not do; and third, I had perceived that we would need to crosstrain as quickly as possible a number of permanent personnel—cooks, messmen, maintenance men, drivers, and mechanics, in mountain and winter warfare specialties. There was no slack in the line to take up, manpowerwise. It was bowstring taut already.

In order to prepare myself and the troops to be physically able to undertake these additional duties, I had launched into my regular physical fitness training program—

all hands not on watch were in front of the headquarters building each morning for calisthenics followed by a run from the main gate to Route 108 for a round trip of four miles initially, expanded to ten miles as the months slipped by. The runs were made at just below seven thousand feet of altitude, which wore us down during the early phases but doubled our stamina once hearts and lungs adjusted to the thin air.

Maj. Curtis James, the training and operations officer who had served with me in the 21st Marines during 1948–49, had told the troops what they could expect from me long before I had arrived. I do not believe that I made a liar out of him.

On 17 September, I had commenced training as a student in Mountain Leadership, a course that lasted just short of three weeks and which taxed me mentally and physically more than anything that I ever had known before. Long days in the field learning the basics—how to mountain walk, how to climb scree and talus slopes, making long and short traverses instead of climbing straight up, learning how to descend as well as climb—all of it a constant, fatiguing, sometimes painful battering of the feet and legs. The basics, too, of rock climbing—of the various holds to be used; the employment of climbing ropes and knots; the use of pitons, piton hammers, and snap links; the use of belays and belay positions, rappels and rappel types. Then into climbing procedures. Free climbing without the aid of ropes; party climbing with two or three climbers tied into a climbing rope 120 feet long, and just a smidgeon of tension climbing.

I just had completed rock-climbing procedures, had done passably well at everything except the navigation of an overhang. Just couldn't seem to snap my overlong body up and over the obstruction as quickly as required. At the end of formal instruction for the day, I was invited to move to the far right of Demonstration Rock, a slab some 300 feet in height and four times that in width, to practice free climbing on a pitch of about 100 feet. I almost had reached the top when my troubles began. . . .

Shelton's voice again. "You want this rope, Colonel. Haven't got all day. Getting hungry. I know that there are some good footholds and handholds on the little overhang on your right. Slide around there and find them—or do you want to come up on the rope?"

The old sting game. Make the student angry. Hit him in his pride. Get under his skin. Make him ashamed. Prod him.

I knew that to remain spread-eagled for much longer could be fatal. It was a long dive to the bottom of the slab, a hard bounce at the end. I *had* to get out of my present position, and I didn't want that damned rope! Sweat popped out. My hearing was deadened by the pounding of my heart. I cautiously slid my left foot to the right, dropped my left hand to a lower hold, twisted my body outboard just enough to pass my left foot behind my right leg, anchored it, let my right hand slide along the edge of the protrusion, found a hold for it, brought my right foot forward and around until I almost was facing in the opposite direction of my start, found a hold for my left hand and pulled hard, found a foothold for my left foot as I moved upward, pushed hard with the left foot, brought the bad right foot up, felt it slide, then catch, found a new handhold for my right hand, and heaved myself up and over the small projection that had been denying my progress. Nerves shot, mentally exhausted, still panting from maximum physical exertion, I lay with the upper half of my body safely over the rock lip, looking neither to the right nor left, my eyes fixed on the gentle slope of stone that ran back to the tree line. No more bad spots. Nothing more to confront me, at least for *this* day.

"I see the Colonel found some holds in that chunk of rock. You OK, Sir?" Shelton's voice came from a position to my left rear, where he squatted back on his heels, head cocked to one side, smiling at me. From his observation post he had followed every step of my climbing route up the long crack in the slab, had seen me work myself into a spread-eagle, had brought the rope to me from a position above, would have given it to me and brought me on up had he believed there was a real danger. Like a ghost he had been close all the way, but not too close, had forced me to go back into the recesses of my mind, dig out the proper answers for my problem from instruction previously given, and come up with a workable solution.

On 6 October 1958, I stood with the remnants of Mountain Leadership Training Class 3-59 to receive my certificate of completion and my sling rope. No student was allowed to wear his sling rope looped across the back of his neck and under his arms until graduation. Not as nice as a metal device to be pinned to the tunic of the service uniform, to be sure, but meriting perhaps more respect in the long run.

For me, 1958 had been a year of symbols—the master parachutist badge presented to me at Fort Benning, the sling rope presented to me at Pickel Meadows—moments of pride and deep humility. When I received my sling rope I was fifty-one days shy of being forty years of age.

The Escape, Evasion, and Survival Course at the Center was designed to acquaint pilots, air crewmen, Marine division reconnaissance battalion, and Force Reconnaissance personnel with elementary capture and prisoner-of-war-camp exposure, escape from confinement, evasion of hostile forces while moving through enemy-held territory to link up with friendly partisans, and survival—living off the land—while evading.

Covered in the prisoner of war compound exercise was capture; confinement under less-than-comfortable conditions; daily and nightly interrogation sessions in specially equipped interrogation rooms, where all interrogations were taped to be played back to the students during the course critique; and an opportunity for the students to organize within the compound, to choose leaders, and to respond to those leaders during the exercise.

Even though the students knew that the exercise would terminate in three days, it was disturbing to see the numbers of them, both officers and enlisted, who would spill their guts on tape, hoping for better treatment in the camp. Name, rank, and serial number was the only legitimate information required, but far too often unit designations, unit special equipment, unit strengths and locations, names of commanding officers, names of wives and children turned up on the replay of the tapes. One could not help but wonder how much detailed information would have been extracted under *real* duress.

The prisoner of war compound had been constructed on the valley floor a short distance from the course classroom area. There were always curious people poking about, prying into things that did not concern them—a bad situation for the instructors, even worse for their students. The compound should have been back in the hills, at a distance great enough to discourage casual visitors. Funding for the construction of a new compound had been approved, but had not been released to the Center for construction to start.

At the end of October a group of official visitors arrived at the Center from the 1st Marine Division located at Camp Pendleton—the assistant division commander, a brigadier; the G-2 and the G-3, full colonels; and a lieutenant colonel from the G-4 section. I had known all of them during my time in the Corps, considered them all well grounded in infantry combat, and had thought they understood the reasons for the training that took place at the Center.

We stood just outside the compound, looking through the barbed wire and the concertinas piled high against it. The compound was illuminated by floodlights—no shadows in which to skulk and hide. From the overhead watchtowers the guards methodically scrutinized every foot of the compound floor, watched and waited for any move on the part of the captives. It was forty degrees as night closed down on us. The visitors wore heavy cold-weather gear over their utility clothing, they stamped their feet and hopped from one foot to the other as though the temperature was frigid. My people were dressed in utility clothing, without jackets or sweaters. We did not think forty degrees was very cold.

Inside the compound the student captives had organized, chosen leaders, and planned an escape attempt, just the way they had been taught to do in classroom instruction. As we watched, a diversion took place while other members of the student body tried to break out of the compound. The visitors moved in closer to observe this turn of events.

The guards had anticipated such a move, had posted just outside the compound a three-man team with a three-inch fire hose at the ready. When the guards posted inside the compound started firing blanks at the escapees, the fire-hose team moved up close to the wire and blasted the students back, rolling them along the ground, drenching them to the bone, quickly dispelling any thought they might have of penetrating the wire. Within minutes they had been corralled, tied up, and left to brood.

I thought the episode realistic; was ready to compliment the course commander, the instructors, and the students on the part each group had played. I never was given the opportunity.

"God *damn* it! What in the hell is going on here? It is below freezing here, and you put a fire hose on them? Trying to kill them? Want to hospitalize all of them? Are *you* authorized to do such stupid things? *Who* authorized you?"

All this from the G-3, from a colonel who was supposed to have seen a lot of combat. I couldn't figure out what he was bitching about. Maybe Ribbon Creek in 1956 had gotten to him, made him overly solicitous, politically nervous—one never knows the motivation when such freak-outs occur. I looked over at the officer in charge. He shrugged his shoulders in disbelief and walked slowly into the compound as if to say "You take it for action, Colonel—it is beyond me!"

I tried to make the point that the temperature was far from freezing, that within a few more minutes the students would change into dry clothing before the exercise continued. The G-3 wasn't having any of that jive. *He* had seen trainees from the division *abused!* When he returned to Pendleton he intended to find *why*—I could be sure of that!

The brigadier, cool and calm, had been with the division, in combat and out, for many years. He wasn't making any hurried judgements. He thanked me for the opportunity to observe the training, received my salute and returned it, bade me goodnight, and secured to quarters. The next day the party departed for Camp Pendleton. I was sure that I had not heard the final word from the G-3—directly or indirectly.

My reporting senior was Maj. Gen. Reginald R. Ridgely, Jr. General Ridgely had been a Japanese prisoner during World War II and had told me several times how much he wished that, prior to his capture, he could have had the advantage of training in a class such as the one taught by Escape, Evasion, and Survival at the Center. As far as he was concerned, the rougher the training, the better it would be for the students, for training never could be as rough as the real thing. Knowing his feelings, I called him and reported the incident at the compound. I was on safe ground. He told me not to be disturbed by all the sound and fury. "Don't worry about it, Averill. *I* command up there, *not* the division. *I* will handle things. Maybe we had better get started on that new compound. Let's locate it up in the hills. Those lads need more *solitude!*"

The incident indeed was brought to General Ridgely's attention by the division G-3, who promptly came a cropper. Not deterred by being stonewalled by the general, he then ordered Lt. Col. John N. McLaughlin, a Korean conflict prisoner of war, to check out the complete Escape, Evasion, and Survival Course to determine whether or not our training methods were too harsh. He was given a free rein at the Center, found nothing horrendous in our training effort, returned to Camp Pendleton, and so informed the division commander, Major General Snedeker. Like General Ridgely, General Snedeker approved of our way of doing things. End of the line. No more trouble.

All that had happened fortunately had been turned to advantage. The need to establish a new compound in a remote area had been underscored dramatically, construction funds were released, and a new compound was built much sooner than we ever had anticipated.

We do certain things to test and evaluate the basic integrity of our people under situations of extreme stress. Sometimes the manner in which this is accomplished seems in the eyes of the uninitiated, both civilian and military, to be extremely brutal and dehumanizing. *Survival* is the name of the game. Survival is often something that must sustain brutality, degradation, and humiliation. Our people deserve to be exposed to these things, even in minimal amounts, in order that they become aware of what they might face in an actual capture situation. It is difficult to cope with the unknown. It is our obligation to lift the veil, to tell them, teach them, and demonstrate to them all that we know of the enemy's methodology.

Busy people at Pickel Meadows. The pattern never changed, winter or summer. With the loss of the aggressor platoon, troops from the mess force, the maintenance section, motor transport, and the headquarters sections constituted the enemy forces required for the field problems. At times there would be no one in the main camp except a communications watch, the officer of the day, the gate sentries, a generator crew, a skeleton mess force, and of course my family. Everyone else was in the boondocks. My family saw little of me during the summer and fall for I, too, was a part of the training force, participating in mountain leadership demonstrations as a guide/rappeller for cliff evacuation and long rappeller—200 feet—during the climbing demonstrations. I also acted as an enemy soldier of the defense force on White Mountain, humping an A-4 light machine gun to the 11,000-foot crest of the mountain and remaining there to run opposition against the students as they attempted to seize a portion of the heights.

The first four months at the Center had convinced me that the overall training package presented there was an asset to the Marine Corps, far too valuable ever to let slip into oblivion. Just to *be* in that beautiful wilderness area was enough to perpetuate the existence of the Center. To be there, pitted against the stresses of nature and the physical and psychological contrivances of man, could not fail to produce a better warrior, a better balanced Marine—an experience immensely profitable to the man and to the Corps. As long as I was commanding officer there, the major effort would be to keep the Center alive for generations of Marines yet to come. In terms of esprit de corps, every mountain, every cliff, every rushing torrent at Pickel Meadows had the value of solid gold. No shortage of military appropriations ever should be allowed to shut down *that* operation!

Christmas Eve—the mountains and the meadows covered with a fresh blanket of snow glistening in the moonlight. Inside the quarters at Pickel Meadows, the tree had been trimmed and lighted. We waited, in the warmth of the holiday spirit and propane gas, for the night to pass into Christmas, our last-born, the twins, the only believers in Santa Claus still left in the family. It was our first Christmas locked into the remoteness of the east slope of the Sierra Nevada, remoteness shared with the unmarried Marines of the command who lived aboard.

Quite without warning, which made its appeal even greater, came the sound of carols sung just outside; then, mixed with the music, the tread of footsteps moving up the wide steps and along the length of the long porch and then a light touch on the doorbell.

When we opened the door, we found the porch overflowing with carolers, the moonlight framing them in silhouette. Behind them in the distance, the peaks at the rim of Yosemite, points of golden light flickering from them, reflecting the sheen of the full moon. As we watched and listened, the old familiar sounds of a childhood Christmas rolled and echoed across the valley, nostalgia stabbing suddenly at the heart, the mind, until moisture glistened, too, as it welled up into the eyes.

Sgt. Maj. Jim Westerman, my leading staff NCO, and his New Zealand-born lady had brought the carolers up from their church in Bridgeport to share the glad tidings with me, my family, and my Marines in barracks whose thoughts were bound to be far from Pickel Meadows on that special night. Sergeant Major Westerman and the people of Bridgeport had presented us with a rare gift of fellowship, of affection; with uncommon perception had opened their hearts to us; had indelibly etched that eve of Christ's birth into our memories, recording in all its beauty the sights and sounds of that fabulous night.

When the time came to leave Pickel Meadows, I was not ready to go. Too many things had happened, too many things still left to do.

Much had been accomplished beyond meeting the commandant's challenge to equal or surpass trainee input, especially in the field of *military* mountaineering. When I came aboard, techniques were being taught in a faultless manner, but their application to military units and military tactics was sketchy at best. The basic reason behind the somewhat glamorous specialist-training syllabus—the ability to move units of relatively unskilled infantry troops into and through difficult mountain terrain by the use of assault climbers and mountain guides—just was not being accorded its true importance. Lectures and classroom work touched on the subject, but there was little practical work.

Such simple things as climbing with a rucksack, a packboard, or the standard haversack, and with a shoulder weapon, were being neglected. Why *don't* we climb with weapons and equipment? Wouldn't we do so in combat? We started climbing the less difficult pitches the way that assault climbers would have to do it for real. No one lost weapons or equipment. No one fell.

Just after midtour we did demonstration climbs for members of a Headquarters, Marine Corps inspection team, with ice and snow on the climbing face—again something spoken of but not practiced. There were some tight jaws among us. Some ice fragments and pieces of rock that pulled out after vigorous probing fell with loud crashes, but there were no climbing casualties. Another notch reached in realistic climbing, additional confidence achieved.

The final and to me the most rewarding exercise of all—a night assault of difficult, rocky pitches, using all of the climbing techniques learned in the course. The White Mountain exercise had proved its value as a vehicle to test stamina and tactical ability during the approach to a mountain objective, but did not include cliff assault and the use of fixed ropes to aid in the attack. During the night assault, a composite platoon consisting of the student body of the mountain leadership class and volunteers from the permanent personnel of the Center—people with absolutely no previous experience in mountaineering—were brought into position to observe the objective, to reconnoiter it visually, and, by the use of scouts during daylight hours and prior to darkness, draw up an attack plan to seize the objective.

In darkness, three teams of assault climbers went into position at the base of a sixty-foot pitch; climbed, carrying weapons and lowering lines to bring up other trained personnel; and established fixed ropes on the pitch and guidelines across the crest of the rock obstacle along which the untrained troops could be brought into the position. As the troops were brought up and over the rock, lines were dropped and machine guns, ammunition, and equipment brought up on them. In total darkness, the assault was conducted without loss of personnel—not even the untrained volunteers—and no equipment dropped or damaged.

It took no great amount of imagination to achieve that training result. It all was written down in the book—in this case the U.S. Army Field Manual on Mountain Operations—and needed only to be put into action. Some of the people who had set up the original training directive for the Center just had not read far enough into the manual or perhaps were not interested in putting their signatures to something potentially dangerous. In any event, an exercise like that was the natural culmination of the special training that had preceded it, and should have been designated a graduation requirement the day that the mountain leadership course began.

No, I had no desire to leave. At the close of the first year of operating at half-strength, we had exceeded the number of trainees established by the commandant. He had kept his promise and funded the Center for another year, leaving in place the same stipulations on manpower. The challenge had been accepted in 1958, the rules had been established, the jousting had begun, and, to the surprise of nobody in my crew, we had won quite handily.

I never had served in a tighter command. It was unique in so many ways, almost like serving in a cavalry outpost during the opening of the West, cut off from civilization by natural surroundings if not by hostile redskins. Like duty in a cavalry outpost, the purpose and mission of the Center, the success of its training objectives, were dependent entirely upon the cooperation of each member of the command, each man's contribution of equal import.

On no other post would Helen and the children become so familiar with the troops or the troops so familiar with them—again a similarity with the Indian fighters, where the ranking officer's family well might be the only one at the post. We left the Center but twice a month, and then for no more than a weekend. Under such conditions of proximity, the command became a part of my family and they a part of the command.

The land itself, with all of its desolate spaciousness, its pristine loveliness, its terrible loneliness, became a part of me, the yearning to remain with it was a twisting, burning pain in my gut. Being king of the mountain made other assignments commonplace and drab. I had glimpsed Shangri-la.

Part Seven

CLOSED CIRCLE

28

The Last Expedition

Following a year of duty under instruction as a student in the Senior Course, Amphibious Warfare School at Quantico, I joined the 3d Marine Division on Okinawa during September 1961, hoping for command of an infantry battalion. No such luck; still too many people on the list to be *qualified*.

I was assigned to Task Force 79, an operational planning staff for the U.S. Seventh Fleet, as an assistant operations officer, my duties to assist in the review and update of current contingency plans for Southeast Asia. Sitting behind a desk, flipping papers all day, was not my forte, but I was stuck with it.

We in Task Force 79 worked under sort of a floating-command arrangement. Whoever happened to be senior in rank on the combined lineal list, between the two major generals commanding the 3d Marine Division and the 1st Marine Aircraft Wing, concurrently was designated as the commander, Task Force 79. During my time on Okinawa, Maj. Gen. John Condon, commanding general, 1st Marine Aircraft Wing, carried the baton.

In 1954, when I reported for duty with the 2d Marine

Division, I had been shunted off to Vieques for a tour of umpire duty. Upon reporting to Task Force 79, I was caught up in the umpire game again, and almost before my gear had arrived I was on my way to the Marine Air Station at Futema. Duty there would have its compensations; aviators always live well. I never had served with an air unit anywhere. The officers and men of Marine Air Group 16 (Helicopter) could not have been a finer group with which to share my first experience in Marine aviation. Umpiring is the same anywhere one goes. I would gain little from it.

At the close of the exercise a real bonanza floated my way. One of MAG-16's squadrons had been moved to the airfield at Udorn, Thailand, in April 1961 for "black" operations across the Mekong in support of Special Forces teams and the Lao units trained and equipped by them. While conversing with Col. John Carey, commanding officer, MAG-16, I learned that he was about to go south to visit his pilots in the black squadron, to check on them and their operations, to see if they required further support from the Group. I mentioned that I dearly would love to go along, whereupon the colonel invited me to accompany him, provided that it would cause no flap with my reporting senior, the G-3 of Task Force 79.

I knew instinctively that the political thing to do was to return to Task Force 79 and take whatever came my way, but the incessant, clamoring need inside of me to see new places, to meet new people, especially against a combat background, was uppermost in my mind and blew away all traces of caution. I made my request. Surprisingly I received no static, was issued travel orders with the stipulation that travel costs be borne by me, and was off to Southeast Asia.

We crossed over Qui Nhon, South Vietnam, at 10,000 feet. In the fall of 1961, Qui Nhon was just another sleepy fishing town, set against a background of azure sea, beaches of beige-colored sand, and tree-covered mountains thrusting up behind it. The cloud cover was eye-catching—typical of Indochina—towering pillars of fleecy white clouds rising more than two miles into the deep blue skies. Transiting Vietnam, watching mile after mile of jungle-covered hills unfold, the immensity of the war in Indochina was revealed. One's eyes could see and register on the obstacles present here for sophisticated battle units, tended to make more plausible the defeat of French units sucked up into this verdant vortex. Thought-provoking. Doubt-instilling.

Then on across Laos, turning north by west, the old French airfields sliding into view, bringing even more sharply into focus the whole French misadventure in Indochina. I wondered how much better, or how much worse, the Americans might fare if committed in strength to an extended battle in that ocean of jungle spread out beneath us.

My first sight of Indochina, my first impulse cautionary, invoked by what I had seen of it the easy way—from the relative safety of the air.

Clustered around the eastern end of the airfield at Udorn were all of the players in the game—Thai military and civilians, Nationalist Chinese pilots and crew members, Chinese aircraft maintenance mechanics, a headquarters group from Air America plus the aircraft under their control, and the squadron from MAG-16. Terry and the Pirates? Could be. All the cast and characters could be found somewhere near the airstrip, all of them strictly compartmented, all of them operating on a need-to-know basis, each group doing its own separate thing. This was my first look at American operations in Southeast Asia. A decade later it would be old hat to me, and—believe it or not—the game still would be played under the selfsame set of rules. In 1961, it all looked very zippy, exotic, and remarkably romantic. Ignorance is bliss.

Our first night at Udorn we showered, courtesy of the squadron's skipper and Air America; donned clean clothing; ate a fine meal; enjoyed the cold beer and the booze at the squadron mess; and stayed up half the night listening to the war stories of the pilots of the squadron. Every day they flew cargo, troop lift, evacuation, and observation missions on the Lao side of the Mekong, supporting those Lao groups who happened to be serving with the American choice of legal government at any given time—a government that could, and did, change overnight. Those young pilots were not trying to snow anyone. Their stories were confined to the facts of their own operations, spiced from time to time with the jungle tales told to them by their Special Forces counterparts advising the Lao.

After midnight, in the relative quiet of the compound, we

crawled into our cots, tied down the mosquito nets, and secured. Just before I dropped off, I thought again of the overflight of Nam and Laos on the way into Udorn; thought, too, of what I had seen and heard that evening. After ten years away from the war zone, it was good to be back, standing at its edge once more, if only long enough to bring back more sharply the memories of its sights and sounds.

The next morning we flew north across the Mekong River—at flood stage so wide that it resembled a lake more than a river—and on to the air space over Wattay Airfield, the runway and its edges pockmarked by the craters of hundreds of artillery and mortar shells, the main runway barely operational from the shelling and the never-ending rain showers. As we touched down, it seemed all too possible that we would lose control, skid, spin out, and end up off the runway. But the bird held steady and true until we had slowed enough to turn off and taxi onto the hard stand.

The rain stopped, the sun came out, the heat and humidity wilting the body as well as the clothing. Wattay, under fire almost constantly from one political faction or another, still maintained its operational capability. Its storage areas were full of cargo to be airdropped—tons of palletized equipment, rations, and ammunition stored just off the tarmac, waiting to be airlifted. Air America was on *this* side of the river, too, their people and aircraft plainly visible and, just by chance on that particular morning, a gathering of representatives of The Company, getting their ducks lined up for the day.

By the time Colonel Carey had finished his business at Wattay, the morning was shot. We lucked into transportation for some local viewing and, between rain squalls, splashed out of the airfield complex and onto the two-lane, beat-up macadam road leading to town.

Vientiane, Laos—an incursion of extreme brevity leaving few impressions on the mind, none of them good. The mark of the French everywhere, from the layout of the town to the architecture of its buildings and their floral landscaping. Vientiane must have been a languidly comfortable place to be posted in the days before the Pathet Lao.

The place that still sticks in my mind was the hospital, every bed in it full, the grounds covered by casualties who could not gain entrance—some on litters, some on ponchos, some laid out on the bare ground in the mud and rain. Off to one side, grouped together like lepers and avoided as stringently as lepers might be, dozens of Meo tribesmen lay in their own blood, no hand lifted to help them. In Laos, as in all of Indochina, the caste system flourished as it had for centuries, the Meo at the bottom of the heap, held barely human in the eyes of the lowland Lao, just as the Montagnards were treated by the Vietnamese across the border.

In the America of 1961, President Kennedy talked about freedom and democracy and how such things were embraced by all the people of Southeast Asia. Opinions differ, depending upon where one sits and what one is privileged to see.

And then south again once more, the rain still hammering at Wattay as we took off, back to Udorn, where the heat, humidity, and boredom were the major problems to confront. A mere thirty-five miles separating Udorn from Vientiane made the difference between life and death, comfort and misery. Those same thirty-five miles would continue to make that same difference for as long as Americans fought in Indochina.

I always will be grateful to Colonel Carey for allowing me to make that journey with him to the bend of the Mekong. It blew a lot of false impressions out of my head, made me aware of some of the realities of war in Indochina where no matter how much the American might desire to be loved, he never would be, but be suffered only for what loot could be extracted from him. Xenophobic is the word generally used to describe the attitude held by the Indochinese. I really would not understand that word, in all of its ramifications, until I arrived in Vietnam after retiring from the Corps.

Operation TULUNGAN, held between 2 March and 12 April 1962, took me into activities other than paper-shuffling, although there was some of that involved also. Modern war depends upon paper far more than it should, but records must be kept, if for no other reason than to cover your butt, and TULUNGAN was no exception to this rule. As a primary project officer, and liaison officer to the other members of the Combined Landing Force, it was my good fortune to be doing more legwork than paper.

TULUNGAN, meaning "cooperation," "mutual assistance," or "hands together"—take your pick—was the code name for the largest SEATO exercise ever held in the western Pacific. The place, Mindoro Island, ten miles south of Luzon—a rugged, mountainous chunk of terrain with 8,000-foot peaks rising sharply from the coastline—and where American troops in quantity had not been seen since World War II when the airstrip at San Jose had been used by American bombers. On our first reconnaissance of the area, several curious natives had sauntered out to the aircraft, sporting bows and arrows and blowguns. Ten minutes by air from Manila, civilization had not quite caught up with some of the inhabitants of Mindoro.

The exercise would be conducted by a Combined Landing Force composed of a Philippine Battalion Combat Team, units of the Philippine Air Force and Marine Corps, Australian Air Force elements, and a U.S. Marine Corps Expeditionary Force consisting of a reinforced Marine division and a Marine aircraft wing plus headquarters and combat support units.

To be placed on the island, in advance of the landing, was a U.S. Marine Corps Battalion Landing Team and a company of Philippine Marines to act as a guerrilla force against the Combined Landing Force. The time spent on Mindoro, training as insurgents, becoming thoroughly acclimated to the heat and humidity, working with and against the difficult terrain every day, becoming familiar with the area of operations, would pay off handsomely during the landing phases of the exercise, would make the assault troops of the landing force look like rank amateurs.

Participating in the exercise, as part of the Combined Landing Force, was the 1st Force Reconnaissance Company from Camp Pendleton, whose members I had worked with during the test jumping of the Istel parachute in 1958. Commanding the company was Maj. James McAlister.

During the early planning and the troop-training phases of the exercise, Jim and I kicked around operational ideas, among them helicopter rappels—a technique originated by S. Sgt. Robert G. Walker while serving with 1st Reconnaissance Battalion, and which I had worked to refine. That kind of work appealed to Jim. He thought we should give it a try.

Where to practice? Since some of Jim's people had not

rappelled before or were rusty in that technique, we first used the side of the water tower at Camp Courtney. Once the review was over, we shifted operations to Futema, secured permission from the commanding officer to use the parachute dry locker, and commenced serious work.

We needed to rig our climbing ropes for a vertical drop, to be able to slide down the full length of the rope, braking only to maintain positive control. Hooking to the top of the parachute hoists, we were able to achieve about half of the distance desired, not what we wanted—too much constriction in space, too much expenditure in time—but it did give us a positive *feel,* gave us a chance to brake once or twice, gave every man the sensation of a vertical drop, quite different from standard rappels off a rock face.

Time to do it for real. One HUS helicopter and crew were made available. A climbing rope was attached to the offset rescue hoist boom and the coil placed inside the passenger compartment. Over the target area, the coil was dropped and the rappeller snapped into the rope, then backed up against the far bulkhead, swung out safely past the landing wheels, and commenced his 100–110-foot drop. We moved cautiously at first, braking off several times before reaching the ground, but gaining confidence with each drop until they were being made with only a couple of brakes on the way down. Finally we all hit it with but a single, well-calculated brake that put us on the ground without a jar and at maximum drop speed. A fast, accurate, completely controlled fall was our objective and we achieved it. Something useful had been accomplished—an insertion technique had been smoothed and polished to a point where it could be completely depended upon.

The pilots that flew us were superlative, holding the aircraft at the specified altitudes; holding steady-on while we snapped in, swung out, and dropped; never pulling us off balance at the point of contact with the ground; giving us every possibility for success. The Marine air-ground team is hard to beat, even when reduced to a handful of each.

Convinced that we had something worth selling, we took the aircraft and the technique to the headquarters of the 1st Special Forces Group; demonstrated for them; let them have a shot at it, just for kicks. They were impressed, became believers, and bought the program, which later became fully accepted Army operational doctrine.

Liaison duty with the Philippine Marine Corps and pre-exercise reconnaissance of the objective area by members of the Combined Landing Force staff kept us moving during the months of March and April 1962. Major General Condon—one of the most forceful and eager general officers I ever had known—was interested in all aspects of the exercise, particularly the short takeoff and landing capabilities of the newly arrived C-130 aircraft. Designated the GV-1 by the Marine Corps, it initially had been purchased as an in-flight refueler. Under existing law the Air Force was tasked with providing troop and equipment airlift for both the Army and the Marine Corps—an impossible arrangement for both the provider and the users. In typical Marine Corps fashion, the GV-1, after removal of the fuel tanks and the insertion of troop seating arrangements, was used quite openly as the primary means of transporting Marine troops and combat equipment—law or no law.

I first had known the C-130 as a jump aircraft during July and August 1957 at Fort Benning. I had seen its short takeoff and landing capabilities demonstrated there, but I never had seen it perform under the conditions it was subjected to in the pre-TULUNGAN days.

None of the airstrips on Mindoro was prepared to take heavy transport, not even the old bomber strip at San Jose. General Condon was not deterred by this and had his pilots slam the GV-1 into and out of highly improbable situations, the aircraft rising to each occasion with verve and vigor. At Mamburao, on the northwest coast, the primitive strip began right at the water's edge, seemed far too short to accommodate the GV-1. We touched down right at the water line, the pilot zoomed in, used up every inch of the strip, reversed his propellers at full throttle, and came to a stop scant feet from the edge of the forest. Ramp down, vehicles out, a ground reconnaissance conducted, return to the aircraft, tie down the vehicles, a turn to seaward made with wing tips brushing the trees, maximum power poured on, and the GV-1 blasted itself back into the air without wetting a wheel.

The Marine Corps needed the versatility of that aircraft—needed it in both its roles—with its primary role tipped more than slightly in the direction of troop carrier.

D Day for TULUNGAN eventually arrived. I wish that in addition to being the largest SEATO exercise ever held in the western Pacific, it also was the best, but that would be far from the truth. Some units, for instance 1st Force Reconnaissance Company, performed their duties in an exemplary manner, carrying out difficult pre-D day missions with dispatch and the highest degree of military proficiency.

As for the Combined Landing Force, the landings took place, the troops went ashore, but the umpires were hard put to give much credit to the landing force beyond its getting onto the beaches. The troops had been aboard ship too long, had not been exercised properly, had not been well briefed regarding the effects of climate and terrain that would be encountered on Mindoro. Not a good thing to see, not a good thing to realize, the troops just were not conditioned to carry out their combat duties in the objective area. Even the division commander got into the act. Coming ashore late on D day, he promptly keeled over from heat exhaustion just getting off the beach, much to the satisfaction of the line troopers who had been ordered, in the interests of presenting a sharp appearance, to button their utility jackets up to the throat, tuck the jacket tails into their trousers, and tuck the trouser bottoms into their boot tops, which resulted in an involuntary Turkish bath. Once the general had passed out from the heat, there was an immediate change—comfort became the watchword in lieu of style.

The Philippine and American Marines playing the guerrilla role chopped up the troops of the landing force in a most spectacular manner. They played their parts with such enthusiasm that the umpires had to call them off in order for the landing force to advance at all. Only at the close of the exercise, when air support could be utilized fully on point targets, did the landing force succeed.

There is an old saying that goes something like "We sweat in peacetime, so that we do not bleed in war." It is a good thought and one that should be utilized, not quoted. The mistakes made during TULUNGAN were not new ones. They had been made in the Solomons, the Central Pacific, on the hills and in the valleys of Korea, would be made again in Southeast Asia. For some strange reason you cannot convince the brass that the only way to train is the toughest way you can, the troops pushed to the point of exhaustion every training day. There is no *easy* way to get ready for combat. Our enemies know this, understand it, and train for one thing—to win.

15 May 1962. A worldwide command post exercise called HIGH HEELS had been underway for more than forty-eight hours, war gaming, contingency plan testing going on at every major military headquarters in the United States and overseas. A test of communication equipment and procedures, of reaction time to hypothetical strategic and tactical problems. Messages in the clear. Messages encoded. Messages by every means of transmission. Reams of paper, gallons of coffee, thousands of sets of bleary eyes watching the paper flow. The men behind those eyes with jumpy nerves, tempers getting shorter by the hour, frustration building, everyone anxious to secure the exercise and get back to routine.

On Okinawa, the 3d Marine Division and its reinforcing units played the game as did we in Task Force 79. Every exercise message came in preceded by "This is HIGH HEELS!" to identify it and separate it from normal incoming messages. At just about midnight, I stretched, pushed myself up from the chair in my work space, and poured myself another cup of coffee. As I did so the radio next to me came to life, broke its temporary silence.

"This is NO HIGH HEELS. I say again, this is NO HIGH HEELS. Activate Joint Task Force One-One-Six. Activate Joint Task Force One-One-Six. This is NO HIGH HEELS!"

Joint Task Force 116 was a task organization made up of U.S. Army and Marine Corps infantry units with artillery support, helicopter support, and tactical air from Marine Corps and Air Force components. Under various contingency plans, the troop list could be tailored to fit the task at hand. Marines could be furnished as a Marine Expeditionary Force (MEF) made up of a Marine division and a Marine aircraft wing; a Marine Expeditionary Brigade (MEB) with a

Marine regiment supported by a Marine aircraft group and artillery; and a Marine Expeditionary Unit (MEU) consisting of a Marine battalion landing team supported by artillery, helicopters, and tactical air tailored to cover the situation. The Army units might run from a brigade to a battle group with their own helicopter support and tactical air furnished by the Air Force or Marine aviation.

Later messages received that night, not seen by peons like me, indicated a deployment to Udorn, Thailand. President Kennedy's advisors were convinced that the Pathet Lao or the Chinese or both were preparing to enter northeast Thailand in force from an area north and west of Vientiane. An immediate show of United States determination to support Thailand was imperative. The effort must be launched as soon as possible.

Major General Condon was on Okinawa as commander, Task Force 79, for the HIGH HEELS exercise. When the message came in to activate, things started to move in all directions. The general was all fired up, wanted to be the man who took the Marine component into Thailand. Initially a Marine Brigade/Marine Aircraft Group was indicated, which put General Condon in command no questions asked. Then, a few hours later, in the interests of a faster deployment, Fleet Marine Force Pacific decreed that a Marine Expeditionary Unit be deployed instead, supported by a composite Marine Aircraft Group. An MEU was commanded by a brigadier, which moved General Condon out of the picture. He was extremely loath to give up his command, fought to hold it, but lost. His disappointment was my own, for I held a line slot in the operations section of a brigade, held nothing with an MEU. I know that my disappointment could not have matched the general's, but it ran a close second.

Seventy-two hours passed and the Udorn deployment, as well as HIGH HEELS, became history. The troops of the Special Landing Force of the U.S. Seventh Fleet—the 3d Battalion, 9th Marines—went ashore at Bangkok, were airlifted from Don Muang to Udorn, and were deployed outside the airfield complex. Marine fighter/attack aircraft arrived from Iwakuni, Japan, and helicopter support was brought in. By sheer coincidence, the U.S. Army component of JTF-116, the 27th Infantry, was already in Thailand on a training mis-

sion with logistical and helicopter support. The Air Force
component arrived shortly thereafter and positioned itself to
support both the 27th Infantry and the 3d MEU. British and
New Zealand air units answered the call under the SEATO
aegis and were positioned at Chiang Mai and Udorn.

Between 17 May and 2 July 1962, I made a nuisance of
myself at Task Force 79 and 3d Marine Division trying to find
a way to be assigned to duty with the 3d MEU at Udorn. No
one at Udorn got sick, killed, or captured—conditions under
which I might have been sent south. As luck would have it, I
would go nowhere until my former bunk mate, Walter Gall,
then serving as G-3 of 3d MEU, came up for rotation stateside. Learning that Walt was rotating, I made one more trip to
the chief of staff, 3d Marine Division. That officer allowed
that I was a persistant cuss, gave me his blessings and a set of
orders to report to 3d MEU by 11 July 1962, and even set up
my air transportation. I got the distinct impression that he
would have done almost anything to get rid of me. I called
Walt on the radio, told him to expect me, received four
inoculations in each arm, and took off for Thailand. After a
few days with Walt at Udorn, he passed the baton to me,
packed his gear, and headed out for the first leg of his trip
back to the Land of the Big PX. He was happy to be leaving
Udorn. I was happy to be there.

The officer who commanded the 3d MEU was Brig. Gen.
Ormond R. Simpson, assistant division commander of 3d
Marine Division. Had extensive research been made for the
proper commander of the 3d MEU, considering its mission,
it is doubtful that another more qualified officer could have
been found.

The general was a thinker, a planner, a diplomat of no
small ability with a hearty, down-to-earth sense of humor
well camouflaged by his austere demeanor. A realist, he had
made the best of the situation in which he found himself at
Udorn, maintaining an excellent relationship with Lieutenant
General Richardson, commander JTF-119 and his staff; with
the local Thai officials; and especially with the command and
staff of the 13th Thai Regimental Combat Team posted at
Udorn.

The east end of the Udorn runway had been partially
inundated when I had arrived there in the autumn of 1961.

Nine months later, there was no visible improvement. So bad was the accumulation of water, with no means of drainage available, that all working and living spaces had to be raised about three feet off the ground—the tents strong-backed with reinforced decking and joined together by a series of duck walks. Seen from a distance or from above, the clusters of tentage resembled lily pads on the surface of a pond. Even the commanding general was staked out on his own individual pad, his flag flying high over the expanse of rust-colored water surrounding his quarters.

The men of the attached Naval Construction Battalion—the Seabees of World War II fame—made a valiant effort to keep a trickle of runoff moving, to keep the bridges from sinking. But they met with only a modicum of success, keeping the roads into and out of the airfield barely trafficable. Every time it rained it was a gamble as to whether the headquarters would be cut off. This was not an ideal location for a command post, but, faced with the requirement for command and control to be located at the airfield, it was the best that could be had.

The Marine infantry component—the 3d Battalion, 9th Marines—enjoyed a much better location on high ground several miles from the airfield. Not plush living by any means—squad tents and pyramidal tents, which held the daytime heat like a sauna bath—but located on a hill that was cooled by desultory breezes and trafficable by foot and vehicle. The area adjoining the bivouac was gently rolling, lending itself to the construction of tactical training areas and live-firing ranges for the troopers.

Enemy forces had not crossed the Mekong at any point along the Thai border prior to my arrival and did not while I was there. In fact none of them ever reached the north bank of the river in appreciable numbers. The Thais were far more warlike—evincing a strong desire to push east and extend Thai territory in Sayaboury Province to the banks of the Mekong. But they were held back by the United States, who wanted no overt incursions into Lao territory by its own forces or those of its allies.

The mission of Joint Task Force 116 was to show the flag, to display a United States presence close to the border in northeast Thailand and by being there to deter aggression by

Communist forces. It was quite apparent that the mission, for
the immediate future at least, had been carried out successfully.

If there was no enemy to contend with, how were the
days and nights filled? With much activity, none of it just
manufactured busywork.

The 3d MEU had a fabulous opportunity to learn very
well the physical attributes of the countryside in the vicinity
of Udorn—of its assets and liabilities in terms of military
operations. Marines had been deployed to Udorn in 1961 and
again in 1962, well might be again, depending upon the
whims of the enemy and the Washington politicians. One
thing was certain—to maintain even a token force such as the
3d MEU in northeast Thailand, 350 miles from a seaport,
took a major logistical effort. The majority of supplies were
brought in by air—very expensive in terms of money and
aircraft availability—with the remainder sent up by road or
rail from Bangkok. It behooved every member of the staff to
take a long look, in terms of future reference, at the traf-
ficability of the roads meeting at Udorn.

To aid the 3d MEU in transport and reconnaissance
missions, General Richardson furnished the headquarters
with an aircraft new to Southeast Asia—the CV-2A, De-
Havilland Caribou, a two-engined light tactical transport
with exceptionally short takeoff and landing capabilities,
carrying a crew of three and thirty-two combat troops. The
Caribous had seen service in Germany and were flown over
the top of the world for service in Vietnam after a brief tour in
Thailand. We never let an opportunity slide by to use this
plane. It made all the difference in road reconnaissance
work, in maintaining contact with troop units out on motor
marches, and, when our ancient R4D was down for lack of
parts, it was used for liaison and liberty runs to Bangkok.
Some of my best hours in Thailand were spent riding the
jump seat between the pilot and copilot, sliding along at 100
knots at 50 feet off the deck, checking out the countryside,
landing to discuss motor patrol activities with participants,
running a Mekong River recon from Vientiane almost to
Paksane, getting to know something about the river and the
Lao towns and airfields on the far side of the waterway.

Four years later, in Vietnam, I would ride in the same seat, but in an Air America Caribou with retired Marine Corps pilots on either side of me and more than a slight chance of Cong rounds slipping through the skin of the bird.

We did our share of moving around. Trips to Bangkok and Korat for liaison visits with the staff of Joint Task Force 116. Visits to the Joint Operations Center, from which all tactical air operations were controlled. Visits to Chiang Mai for liaison with the British air units based there, and to units of the 27th Infantry for firepower demonstrations and an introduction to the Bell HU-1A helicopter, already in use by Army elements but brand new to us—its speed and maneuverability something to marvel at after flying in the Sikorsky HUS utilized by the Marine Corps.

And there was one more place of visitation not touted to the general public. Permission had been secured through the headquarters of General Harkins, commander, U.S. Military Assistance Command, Vietnam/Thailand, to send into Vietnam, on a temporary basis, junior officers and NCOs from the 3d MEU to serve with the advisors to the Vietnamese Marine Corps during reconnaissance and combat patrols, ambushes, and defensive operations. The stay in Vietnam ran from ten days to two weeks. No special proficiency was expected in that length of time, but rather a good exposure to terrain, climate, and weather, with occasional exposure to a real-live firefight. It all came under the heading of unit training, and it was worth every hour of its duration. Those lads coming back from the Nam visitation might not have seen the elephant, but they had stepped in its tracks.

During the same relative period, a Marine Corps air task unit known as "Shoofly" (HMM-362), operating out of Soc Trang, 100 miles south of Saigon in the Delta, was relieved by HMM-163 after flying fifty Vietnamese troop-lift missions which involved more than a hundred landings against the Cong. During the tour, which commenced in April 1962 and ended on 1 August of that year, HMM-362 suffered no casualties.

By the end of autumn 1962, both air and ground units of the Marine Corps would have been exposed actively to what would become the second Indochina War.

On 23 July, the declaration and protocol of the neutrality of Laos was signed and proclaimed by the fourteen-nation conference meeting in Geneva. The signing of those documents would have a direct bearing on our existence at Udorn, for the U.S. Military Assistance Advisory Group, Laos, no longer could remain in that country, must come back across the Mekong and relocate. Temporarily that location would be at Udorn. In preparation for that move, the 167th Signal Company, U.S. Army, commenced phasing in troops and communications equipment.

On the heels of the news concerning MAAG, Laos, came rumors of the withdrawal of JTF-116 from Thailand. Again the administration in Washington was getting jumpy, this time because it feared international criticism for maintaining combat troops so close to the now-neutral country of Laos after the signing of the protocols at Geneva. At first we did not believe those rumors, but soon dispatches from Commander Task Force 79 arrived to confirm their validity. No dates or times were set, just be ready to execute upon signal.

Commencing on 23 July, planning was initiated—plans to go by sea-lift, plans for total airlift, plans for combinations of lifts, all of them sent out to Commander Seventh Fleet and Commander Task Force 79.

Before *any* plan could be approved, Washington forced our hand. By 27 July we were on standby to move—how, no one really knew. Air control units from 1st Marine Aircraft Wing and a detachment of Air Force controllers had arrived at Udorn, ready to initiate a major airlift, so it seemed apparent that a combination of air- and sea-lift would be the eventual answer.

Then the word came down. Move all *combat* troops out of Thailand within ninety-six hours. Presidential order—don't drag your feet—get cracking! We had neither the facilities nor the capabilities to meet those orders at the time they were received; but, as so often happens, fate intervened.

Just as we were preparing to execute, knowing full well that it would be impossible to meet the established deadline, a massive typhoon moved in on Okinawa, sending all flyable aircraft scurrying south to the Philippines to ride out the storm. In the array of aircraft descending on Clark Air Force

Base, Sangley Point, and Cubi were C-123s, C-124s, and C-130s. Messages went out requesting participation of these aircraft in the lift. Messages came back—*can do!* Thanks to the Okinawa typhoon, we now had more than enough aircraft to carry out the withdrawal—might even make it in time!

As with an amphibious operation, if you have not participated in an extended airlift, you never can understand its complexities. Every member of the 3d MEU staff, from the chief of staff on down, took part in the lift on a full-time basis. The field stayed open night and day. The Marine Corps and Air Force control units handled the incoming and outgoing aircraft; the air crews of the individual planes and the logistics personnel handled the loading of troops and equipment; the MEU staff handled the clearance and dispatching—an all-hands evolution, with no time for anything except the task at hand. We were blown around by the constant prop wash, went partially blind trying to read manifests and almost deaf from the sound of aircraft engines and the blaring of bullhorns.

We had been allowed ninety-six hours in which to whisk the combat troops out of northeast Thailand. When the last transport carrying the last combat trooper took off from the airfield, sixty-nine hours had elapsed.

We left Udorn by air on 3 August, leaving behind a rear echelon to move the heavy equipment to the railroad in Udorn, for further shipment to Bangkok. After five days in Bangkok, checking on the arrival and loading of our assigned shipping, we closed down the command post in the Hotel Rama, flew to Clark Air Force Base, spent the night, and on the following morning commenced the final leg of the Thailand experience. Almost home—the 3d MEU still functional—paperwork still to be completed before closing out.

Had my sojourn in Thailand been worth the honking and stroking it had taken to get there? Had being with the 3d MEU been worth the time and energy expended? Would I do it again the same way? To all three questions—affirmative.

As long as Marine units were deployed to areas of potential contention, I always would desire to be with them. It is under such conditions that our pay is earned, our trade learned. It is not in me to rest easy without getting a taste of such deployments—to see firsthand where an action might take place should the right circumstances prevail, to learn as much about the target area as possible for future reference.

In Korea we used to say, "It isn't much of a war—but it is the only one that we have!" That is exactly the way I felt about the deployment of the 3d MEU to Thailand—as long as it was all we had, it was the place I wanted to be.

29

The Cadet School

Closed circle. For me, boot camp at Parris Island had ended during October 1941. Twenty-one years later, in November 1962, another trick at the wheel—at the Marine Corps Recruit Depot, San Diego, California. This time I would not be in ranks, would be able to call the tune. It promised to be interesting.

My initial assignment was that of Operations and Training officer, Recruit Training Regiment. A good way to break in, to get the lay of the land—a chance to observe up close the daily training activities of the three recruit training battalions and the special training units of the regiment. I had two outstanding staff NCOs to help me with the paperwork and the scheduling, which left me free to take a long, searching look at both the trainers and the trainees; to form my own opinions, good and bad, of the training effort of what we at Parris Island always had called the San Diego boot camp— the Cadet School.

So different in so many ways from Parris Island. The Marine Corps Recruit Depot, San Diego, was set right in the middle of a transportation, business, and residential complex. The main gate opened onto the steady swish, swish, swish of swiftly moving traffic. From any portion of the training area, civilian sights and sounds assailed the eyes, the ears. At any time of day or night, commercial jet aircraft wheeled overhead, landing and taking off from nearby Lindbergh Field. Not in the least bit similar to the somber, threatening swamps surrounding Parris Island. There, no one tried to go over the fence. It was far safer to stay inside the wire. At San Diego the recruits went over the wire on a regular basis, to be quickly captured by civilian and military police, but it was in them to give it a try. *Their* world could be seen every day at San Diego. At Parris Island the old world was gone, with nothing but the new world to embrace.

Different, too, from what I had known was the whole supervisory machinery of recruit training. In 1941 we seldom saw an officer—maybe one or two at inspections and the final parade—but never on a daily basis. In the boot camp of 1962, recruits saw them every day. They might see the company commander, surely would see a new addition from my time— a lieutenant, called a series officer, responsible for a series of platoons, who had been plugged into the supervision game since Ribbon Creek, referred to by some as the most important link in the supervisory chain and who was the direct supervisor of the drill instructors in charge of the three to four sixty-five-man recruit platoons in a series.

And there were special platoons that could handle just about any problem a recruit might have. You could get fat if you were skinny, skinny if you were fat, strong if you were weak, and there was even a resident psychiatrist if you had blown your mind. It all took time, supervisory personnel, and money, with somewhat dubious results. In my boot camp, if you screwed up they sent you back to a beginning platoon to try once again. If you failed that time, they sent you to Casual Company, issued you a nine-dollar civilian suit, gave you a bus ticket, and sent you home in disgrace. That approach was far more economical than the new, and it weeded out the incompetents early in the game.

But *some* of my boot camp remained, thank God! Nothing could ever change the chant of the drill instructors moving their charges from place to place—the Wahn-Hup-A-Ree-Ho—Wahn-Hupper-Ree—Wahn-Ree—Wahn-Hupper-Ree resounding across the length and breadth of the grinder. In 1962 the Corps still was armed with rifles, the M-14, with which the marching manual still could be rendered smartly. And there were those indefinable things that mean so much, that make us so different from the other services. The parade flags; the flash of swords in the sunlight as salutes are given and returned; the always-impeccably-turned-out depot band marching with that beautiful, rolling gait, the music of the old familiar marches more nostalgic than ever, pulling, binding, cementing the brotherhood. The Hymn completely compelling as always, accelerating the heartbeat, shortening, sharpening the breathing process as each note struck at the ears.

They might change the methods of bringing a recruit along, but they never could change the inexplicable mysteries, the ingrained loyalties perpetuated by the Eagle, Globe, and Anchor; the Motto; and the strains of the Hymn. Those things are indestructible, will remain constant through generation after generation of Marines for as long as there is a Corps.

One might suppose that the supervisory personnel of the Recruit Training Regiment, both commissioned and noncommissioned, would be of the caliber that would of their own volition surpass the recruits in every facet of training, from close-order drill to physical fitness. During my time as Operations and Training officer of the regiment, I found to my consternation that this was not universally so. When my observations concerning this were tendered to higher echelon, they were noted, initialled, and filed. No response. It seemed to me that no one really gave a damn, the old saw, "Don't do as I do. Do as I say!" the apparent watchword. Beyond reporting the weakness and recommending corrective action, there was little that I could do. Staff officers do not establish or enforce policy.

In the summer of 1963, I was sent to Quantico to attend a counterinsurgency course for senior officers. While attending that course, I made my first contact with The Company.

An old friend from World War II was attending the same course. It had been years since we had been together and he took me to his home in McLean, Virginia, for dinner one evening. After the meal he asked me if I would like to come cross-service and work for The Company on a temporary basis. The assignment would be in Vietnam, at the city of Hue, training Vietnamese airborne troops for special operations controlled by The Company. The assignment would last for about two years and my family could accompany me. It sounded great. When would we start?

The next two days, I begged off classes at Quantico and with my friend drove out to Langley, where introductions were made and initial paperwork was accomplished. Testing, also, to include the polygraph, which scared me witless. At the end of those two days, things looked good.

Not so. We both had been too eager, too enthusiastic. The billet at Hue had been cancelled; no one would be going there. An attempt to line me up for a European billet failed. Back to square one. In spite of the standoff, the time had not been wasted. They were interested in me, I in them. In less time than might have appeared likely to either party, we would powwow again for mutual benefit.

I had asked to command the first available recruit training battalion. The first one up for grabs was the 1st Recruit Training Battalion, and I locked onto it like a hungry salmon.

My company commanders, series officers, drill instructors, and my headquarters officers and enlisted men were typical of the times. All of them, without exception, possessed the potential to become excellent supervisors in their fields of endeavor but never had developed that potential. No one ever had deliberately ground them down, worked them over, driven them beyond their own comfortable, self-imposed limitations concerning stress and strain. It was time they learned what soldiering was all about—what went into leadership by example. The recruits deserved the best in leadership and supervision. I fully intended that they should have it, intended that they should look back on their boot camp with the same pride and satisfaction that I looked back on mine.

Over the years it had become my practice, upon assumption of the command of a unit, to break out the troops, introduce myself, and let them know in cogent terms just what lay in store for them. Just as quickly as I could, I broke out the 1st Recruit Training Battalion and let its members know what I stood for and what I expected of them as recruit producers and as United States Marines. I told them that I expected them to outmarch, outdrill, outrun, outperform their recruits in every way, and that it was my desire that they bring themselves into that state of training excellence soon. I further told them that they could expect to see me in the recruit areas at all hours of the day and night, that I would make unannounced visits to those areas, that I did not want to find those on watch asleep or holding down space in any but their assigned areas. All hands were duly warned. They had no reason for complaints in the future.

I was as good as my word. Commencing that night I visited the recruit living spaces at midnight, at 0200, at 0400, and at reveille. The next night I went in at 2300, again at 0100, at 0300, and at 0500. During the days I hit all of the scheduled training areas, including the physical training area. I was told later by one of my senior drill instructors that during those early months the drill instructors had made up their own watch list, had posted their own sentries to spot me, to check on my direction of approach, and to be on station when I arrived. In any event, the additional hours paid off, and I could feel free to spot-check an area after hours anytime, knowing that my people would be one step ahead of me. If you keep your promises, you have a much better chance of getting the desired results.

At the same time we took up the matter of physical training and distance runs. Since the recruits had to master a three-mile run, it seemed logical to me that their supervisors should be able to outdistance them. Six miles in fifty-four minutes was the goal established and that is what we immediately shot for. There were some worn-out, nauseated, fatigued officers and men staggering in after those initial attempts, but after a reasonable length of training time, the goal was finally attained.

For physical training we relied upon the old standbys. Six pull-ups (not chin-ups), fifty sit-ups in two minutes, thirty-five push-ups against no time limit, and twenty-eight squat-thrusts in one minute. Meeting the required numbers of repetitions against the required times according to Field

Manual 21-20 placed one in an average to good category of
physical conditioning—nothing great, but still ahead of recruit requirements.

The attainment of those training objects took time,
effort, and for some a great deal of pain, but it paid off. In
order to keep things moving—no slack in the line—a new
running course was established, not to supercede the six-
mile course, which was run in utility clothes and combat
boots, but rather to augment it. Four miles, wearing a steel
helmet, a pistol belt, carrying a haversack loaded with fifteen
pounds of sand, a full canteen, and a training rifle weighing
ten pounds. Time limit—four miles in thirty-six minutes.
Again some whipped Marines, some sick ones, some who
passed out during the run. But I finally was getting through to
them, getting their undivided attention, proving to them that
it could be done.

Our little excursions around the training areas also had
gotten the attention of the commanding general, who graced
us with his presence one morning just as we were about to
take off on a four-mile jaunt with full equipment. I am almost
certain that he had come into the area hoping to observe
something illegal, something outside the purview of approved
training practices. I was there, as always, had on full equipment, was carrying a rifle, was about to lead the run. I had
learned long ago that if *you* lead, if you submit yourself to the
same hardships of the troops, there can be no criticism, no
fault found—and there was none that morning.

Of course there was a lot of static about the program at
first, just as there had been in the other units I had commanded, but in the end the same results accrued—intense
esprit de corps, a deep and abiding sense of accomplishment,
a tremendous personal pride.

During July 1964, Col. Glen Martin, my first battalion
commander in Korea and the officer who had relieved me at
Pickel Meadows, visited the depot as part of the inspector
general's team out of Washington. After kicking around the
good old days, the colonel posed some strange questions, the
answer to which he should have known from our past association. Was I enrolled in off-duty study classes in any of the
local universities or colleges, taking courses that could lead

to a degree? Was I by chance doing it by correspondence? No, Sir. Neither. Why? The answer was that I was in the selection zone for promotion to full colonel, would be coming up before the board the following month.

So what? In 1967, before a board with an attrition rate of 60 percent, I had been found qualified and selected for promotion to lieutenant colonel—without a college degree. I just couldn't believe that formal education could carry that much weight in selection to colonel. I firmly was convinced that my tours of combat duty, my time with troops, would more than compensate for the lack of a degree. It seemed to me that my chances were good, and I made that comment to Colonel Martin.

I know that he did not want to lay it on me, but he would have been less than a friend if he had not. He told me that if I did not hold a degree, if I was not actively seeking ways to procure one, that I could hang it up. I would not be considered eligible for promotion to colonel.

I only could hope that the colonel's information was in error, that he somehow had read it wrong. I took a long breath, crossed my fingers, and prayed for a miracle.

I did not have long to wait. In three weeks the list came out. Doubtful, apprehensive, I scrutinized every page of the list and then went back over it again. No Averill on *that* list. Later that evening I called Communications to see if by chance a page might have been missing. No. List complete. I just was not on it. Colonel Martin had been right. It knocked me for a loop, confused me. I had seen all of my fitness reports—all of them as good as one might want them to be—and just a couple of weeks ago the commandant of the Marine Corps had put his arm around my shoulders and personally congratulated me on maintaining an exceptionally high percentage rate in the transfer of Reserve recruits into the Regular Marine Corps, while undergoing recruit training—a direct reflection upon the training methods utilized in the battalion. Due to these all-too-cosmetic achievements, I had allowed myself to assume a completely unwarranted sense of personal security as far as promotability was concerned.

Well, hell! It *hurt,* but what was there to be done? Not much. The Marine Corps never had promised me anything except to run with the ball—and a good run it had been. I never had failed to give the Corps my best, in combat and out. It had reciprocated by taking me as far along the line as reasonably could be expected—had let me go up the ladder until I reached a point where, in its estimation, my liabilities exceeded my capabilities. I would be considered the following year. I had no illusions about being promoted then.

Two other things of some importance to me occurred during the late summer and early autumn of 1964.

Within a week of my failure to be selected for promotion, I received a phone call from Camp Pendleton. My contact with The Company was there for annual Reserve training. We had dinner together at my quarters in San Diego. During his visit with Helen and me, there were many spook stories, much interest in my future plans predicated upon my passover. Would I stick around in the Corps and wait for another chance? That was my plan. Go to bat one more time and take it from there. He left us that night with the inference that the door to spookdom was open more than a crack.

My oldest son Mike sailed for Okinawa that autumn with a battalion landing team from the 1st Marine Division. He had enlisted in the Reserve following graduation from high school, taken his boot training at San Diego in a battalion other than mine, coasted for awhile after completion of training, and enlisted later in the Regular Marine Corps. He would land at Danang early in 1965 with the first Marine units to serve there, would be the first of my immediate family to fight in Vietnam.

30

Spinning In

The John F. Kennedy Center for Special Warfare, Fort Bragg, North Carolina, July 1965. A new assignment—as Marine Corps liaison officer to the Center. It would be one of the best, and also the most brief, of any tour of duty in my time in the service.

The people at the Center were my kind of people—chargers, able, eager to get on with a new concept sponsored by no less than the president of the United States, whose untimely death had not diminished the interest in special operations or the use of Special Forces in unconventional warfare. My predecessor had carried out his duties in a superlative manner, had made the name Marine the subject of respect and admiration among the Special Forces officers and men with whom he had served. I had only to follow his lead; the spadework already had been done.

In the summer of 1965 the Center was filled with returnees from Indochina. In addition to being blessed with experienced personnel, the Center was also the terminus of all reports and major message traffic emanating from Vietnam, Laos, and Cambodia. If you really were interested, you could

be guaranteed a play-by-play description of Indochina operations. At the Center there was no cool detachment but rather
a heavily personalized interest in what every "A" Team was
doing on a daily basis. The atmosphere was electric, charged-
up twenty-four hours a day. I was both pleased and content to
be there.

While attending a liaison officers' conference at Quantico, I received my second pass-over for promotion. On the
afternoon of my arrival there, the list was published. No
Averill on its pages. Some of my friends, passed over along
with me the previous year, were picked up for promotion. I
was happy for them—good people who deserved to be picked
up, who never should have been passed over in the first place.
I allowed myself to flip into emptiness, phase one, for a short
time, but saw no reason to indulge myself. It was over for
me—a fact I now must learn to live with.

The second pass-over was followed by a letter dated 8
September 1965, informing me that the secretary of the Navy
had selected me to be retained on the active duty list as a
lieutenant colonel until I had completed twenty-six years of
commissioned service, with a chance of selection to colonel
each year of the period. Retention would have allowed me to
remain on active duty until 30 June 1969. I just couldn't do it.
The Corps, after two pass-overs, had made the message
abundantly clear. No, it was better to go out under a full head
of steam, to step aside gracefully, to let the youngsters slide
on up and be promoted. Better to forget the possibilities,
accept the probabilities. *If* I was promoted to colonel, the
only duty I really would desire would be the command of a
regiment. With only nine infantry regiments in the Corps,
what chance would I have to command after two or more
pass-overs? Poor—very poor! And if I failed promotion, what
assignments would I draw? Nothing but dregs!

And I must be honest and admit there were attractions
elsewhere. If the Corps did not want me, there were still
those who would buy my sword. The people at Langley had
been locked onto me for months. The second pass-over had
not been out a day before a call came from them. Was I about
ready to come aboard? They had a job for me.

*   *   *

Shortly after my return to Fort Bragg, the commandant decided to activate the Marine Corps Reserve for duty in Vietnam. An immediate freeze on Regular officer retirements went into effect. How would it look if the Reserves went over to Nam and the Regular officers went home? I went back to Washington, went directly to General Weede for clarification, laid it out in spades. The Corps doesn't want me, but won't let me go. What kind of insanity is this? General Weede, cool as ever, had the answer. Go back to Fort Bragg. Write a letter to the commandant requesting retirement to accept a classified assignment with another government agency. When the letter arrives, I will walk it through the secretary of the Navy for you. I trusted him, as I always had. He honored that trust by doing precisely what he said he would. My retirement orders, effective 1 December 1965, came down to Fort Bragg.

During October, with the help of Brig. Gen. Joseph W. Stilwell, commandant of the Center, who for some reason had taken a genuine interest in me, I processed in at Langley, completed a battery of tests, went back on the polygraph again, and nailed down my pay and allowances. When I left for Fort Bragg, everything had been accomplished but for swearing in and signing the contract.

On 22 November I moved my family from our quarters on post into a newly completed home in Fayetteville, registered three children in new schools, and prepared to tilt with civilian life.

Twenty-four years, three months, and nineteen days— nearly a quarter of a century. For some, far too long—an eternity—chafing to have it all finished, wrap it up, and go civilian. For me, but a beginning, not nearly enough. The sting of being passed over could not be dispelled, but the lure of a fascinating new career was there—never a real substitute for the Corps, but one that could offer me momentary respite—that could, with the passage of time, win my admiration and loyalty. And it saved me from immediate exposure to the grim stolidness of straight civilian life.

As the days slid on by, separation more imminent, my emotions were far from clear, my love of the Corps and its people tearing at me, not wanting to give up the old life and what it had meant to me, logic telling me coldly that it never could be as it had been before.

On 1 December 1965, with no formal ceremony—no flags flying, no band playing the Hymn—in the office of General Stilwell I accepted my retirement orders. I had entered the Marine Corps without fanfare. I would leave it in the same fashion.

How had the journey through the Corps been for a "sand blower" from Maine? It had far exceeded my greatest expectations. I had come into the Corps dreaming that I might make sergeant when I shipped over, might one day stand a chance of making Marine gunner. Instead there had been corporal's stripes and Regular commission—a chance to go for broke. I had visualized involvement in skirmishes such as the Marines had fought successfully in Haiti, Santo Domingo, and Nicaragua. Instead of skirmishes, the toughest war ever fought by the United States happened along, giving me a chance to learn my trade at the platoon and company level against the meanest, most professional enemy that this country ever would know. Just five years later in the hills and mountains of Korea, I was given the chance to do battalion operations against the Chinese and the North Koreans, the latter, in my estimation, coming very close to the Japanese in ferocity and tenacity.

My peacetime service, especially in the Fleet Marine Force, could not have been better. In spite of altercations between some of my commanding officers and me, I can recall only one instance in which I was given a direct order to halt or modify my training programs because, as it turned out, there had been congressional interest, and the commandant had been scolded by a senator. That incident did not really upset me, for I was scheduled to leave that station in less than two weeks anyway.

Certain things move a man, get under his skin, get him moving, make him aware. Three things happened to me when I was a corporal and became touchstones, stayed with me for the rest of my life.

The first happened at Lakehurst. Harold Hansen, a corporal as tall as I was short, had come with me from Parris Island to undergo jump training and, like me, had been suckered into rigger school. One evening in the barracks, as I sat working on my leather gear, he questioned me about my ability to lead a squad in the Fleet Marine Force. Could I do it if I were dumped into a situation that required it?

I will be truthful. Just getting through jump school and rigger school took my full issue of concentration. We were at war, but the Marines had yet to be committed. It all seemed far away, out of sight. Hansen's question got to me, stung and burned me. I knew I was not ready, not prepared at that time to do a successful job with a squad and I told him so. His answer was succinct: "Don't you think that it is about time to get ready?"

From that day forward, I constantly was aware of my tactical imperfections, my lack of preparedness. From then on I did my best, not only to know my own job in detail but also that of the next man up the ladder in rank.

The second thing occurred at Quantico, when I was under instruction as a candidate for a commission. I asked a salty gunnery sergeant what one must do to be a good Marine. His answer was short: "Don't ever miss a campaign!"

I did my best to follow that advice for as long as I wore the uniform. Wherever the action was or might be taking place, that is where I wanted to be. Sometimes I bugged people too many times. Sometimes I stubbed my toes badly, as when I went to Washington, D.C., from Quantico to enlist Colonel Krulak's aid in getting back to Korea for a second tour. General Shepherd just had put out the word that no officer would go back for seconds until all had been out once. Colonel Krulak had gone to bat for me, had tried to slip me through, but had been stopped. My next communication from the colonel was a one-page note which read, "My advice to you is to get into the traces and pull!"

Then the third, and most important. I asked another gunnery sergeant at the schools the same question—what must one do to be a good Marine. His answer, pondered slowly and deliberately, was another question. "Lad," he said. "If you can answer *yes* to the question 'Are you the kind of Marine that you would want your son to serve under in combat?' you will *be* a good Marine!"

That question stayed in my mind and in my heart forever. It became my watchword, my goal. All of us can find a yes answer to that question, but not through routine effort. It has to be the single, uppermost thing in one's mind night and day, in peacetime and in war. Through my wars it was the measuring stick of my own ability. To have the answer come up in the affirmative meant more than anything else in the world to me. Sometimes I felt that I must have hit the mark, had come close to the bull's-eye. If I missed, it was not from lack of effort.

There were positive indicators every once in a while, and they made me feel good. Once I was going over a captain's fitness report with him. It seemed to be marked much lower, in his estimation, than it should have been, and he was trying to convince me of that. As we went over each item carefully, I advised him of the improvements that must be made in order to attain higher marks on the next report. *"Next report!* What about *this* one?" I told him there would be no change in the markings. He hung his head for a moment, then looked up with an embarrassed smile. "Major," he said. "You are a real son of a bitch—but if we are going to go to war, I want to go with *you!"*

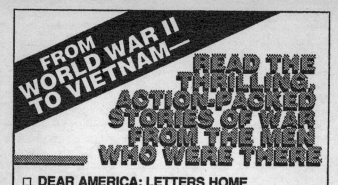